PASTOR
to
PASTOR

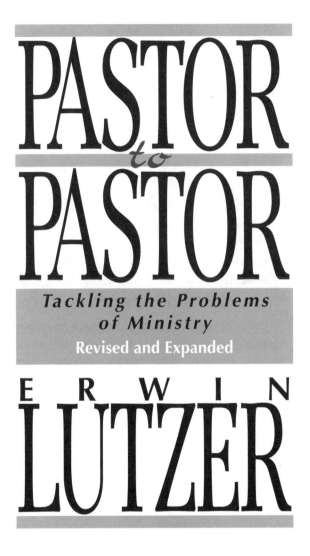

PASTOR *to* PASTOR

Tackling the Problems of Ministry

Revised and Expanded

ERWIN LUTZER

kregel
PUBLICATIONS

Grand Rapids, MI 49501

Pastor to Pastor: Tackling the Problems of Ministry

Copyright © 1998 by Erwin Lutzer

Published in 1998 by Kregel Publications, a division of Kregel, Inc., P.O. Box 2607, Grand Rapids, MI 49501.

Unless otherwise indicated, Scripture quotations are from the *New American Standard Bible*, © the Lockman Foundation 1960, 1962, 1963, 1968, 1971, 1972, 1973, 1975, 1977.

Scriptures quoted from the *Holy Bible*: *New International Version*® copyright © 1973, 1978, 1984 by International Bible Society. Used by permission of Zondervan Publishing House. All rights reserved.

Library of Congress Cataloging-in-Publication Data
Lutzer, Erwin W.
Pastor to Pastor: tackling the problems of ministry/ Erwin W. Lutzer.—Rev. and expanded.
    p.   cm.
Includes bibliographical references.
1. Clergy—Office. 2. Pastoral theology. I. Title.
BV660.2.L86 1998
253—dc21   97-41096
                                                       CIP
ISBN 0-8254-3164-6

Printed in the United States of America

4 5 6 7 8 / 10 09 08 07 06

Contents

6 CONTENTS

Foreword

Numerous books are available to guide us as we face and solve personal and church problems. I have read many of those books and have found them helpful in one way or another.

Then, why another one?

Because this one aims for a much higher goal than simply the answering of questions or the solving of problems.

Personal spiritual growth: that is Erwin Lutzer's great concern as he shares these insights with you. The goal is not just the solving of church problems, as important as that is, but the spiritual development of both minister and congregation. After all, each problem we encounter is an opportunity for both pastor and people to face the situation honestly, seek God's wisdom diligently, and obey His will trustingly. The result? Spiritual growth all around!

Something else makes these chapters unique: they come from the heart and mind of a man who is a pastor, theologian, teacher, and philosopher, a man who has a heart for revival and renewal in the church. Erwin Lutzer draws from a wealth of learning that has been filtered through the grid of personal experience. No ivory tower ideas here, and no pious evasions!

Don't speed-read this book. Pause, ponder, pray, and grow!

Warren W. Wiersbe

• 1 •

The Call to the Ministry

Do We Need One?

Suppose Charles Spurgeon and Billy Graham had chosen careers other than preaching. Would it have been all the same to God?

I don't think so. Though the idea is not popular today, I believe God still calls individuals to specific ministries, particularly preaching and teaching His Word.

During the past twenty years, missionaries have been telling us that there is no need for a specific call. Christ commanded us to preach the gospel; so, if we qualify, we should go. We shouldn't waste time waiting for a signal from heaven.

In *Decision Making and the Will of God*, Garry Friesen teaches that God has a sovereign will (His overall plan) and a moral will (His guidelines for life and belief) but no individual plan for every believer that we must "find."[1]

He asks us to remember how difficult it was to "find the will of God" when we had to make a particular decision and explains why that happened: we were looking for something that did not exist. We were seeking for a form of guidance that God did not promise to give.

Friesen exhorts us to make decisions on the basis of wisdom. We should gather all the information we can, weigh the pros and cons, and make our own decisions in faith. Of course, an important part of this is to consult with those who know us and to seek the insight of others.

He then asks about all the men called by God in the Scriptures. Because God spoke audibly to them, they had no doubt as to His will for them. God told Jeremiah directly that he was chosen for a specific ministry (Jer. 1:9–10). But God doesn't do that today, so those examples don't apply. We're expected to be obedient to God's moral will, but after that the decisions are ours. Any one of a number of choices would be fine with God.

There's some truth in that. Many of us grew up thinking we had to pry into the secret counsels of God whenever we had a decision to make. We tried to read His diary, but the print seemed blurred. His will was a mystery wrapped in an enigma. Doubtless we should have just gone ahead and made a reasonable decision. As one pastor told a friend, "Get a pure heart, and then do as you please."

We also believed that being called to the ministry required a Damascus-road experience. Short of that, we felt obligated to choose a "secular" vocation. I can remember many young men in Bible college and seminary discussing whether they were "called." Many of them hoped they were called but they weren't sure.

Furthermore, emphasizing a call to the ministry tends to exaggerate the distinction between clergy and laity. Every believer is a minister of God. To say that some Christians are called to specific ministries while others aren't seems contrary to the biblical teaching that each member of the body of Christ is important.

Friesen's position would also explain why some people have felt called to ministries for which they were ill-suited. Put simply, they were mistaken. What they thought was the Holy Spirit's leading was nothing but a personal hunch. You may have heard about the man who was called to preach; unfortunately, no one was called to listen! One man, burned out at age forty, concluded that he had never been called to the ministry; he entered the ministry only to satisfy his mother. As a youngster he showed great promise in public speaking and church ministry, so she encouraged him to become a pastor. Now he concludes that was a mistake.

Despite the fact that we don't know as much about the "call" as we would like, I still believe that God gives a call to some people that is more than just a general call given to all believers. There is a call that is more than simply being gifted for ministry and even more than just a desire to preach or teach. Charles Bridges has a point when he says that ministerial failure can sometimes be traced "to the very threshold of the entrance to the work."

The late J. Oswald Sanders was right when he wrote, "The supernatural nature of the church demands a leadership that rises above the human. The overriding need of the church, if it is to discharge its obligation to the rising generation, is for leadership that is authoritative, spiritual and sacrificial."[2] Spurgeon, Graham, and hundreds of other preachers have said that they chose the ministry only because God chose them for it. Apparently Timothy didn't have an audible call. Yet I can't imagine Paul telling him that he could leave the ministry if he wished without also leaving the will of God. On the contrary, Paul urged him to fulfill his ministry. And when Timothy began to wonder about his call, Paul urged, "And for this reason I remind you to kindle afresh the gift of God which is in you through the laying on of my hands" (2 Tim. 1:6 NASB).

I don't see how anyone could survive in the ministry if he felt it was just his own choice. Some ministers scarcely have two good days back to back. They are sustained by the knowledge that God has placed them where they are. Ministers without such a conviction often lack courage and carry their resignation letter in their coat pocket. At the slightest hint of difficulty, they're gone.

I'm disturbed by those who preach and teach without a sense of calling. Those who consider the ministry to be one choice among many tend to have horizontal vision. They lack the urgency of Paul, who said, "Necessity is laid upon me." John Jowett says, "If we lose the sense of wonder of our commission, we shall become like common traders in a common market, babbling about common wares."[3]

Since God called numerous individuals to specific ministries in Bible times, it is only reasonable that He would do so today. Though He doesn't call audibly now that the New Testament is complete, we have an adequate basis by which to test the inner guidance of the Spirit.

Characteristics of the Call

Let me risk my own definition of a call. *God's call is an inner conviction given by the Holy Spirit and confirmed by the Word of God and the body of Christ.*

Notice the three parts to the definition. First, it is an inner conviction. Feelings and hunches come and go. They may be based on impressions we had as children when we romanticized the idea of becoming a missionary. Or maybe we idolized the role of a pastor.

But a God-given compulsion is not deterred by obstacles. It gives us the single-mindedness needed for effective ministry. Some of us have had this conviction from our youth; others had a growing sense of urgency as they have studied the Bible; and still others perhaps had a less distinct but no less sure sense of direction. But the bottom line is the same: a strong desire to preach, join a mission team, or perhaps train others in the Word.

Of course, we don't all have to be called the same way. Circumstances and temperaments vary. I've already mentioned that for some people this conviction may be sudden; for others, it may be gradual. A person may sense no call at all until he is encouraged by discerning members of the body of Christ. Yet, despite those differences, there is a sense of purpose. Yes, "Woe is unto me, if I preach not the gospel!" (1 Cor. 9:16 KJV).

Second, the Word of God must confirm our call. We have to ask whether a person has the qualifications listed in 1 Timothy 3. Is he mature? Does he have the necessary gifts? Has he labored in the Word of God and in doctrine? Or might he have disqualified himself through moral or doctrinal compromise? Character is not all that is necessary, but it is the basic indispensable ingredient.

No doubt mistakes have been made when the scriptural qualifications have been overlooked in deference to a call. For a man to say that he's called is for some people reason enough to thrust him into ministry. But the church should not be hasty in ordaining those who are deemed called to such work. Though some people might have such a compulsion, they might have disqualified themselves, or their own perception might be mistaken.

On the other hand, churches have sometimes erred by refusing to ordain a man whom they deemed unfit for ministry. Perhaps the expected gifts were not present; perhaps the candidate did not appear to have the determination needed for ministry. And yet, as time went by, the man might have distinguished himself as a faithful minister. Even with the best of intentions we fail. But as was already mentioned, character must always be at the center of any evaluation of a call.

Certainly the qualifications of 1 Timothy 3 are more descriptive of the man's present character than his past character. But often his past, particularly since his conversion, is also relevant. If the man fails the test of the Scriptures, he must be excluded from ministry. Perhaps at a later time his call can be realized in another way.

Third, the body of Christ helps us understand where we fit within the local church framework. The leaders of the church in Antioch were ministering to the Lord and fasting when the Holy Spirit said, "Set apart for Me Barnabas and Saul for the work to which I have called them" (Acts 13:2 NASB). The body enables its members to find their spiritual gifts and is a testing ground for further ministry. Those who are faithful in the least may later be entrusted with greater responsibility.

God might choose to confirm the call by special coincidental happenings or human mediation. I think of John Calvin's spending the night in Geneva when the fiery preacher Farrel pointed his finger at the young scholar and said, "If you do not stay here in Geneva and help the reform movement, God will curse you!" Unusual, I'd say, but would anyone disagree that Calvin was called of God to minister in Geneva? This incident was, of course, properly speaking, God's leading to a specific geographical location, but let us never limit the means God might use to get our attention and help us understand that His hand is upon us for special service.

My own call to ministry was confirmed when my pastor asked me to preach occasionally when I was in Bible school. The affirmation I received resonated with what I believed to be the leading of the Spirit within my heart and mind. I felt "called" as a child to preach, but if the body of Christ had not confirmed my conviction, I could not have pursued the ministerial path.

Often a person senses a call to the ministry but has no leading to a particular organization or church. Again, God uses the body of Christ or a mission board to clarify the next step. Often we are unaware of God's leading, but looking back we can see His hand of guidance on our lives. Indeed, some people who were initially unsure of their call have nevertheless done an effective work for God.

Though the details are different in each case, the end result must be the same: a sense of the divine initiative, a commission that leaves a man or a woman with a settled assurance that he or she is doing what God desires.

Our Response to the Call

Our response to God's call should be one of amazed humility. Each of us should have a sense of authority and boldness. We should be characterized by unusual earnestness and diligence in study and prayer. Jowett perhaps overstated it only slightly when he wrote, "The call of the Eternal must ring through the rooms of his soul as clearly as the sound of the morning-bell rings through the valleys of Switzerland, calling the peasants to early prayer and praise."[4] Spurgeon discouraged men from entering the ministry. He told them plainly that if they could take another vocation they should. He wanted in the ministry only those who felt strongly that they had no other alternative. Luther warned that one should flee the ministry, even if he were wiser than Solomon and David, unless one was called. And "if God needs thee, He will know how to call thee."

How do I account for those who have dropped out of the ministry? Should they feel as if they have failed in their calling? It's possible of course, that some of them have failed. But that doesn't mean God can't use them in other vocations, for He is always working in spite of our failures. Many fallen pastors can be restored as brothers, but they have disqualified themselves from spiritual leadership. Others simply might have considered the ministry as one opportunity among many and therefore lacked the passion that would make them deeply committed to God.

But there may be other explanations. Perhaps such ministers were called, but the body of Christ failed them. Young men have been ruined by critical congregations.

Others may not have failed at all, but worldly standards of success would interpret their ministry that way. Isaiah had a marvelous call, but from a human perspective, he failed in the ministry. Indeed, God told him that practically no one would listen to what he had to say.

Then again, some ministers may be like John Mark; discouraged, they give up at first, but they may become effective in a later ministry.

We do not know all of the contingencies, but let us not allow those difficulties to rob us of a divine sense of calling that gives us our courage and authority. And, as the old saying goes, "If God calls us to preach, let us not stoop to become a king."

• 2 •

A Congregation's Expectations

Can We Adjust?

"If you have the reputation of being an early riser, you can sleep until noon."

I don't remember where I read this bit of insight, but it reminded me that a congregation's perception of its pastor influences, for good or for ill, the effectiveness of his ministry. If he's perceived as dishonest, inept, or indiscreet, his words and actions will be interpreted through a negative grid. If he's thought of as godly and competent, he will be given the benefit of the doubt even when he fails.

Often, this situation puts him at a disadvantage. If he should lose the congregation's goodwill, his ministry might soon be over. But if he consciously attempts to establish and maintain a correct impression, he courts spiritual disaster. We all stand in need of perspective in this matter.

The Pressures of Public Ministry

Pastors are continually open to public evaluation. Preach nine good messages and one blooper, and some people will remember only the message that bombed. Walk past a deacon without acknowledging him, and you might rankle his feelings. And if a disgruntled church member begins some gossip, a little leaven could leaven the whole lump.

We're also under pressure because few members of the congregation know the demands of our schedules. One pastor asked his deacons to outline how they thought he spent his time. Although he was working a seventy-hour week, they had difficulty coming up with a forty-hour week. We've all laughed at the child who says to the pastor's kid, "My dad isn't like yours—he works for a living." But it hurts just the same.

⚘ Once you've gained a reputation, you're more or less stuck with it. I read about a pastor who was at a baseball game when a church member needed him. The irate parishioner spread the story that the pastor spent all his time at the ballpark. Although the pastor nearly ruined his health and family working overtime to correct the false impression, it lingered.

Such perceptions, whether true or false, can wield awesome authority over us. If we are self-conscious, always wondering how well we are liked, we'll soon be slaves to the pulse of our popularity. We will do everything with an eye on our ratings.

At that point, we'll lose our authority to minister. "The fear of man brings a snare" (Prov. 29:25 NASB). We'll desire to remain neutral in disputes, trying earnestly to agree with everyone. We will not administer church discipline for fear of criticism. We'll back away from any unpopular stand, even when it's right. Many pastors are intimidated by confrontation.

I'm not saying we should be insensitive. We've all met the pastor who takes pride in "not caring what anyone thinks" and callously disregards the feelings of others. I'm talking about a lack of boldness even in matters that are clear in the Scriptures.

We'll also find it difficult to rejoice in the success of other pastors. Television has brought the superchurch to our parishioners' living rooms. Comparison is inevitable. We've all had to chime in enthusiastically when we heard glowing comments about the great blessing that "so and so" has been to the life of one of our members. We want to rejoice, too, but the joy doesn't come easily. We may even take secret delight in another's failure. One assistant pastor, who was an apparent threat to the senior pastor, told me, "Nothing would delight him more than if I were to blow it."

When we're overly sensitive to what others think, we'll also live with guilt—the nagging feeling that we could be doing more. Since by definition our work is never finished, we then carry it home with us. My wife would tell you that sometimes I'm not at home even when I'm physically present. I'm preoccupied with the pressures of the day and the ones I'll face tomorrow.

In the process, our faith is eroded. Christ directed this question to the Pharisees: "How can you believe, when you receive glory from one another, and you do not seek the glory that is from the one and only God?" (John 5:44 NASB). The desire for human praise and the faith to minister cancel each other—seek the one and the other eludes you.

When in conflict with the Pharisees, who were somewhat less than enthusiastic about His ministry, Jesus said, "And He who sent Me is with Me; He has not left Me alone, for I always do the things that are pleasing to Him" (John 8:29 NASB).

How can we be that free, that single-minded?

Freedom to Serve

Our Lord was free from men's opinions about Him. Though He cared what they thought because He knew that their eternal destiny depended on whether they believed in Him, His actions were never calculated to gain their praise. The will of the Father was all that mattered. And if the Father was pleased, the Son was pleased. That was why He was just as content when washing the disciples feet as He was when preaching the Sermon on the Mount.

I've known pastors who were like that—surrendered, secure, and free from actions motivated by a desire for human praise. They felt no need to prove themselves or be in the limelight. No grudging admissions about other people's successes—just freedom and joy in the work of the Lord.

What characteristics could we expect if we were brought to such a place of surrender?

First, we would not let people push us into their mold. We all live with the tension between what we are and what others want us to be. We'd like to fulfill the exalted expectations that many people have for us, but we can't. If we know ourselves realistically, both our strengths and weaknesses, we'll not think that we are God's gift to every human need.

Christ faced this tension, too. After He fed the multitude, the crowd sought to crown Him king. But He went off by Himself, refusing to consider the offer, even though He knew that this was a disappointment to His followers. His miracles generated expectations He simply could not fulfill at the time.

Yet before His death He could say He had finished the Father's work, though hundreds of people were still sick and thousands more had not believed on Him. But the pressure of those needs did not blur His vision to please only the Father.

The more blessed people are by our ministry, the greater their expectations of us will be. If we let them, they will lead us to believe that we're the only ones who can lead people to Christ, counsel the emotionally troubled, or visit in the hospital. We do well to heed the words of Bunyan: "He that is low need fear no fall."

And if we believe that we are God's answer to every need, we'll also accept every invitation for lunch, attend all committee meetings, and take outside speaking engagements when asked—all at the expense of our families, our health, and, most of all, our relationship with God.

Let's not let our successes propel us into a role that is beyond our strengths and abilities. Our self-image must always be adjusted to fit reality. Saying no graciously is an essential characteristic of a man who has submitted his will to God.

Second, we would profit from criticism. No one likes criticism, particularly when it's unfair. Furthermore, we usually don't get a chance to give our side of the story without risking additional misunderstanding. Yet sometimes, even when the criticism is valid, our pride prevents us from learning from the experience. When we think of ourselves more highly than we ought to think, we may believe we are beyond rebuke.

Paul also received criticism. He was under fire for going to the Gentiles and was imprisoned because he refused to compromise the inclusive claim of the gospel. Sometimes the condemnation was personal and vindictive: "His letters are weighty and strong, but his personal presence is unimpressive, and his speech contemptible" (2 Cor. 10:10 NASB). But he was undeterred. He knew that God would vindicate him.

Every leader has his critics. If we are especially sensitive, if we cannot tolerate differences of opinion, and if we refuse to learn from criticism, we're still clinging to our reputations.

Many lies were published about revivalist George Whitefield to discourage the crowds from hearing him, but he responded by saying that he could wait until God rendered the final judgment. Such a man of faith cannot be destroyed.

Third, we would not be afraid to let our humanity show. Our congregations believe that we are different—free from the emotional and spiritual struggles of others. After all, if we are not walking in uninterrupted victory, who is left to lean on? Heroes are in short supply, and a pastor who has been a blessing to his flock is a good candidate to fulfill the role.

If we refuse to talk about our failures and share only our victories, we'll reinforce that distorted perception. Eventually, it will give way to myth. One pastor confessed in exhaustion, "My congregation expects me to be perfect." I suggested to him that he be willing to help his people "demythologize" him by discretely letting at least a few of his faults show.

Our lack of authenticity creates a burden that is too heavy to bear. Struggling under its weight, we'll assume we have, indeed, arrived spiritually and, hence, be blind to our shortcomings or kill ourselves trying to live up to others' expectations. We'll also tend to withdraw, fearful that people will get to know what we're really like.

Yet what pastor hasn't done some things of which he's ashamed? If our congregations could open our minds for inspection, we'd all resign in shame and disgrace. We can help our people better when we let them know that we stand with them in the quest for righteousness, neither above nor off to the side, where the arrows of Satan and the passions of the flesh can't touch us. Honesty communicates much better than a false sense of perfection.

One church member wrote a letter to his pastor asking in part, "Are you as human as we are? Have you struggled with some of the same problems we face during the week? Is there discord in your home? Heartache? Anguish? Won't you share that with us, too, as you share your doctrine, your theology, your exposition?"

Finally, we would not see the success of another as a threat to our own ministry. When the Holy Spirit came upon the seventy elders during the ministry of Moses, two men continued to prophesy. Joshua, jealous for Moses' reputation, suggested that Moses restrain them. But Moses replied, "Are you jealous for my sake? Would that all the Lord's people were prophets, that the Lord would put His Spirit upon them!" (Num. 11:29 NASB).

Here was a man who could rejoice in the success of others. He did not want to keep his gift to himself, nor did he have to defend his call to the ministry. Many pastors struggle over the success of another, especially if that individual is on their staff. The fact that God sometimes uses those who are less gifted, or even less authentic than we would like, brings the sin of envy to the surface.

But the person who has died to himself will bow humbly, resisting the temptation to envy simply because God is generous. In the parable of the workers in the vineyard, the landowner said to those who had worked longer hours and grumbled about equal pay, "Is it not lawful for me to do what I wish with what is my own? Or is your eye envious because I am generous?" (Matt. 20:15 NASB).

It's God's prerogative to bless some people more than we think He should. Apart from such grace, we'd all be lost. Friends of John the Baptist were concerned because some of his disciples were leaving to follow Christ. John responded, "A man can receive nothing, unless it has been given him from heaven" (John 3:27 NASB).

If we believed those words, we'd be free from all comparisons, competition, and self-consciousness in the ministry. We'd serve with a glad heart, accepting our role.

Later, John added, "He must increase, but I must decrease" (v. 30).

Even if our ministry should be diminished, we can accept it more easily if Christ is honored through submission to His will. Since our ministry is God-given, we can neither take credit for it nor insist that it continue.

If we have become men pleasers, let's repent. Such an attitude is an affront to God. Subtly, we are preaching ourselves, not Christ.

If you have the reputation of being an early riser, you can sleep until noon. But God knows when you get out of bed, and His perception is the one that really counts.

· 3 ·

Surviving a Skirmish

How Should We Relate to the Board?

Perhaps the most sensitive pressure point in a church organization is the relationship between the pastor and the church board. The details differ, but the story is the same: the pastor wants to take the church one direction, and the board wants to take it another. The pastor believes he receives his orders from God, so the board had better follow him. But the board is unconvinced and digs in its heels, settling down for a long power struggle.

Division can come over anything from the building program to the order of the morning worship service. Pastors and boards have parted company over whether wine should be served for Communion, divorced people should teach in Sunday school, or the carpet should be blue or red.

The issue is often irrelevant; it's who wins that counts. What's at stake is power, and the question of who's in charge must be settled. Eventually, the issue will be settled but often at the expense of a split.

As pastors, we sometimes bring division on ourselves. For some pastors, submitting to the board is a sign of weakness, a denial of a God-given mandate. Some of us think that to be called of God is a guarantee that we know God's will for our congregations. Furthermore, we may think that God blesses only those pastors who stand up for their views regardless of the cost. Our desire to vindicate ourselves is powerful. If our egos are not subdued by the cross, we'll even be tempted to misuse Scripture, warning our detractors that they had better not "touch the Lord's anointed."

The more dictatorial the pastor, the more necessary it will be for him to win on every issue. He interprets even minor matters as a referendum on his leadership, so he must get his way every time. And if the board doesn't grant his wish, he'll resort to pressure, bypassing the board to appeal to the congregation or coercing other leaders in the church. Or he will write an unauthorized letter to the congregation in defense of himself, often in the interest of truth, for the sake of "setting the record straight." Unfortunately, few pastors today are willing to leave some disputes for the Lord to set right at the judgment seat. Such a pastor may not realize that what he gains in the power struggle he loses in credibility and respect.

Peter had a different understanding of the elder's role: "Shepherd the flock of God among you, not under compulsion, but voluntarily, according to the will of God; and not for sordid gain, but with eagerness; nor yet as lording it over those allotted to your charge, but proving to be examples to the flock" (1 Peter 5:2–3 NASB).

Christ taught that the primary quality of leadership was servanthood, not a dictatorial spirit. The Gentiles sought superiority and control; believers should seek humility and submission. The only clear instance of one-man rule in the New Testament is that of Diotrephes, who loved to have the preeminence (3 John 9).

I'm not suggesting, however, that the board is always innocent. I've heard many horror stories of church boards that have driven their pastors to unnecessary resignations. But I'd like to suggest some basic principles that can help us in negotiating the inevitable differences that arise.

The Principle of Accountability

Everyone on the board (including the pastor) must be subject to the board's consensus. After having conducted an exhaustive study of every relevant New Testament passage on the topic, Bruce Stabbert states in his book *The Team Concept*, "In all these passages, there is not one passage which describes a church being governed by one pastor."[1]

Of course, in Baptist polity, deacons usually assume the responsibilities that elders held in the New Testament. But the principle of plurality of leadership still applies, regardless of how churches are organized. The pastor, therefore, has no authority to act independently of his board. He cannot override its vote by an appeal to his divine call simply because all the elders have equal authority. They, too, have a divine call, albeit to a different role and responsibility.

Nor should the pastor threaten to resign unless the controversy merits his resignation. More than one board has called a pastor's bluff and forced him to eat his words or follow through with his threat.

But what if the board is obviously wrong? If the matter involves eternal truth, such as important doctrinal or moral issues, the pastor must warn the offending party of the consequences. There are times when a split may be necessary. As the apostle Paul taught, "For there must also be factions among you, in order that those who are approved may have become evident among you" (1 Cor. 11:19 NASB).

But I've seldom heard of a split because of doctrinal or moral error. Usually it's because of the building program, the pastor's leadership style, or floundering church programs.

When difficulties arise, the pastor often feels slighted, unappreciated, and misunderstood. The innate desire we all have to justify ourselves may take over, and the pastor determines that he will not leave until justice is done.

Paul, however, admonishes us not to avenge ourselves but to let God settle our accounts. Blessed is the pastor-elder who can accept wrong without compromise but also without retaliation. To clarify a matter is one thing, but to persist in being defensive is quite another.

However much he may try to convince the board of his viewpoint, the bottom line is that he must submit to its authority unless a clear point of Scripture is at stake. It's better to leave than to stay to prove a point or to get "justice."

Leadership Through the Board

The pastor must share his vision with those to whom he is accountable. In this task, time and patience bring fruitful dividends when the board acts as one in making decisions for the benefit of the body.

But that kind of unity comes only through prayer and hard work. If the previous pastor had a tarnished reputation, the board will need time to develop confidence in the new pastor's integrity. There will be a trial period until mutual confidence is established.

When a group decision is made, there is also shared responsibility. Does that mean the pastor shouldn't be a strong leader? Not at all. Most boards expect their pastor to take the initiative, to give the ministry direction. In 1 Timothy 5:17, Paul writes, "Let the elders who rule well be considered worthy of double honor, especially those who work hard at preaching and teaching."

The New Testament allows for strong leadership within the plurality of elders. However, if the pastor dictates to the board, and it is not an integral part of the decision-making process, its members may eventually polarize against him. A board may have diversity of opinion about a proposal, of course. But the pastor and the board must be willing to pray and wait until a consensus emerges.

A word of caution: Sometimes a board doesn't stand behind its decisions if members voted yes just for the sake of pleasing the pastor or for the sake of unity. I know one instance in which the board voted unanimously to ask for a staff member's resignation, but individual members reversed themselves after going home and talking it over with their wives. The ability to sense whether a board is sold on an idea or just going along for the ride is an art.

The Board's Responsibility to the Board

The board must keep its members from becoming unruly. The following scenario has happened a thousand times. One board member, usually the unofficial "church boss," itches for recognition and control. He begins to oppose the pastor and pretends to speak for others. The other board members are intimidated. After all, they reason, he's been in the church for years, and his wife plays the piano. So they sit by, hoping the problem will go away. But it only gets worse, and discord spreads.

In one church, an elder ruined the ministry of three pastors by using the same strategy. He would befriend the pastor in the first year and then turn against him in the second. Because of his influence, he'd generate enough opposition to force a showdown. The board was at a loss to deal with the problem, so the members let it go on.

Unfortunately, the board usually believes the pastor is expendable. Pastors come and go, but the elder stays forever. The board must have the strength to discipline its own members. If not, church leaders adopt a double standard, and the work of God is hindered.

Paul gives some specific instructions for confronting an elder. An accusation should not be received except on the basis of two or three witnesses, and if an elder continues in sin, he should be rebuked publicly (1 Tim. 5:19–20). The pastor must enlist the cooperation of other board members when calling a fellow elder to accountability.

If Satan can't get a pastor to ruin his own reputation, he will try to create friction between the pastor and the board. Without unity, we can conquer neither the world nor the devil. As Benjamin Franklin said at the signing of the Declaration of Independence, "We must all hang together, or assuredly, we shall all hang separately."

Let's redouble our effort to obey Paul's admonition to be "diligent to preserve the unity of the Spirit in the bond of peace" (Eph. 4:3). Anything less will cause the body of Christ to work against itself.

Let the hard work begin.

• 4 •

Problem People

Confrontation or Compromise?

A friend of mine, fresh out of Bible college, became the pastor of a small country church. One day, the elders asked him to visit a wealthy member who hadn't been attending regularly but continued to contribute to the church coffers.

"We don't think he's even a Christian," they said. So at their insistence, he visited the old gentleman and asked him point-blank if he was saved. The man became incensed at the pastor's audacity to suggest that he, a self-made man, was not a Christian.

Several weeks later, the church building burned. The congregation met in a schoolroom to decide what to do. After they decided to rebuild, the man whose salvation had been questioned stood up.

"This young man had the nerve to question whether I was a Christian," he stated. "What do you suggest we do about it?"

He sat down with an air of importance, waiting for a response. Silence.

"I move we terminate him as pastor," the man said.

There was some discussion, but not one of the elders rose to defend their pastor and explain that he had been acting on their request. Later, a vote was taken, and the young man was given two weeks to resign.

After the meeting, no one came to speak to him except a school janitor who overheard what had happened over the public address system. The pastor left the building and began walking in blinding rain mile after mile, scarcely aware of where he was going.

That was thirty-five years ago. He has never pastored another church. He has served the Lord as a layperson, but that one devastating experience could never be erased from his memory.

Techniques of Opposition

Most of us haven't had such an experience. But perhaps we've had board members who supported us in meetings but criticized us to others on Sunday. We've all had to work with people who are negative, critical, and obnoxious. In one church, a man takes notes diligently with the intent of keeping the pastor straight on his theology. After each service he confronts the pastor, explaining how he could improve his preaching.

Recently, a pastor told me about a parishioner who opposed his ministry. The critic would approach a member of the congregation and throw him some bait.

"You know, I've met people within the congregation who question whether the pastor should . . ."

If the person said he strongly supported the pastor, the man would back off. Because he claimed to be speaking for others in the congregation, he faced no personal risk. But if the person expressed some agreement, the critic would sow bitter seeds of discord. He was a garbage collector. He went from person to person gathering grievances. Eventually, he stirred up enough trouble to force the pastor's resignation.

Ironically, sometimes the person who befriends the pastor when he first arrives is the one who later turns against him. The man is attracted to the pastor because he wants to brief him on the way things really are. But if the pastor doesn't agree with him right down the line, he will soon become his adversary. To see the pastor succeed would be his greatest disappointment.

The problem person sees himself not as difficult to live with but as a loyal member of the congregation just doing his duty. Many such a person has sent a pastor to an early grave either unaware of his destructive influence or sincerely thinking that the pastor deserved to be punished. Remember, disgruntled people always cloak their actions with verses of Scripture; they speak of having the "pastor's best interests at heart." Spirituality and the Bible are both pressed into service to justify self-serving or unwise behavior.

This problem is difficult because most problem people will not face the pastor directly to resolve their disagreements. They ignore Christ's teaching about going directly to the person with whom one has a dispute (Matt. 18:15–17). They prefer to give their speech at a public meeting where they can claim to speak for others—and at the same time poison the atmosphere of the whole church. The pastor may find it difficult to defend himself for fear he might be viewed as unspiritual. And even if he does have a legitimate defense, the damage has been done.

One elder who was silent when the board voted to borrow money for a building program stood at a congregational meeting and insisted that the church was in sin because it had chosen to borrow money. The division that resulted took about a year to resolve. Of course, it never dawned on him that he was in sin for publicly chastising the church rather than voicing his concern in board meetings and working though proper channels of authority.

Handling Dragons

How shall we cope with difficult people in our congregations? First, we must listen carefully to what they are saying—they might be right. Some pastors are so sensitive to criticism that they tend to reject all negative comments. But even if we think the person has been unfair, there may be some truth to what he has said.

Many a potential problem has been diffused by simply giving our friend an honest hearing. In fact, he may be doing us a favor. "Reprove a wise man, and he will love you" (Prov. 9:8 NASB). Others in the congregation may have the same criticisms but haven't felt free to tell you. In *Well-Intentioned Dragons*, Marshall Shelley writes, "Solitary shots should be ignored, but when they come from several directions, it's time to pay attention. As someone else once said, 'If one calls you a donkey, ignore him. If two call you a donkey, check for hoof prints. If three call you a donkey, get a saddle.'"[1]

After you've heard the friend's criticism, you must see the problem in perspective. You can receive a hundred compliments, but it's that one criticism that sticks in your mind. Many a pastor has spent a sleepless night because of a single negative remark.

But now is the time for sober analysis. Is the criticism at least partially correct? Is it because of a difference in style or leadership philosophy, or might it be a personality conflict? If you've hurt someone's feelings, even unintentionally, humble yourself and ask forgiveness. If you can resolve the difference by a personal meeting, by all means do it.

One pastor with an opposing board member sensed trouble for months, but he refused to take the man out for lunch because he feared direct confrontation. His refusal only increased the alienation. Finally, reconciliation became impossible.

Not all disagreements are necessarily bad or evidence of carnality. Remember, Barnabas wanted to take Mark on the second missionary journey, but Paul disagreed, reminding him that the young man had deserted them in Pamphylia. Luke wrote, "And there arose such a sharp disagreement that they separated from one another, and Barnabas took Mark with him and sailed away to Cyprus" (Acts 15:39 NASB).

Sometimes there is no easy answer to who is right or wrong. If possible, work out a solution to accommodate the critic's legitimate complaints. Maybe you could change the order of worship from time to time or begin to teach that Bible class. Many a potential trouble-maker has been diffused by reasonable compromise.

But there are some critics (Shelley calls them "dragons") who will never be satisfied. We've all had critics who criticized us (and everyone else) to satisfy their own deep personal problem; they might have ego needs that defy resolution. They are like the drunkard who'd had strong-smelling cheese smeared on his mustache before he left the saloon. As the man staggered into the clear night air he muttered, "The whole world stinks!"

With such a person, you must make a choice. Ask yourself, "How deeply do I feel about this matter? Can I live with the situation, accepting it from God as His means of personal refinement?" Spurgeon said, "Get a friend to tell you your faults, or better still, welcome an enemy who will watch you keenly and sting you savagely. What a blessing such an irritating critic will be to a wise man, what an intolerable nuisance to a fool!"[2]

Taking a Stand

But perhaps you think the matter is important enough to put your reputation on the line. If there appears to be no resolution, and if the disagreement interferes with your ability to minister, then you must throw the matter into the lap of the board and be prepared to accept the consequences.

Scripture teaches that those who walk disorderly should be disciplined. Paul wrote, "And if anyone does not obey our instruction in this letter, take special note of that man and do not associate with him, so that he may be put to shame. And yet do not regard him as an enemy, but admonish him as a brother" (2 Thess. 3:14–15).

If the board backs you decisively and admonishes those who sow discord, you can continue your ministry with confidence. If you have built solid relationships with board members, they will be prepared to give your viewpoint due consideration. But if the board thinks the criticism is justified, or if the men are too weak to stand against those who would polarize the church, you may have no recourse but to resign. Seldom does the decision to "stay no matter what" have a good result.

Unfortunately, board members tend to side with those who've been their friends in the church for many years. It's particularly difficult when the troublemaker is married to the choir leader or is related to four other families in the congregation. Unfortunately, most of us cannot handle problems with complete objectivity; friendships, old loyalties, and partial information often cloud our ability to act as we should.

In one church, the entire board opposed the pastor because of the persuasive power of one woman who had indirectly controlled the church for years. In a vendetta against the pastor, she even suggested that he should divorce his wife, though they had been happily married for thirty-eight years! Yet, board members were so mesmerized by her that they accepted her criticisms, and the pastor was forced to resign.

In such situations, a pastor can either carry his hurts with him and poison his future usefulness to God or come to terms with the injustice. This particular pastor committed the matter to the Lord, believing that God would ultimately untangle the mess at the judgment seat. He has been blessed in special ways and will undoubtedly be used of God in the future.

Peter Marshall said, "It is a fact of Christian experience that life is a series of troughs and peaks. In His efforts to get permanent possession of the soul, God relies on the troughs more than the peaks.

And some of His special favorites have gone through longer and deeper troughs than anyone else."[3]

Remember, when we encounter dragons who are believers, God loves them too. He can use us in their lives, but He can also use them in ours. There is no one correct answer to all situations. But Shelley does state one cardinal rule: *When attacked by a dragon, do not become one.*

As my friend said, "God will have to untangle many things at the judgment seat." Sometimes it's best to leave the problem with Him rather than try to solve it ourselves.

• 5 •

Preaching

How Can We Reach Their Souls?

Charles Spurgeon once walked into a new auditorium and tested the acoustics by shouting, "Behold the Lamb of God, which taketh away the sin of the world." A workman who overheard him was smitten with conviction and was converted.

Some preachers get a better response than others. If ten pastors preached the same message verbatim, the results would not be the same. Some pastors exude instant charisma; others are more yielded to the Spirit or have greater gifts. It's not just *what* is said but *who* says it that makes the difference.

Sermons with good content may fall flat for many reasons. Perhaps the most common reason is that they are delivered with an absence of feeling. We've all fallen into the rut of preaching unfelt truth. We've rattled through a message as if it were a stock market report at the end of a lackluster day of trading. Vance Havner said, "I've never heard a sermon from which I didn't get something, but I've had some mighty close calls."

When I was a teenager, I wondered why the pastor didn't simply mimeograph his messages and mail them. That would have enabled us to get the truth without the effort of going to church. Now I wonder if I entertained such thoughts because the pastor preached so nonchalantly that his personal delivery added little to the message.

Preaching is not just giving a message. "Is preaching the art of making a sermon and delivering it?" asked Bishop William A. Quayle. "Why no, that's not preaching. *Preaching is the art of making a preacher and delivering that!*"

It's the preacher's delivering himself that is absent from so many of our pulpits on Sunday mornings. Many preachers have no fire in their bones.

Michael Tucker, a pastor in Colorado, writes of an effective preacher: "Preaching must pump his heart until he lives and breathes the message. The message will hound him, drive him, even explode within him. So great will be the desire to preach that he will find it difficult to wait for the time to deliver the message of God."

George Whitefield preached with intensity. He wrote to a friend, "Speak every time as if it was your last. Weep out, if possible, every argument, and as it were, compel them to cry, 'Behold how he loveth us!'"

Jesuit theologian Walter Burghardt deplores the perfunctory remarks made by priests in their homilies. He laments that the laity of the Roman Catholic Church is "puzzled by our ability to declaim about the divine without a shred of feeling or emotion." His words apply to many evangelical ministers, too.

Three Styles of Preaching

Richard Owen Roberts, author of the book *Revival*, speaks of three levels of sermon preparation. The first level is mouth-to-ear preaching. That's when a man is greatly concerned about the choice and organization of his words. He's conscious of the need for good illustrations and vivid descriptions. He's careful to work on key phrases and unique expressions. A typical listener responds, "What a lovely sermon. I really enjoyed it!"

Then there is head-to-head preaching. It stimulates thought and challenges the minds of the listeners. The preacher aims at being well organized, theologically accurate, and enlightening. At the door he hears, "That was a great sermon. I never thought of that before."

In soul-to-soul preaching, the preacher spends hours preparing his message but equal time preparing his soul. Only that kind of preaching results in conversions and personal holiness.

That explains why some of the most effective preachers are not the most eloquent. Some preachers who have only ordinary gifts are used in extraordinary ways because they deliver not only the message but also themselves. Quite literally, they become the message they are preaching.

The Three Persons Participate in Preaching

How can we preach in such a way that we stir the emotions and move the will? Shouting won't do it, nor will dramatic stories. We must become intimately aware of the three personalities involved in the preaching event.

The first such personality is God. Peter wrote, "Whoever speaks, let him speak, as it were, the utterances of God" (1 Peter 4:11 NASB). A preacher speaks on God's behalf; if the sermon is boring, repetitious, or perfunctory, that's the way the congregation will perceive God's message.

Does God have a relevant word for today? Has He spoken with clarity about the issues that face the members of our congregations? Can He demolish walls of hatred and suspicion among families and believers? All of these and a hundred other questions are being answered when we speak on His behalf.

We can't represent Him effectively unless we spend time meditating on His attributes. We must stand in awe of His holiness as displayed in that thunderous revelation at Mount Sinai, of His sovereignty in creation and history, of His love as shown at the cross.

For thus says the high and exalted One
Who lives forever, whose name is Holy,
"I dwell on a high and holy place,
And also with the contrite and lowly of spirit
In order to revive the spirit of the lowly
And to revive the heart of the contrite."
(Isa. 57:15 NASB)

We must be diligent in rekindling our emotional fires for preaching by grasping anew the wonder of our privilege as messengers of the Most High. We must know Him well before we can effectively represent Him to others.

The second person invoked in the sermon is the listener. Let's discard the idea that if we talk others will listen. People do not come to church with open minds. Haddon Robinson, of Gordon Conwell School of Theology, says, "Heads are neither open nor hollow. Heads have lids, screwed on tightly, and no amount of pouring can force ideas inside. Minds open only when their owners sense a need to open them.

Even then, ideas must still filter through layers of experience, habit, prejudice, fear, and suspicion."

Anger, for example, may prevent a person from listening. A parishioner's teenage son fell asleep at the wheel of his car and was killed. The insensitive pastor said to the distraught father, "Don't expect me to take the funeral, because I'm going on vacation." The father told me later, "Even though he was a good preacher, after that remark I never heard a word he said in his sermons."

That anecdote illustrates an important principle of communication: You can preach up a storm, but if a person is not disposed to listen, it penetrates no farther than water on a marble slab.

Or maybe the parishioner is thinking about the pressures of the past week, family problems, or financial reversals. Add to that the depravity of the natural mind and Satan's ability to snatch the Word of God from people's hearts, and it's a miracle that communication takes place at all.

We can't pry through this grid unless we genuinely love our people and bear their needs close to our hearts. Information alone will not change their attitudes and behavior. They must see us bleed along with them. We must enter into the hurts of their world.

Finally, there is the preacher. He must apply the truth to himself before he shares it with others. That is difficult for those of us who preach two or three times a week. But we cannot afford to pass on truths that are supposed to work for others but haven't worked for us. We must share ourselves so that people can see we are a part of the message we are bringing. Our people want to know that we are human, that we share in the griefs and hopes of mortals.

Expressing honest feelings isn't easy. Bombarded with human need, we insulate ourselves from the emotional overload we encounter daily. We are unable to weep for those in need as Christ did when He stood on the Mount of Olives and wept for Jerusalem. Seminary has trained us to think deeply but not to feel deeply. One writer well says that "a preacher must think clearly and feel deeply and cause his hearers to do the same."

The effectiveness of our preaching would rise dramatically if we followed a simple rule: Let's not preach beyond our experience. When we share the message God has given us, we should know it well enough that we can concentrate on its content rather than worry about remembering its outline. Only then can we say with authority, "Thus says the Lord."

Perhaps we ought to follow John Owen, a Puritan scholar and pastor of the seventeenth century, in taking a vow before we step into the pulpit: "I therefore hold myself bound in conscience and in honor, not even to imagine that I have attained a proper knowledge of any one article of truth, much less to publish it, unless through the Holy Spirit I have had such a taste of it, in its spiritual sense, that I may be able from the heart to say with the psalmist, 'I have believed and therefore have spoken.'"[1]

When I taught homiletics at an evangelical seminary, I wanted to illustrate to the class how dependent we must be on God when preaching, especially to the unconverted. So I held the class in a cemetery and began by reading Ephesians 2:1–6, "And you were dead in your trespasses and sins. . . ." Then I asked one of the students to preach to one of the dead, telling a man who had long since been buried that the day of resurrection had come. When he refused (thinking that I wasn't serious), I did it myself. "Jonathan!" I shouted at the grave stone, "It is the day of resurrection!" Thankfully, there was no response!

Then I turned to the students and said, "I felt very foolish doing that. I knew that Jonathan, buried in 1912, would not rise. But that is how foolish we are when we preach the gospel, except for one fact: God might graciously grant a resurrection!"

Paul continues, "But God, being rich in mercy, because of His great love with which He loved us, even when we were dead in our transgressions, made us alive together with Christ (by grace you have been saved), and raised us up with Him, and seated us with Him in the heavenly places, in Christ Jesus" (Eph. 2:4–6 NASB).

I reminded the class that God asked Ezekiel to speak to dry bones, and God then created flesh and breathed life into the corpses. Then we knelt in the cemetery to ask God to give us the grace to preach the gospel with a sense of helplessness, with a conscious dependence on God and His grace. Only He can raise the dead; only He can grant them the ability and the faith to believe.

In brief, my philosophy of preaching is to expect people to be changed forever because of the ministry of the Word. Of course, that might not always be achieved, but if we aim at anything less, I fear we shall hit it! If we spend as much time preparing our hearts as we do our minds, our congregations will know that they have heard from God. Our utter dependence upon His grace will show.

Let us pray that God will make preaching the agent of transformation God intended it to be.

> Get yourself up on a high mountain,
> O Zion, bearer of good news,
> Lift up your voice mightily,
> O Jerusalem, bearer of good news;
> Lift it up, do not fear.
> Say to the cities of Judah,
> "Here is your God!"
> (Isa. 40:9 NASB)

When we preach, God just might do a miracle!

• 6 •

Christian Loafers

Can We Get Them in Step?

Faithfulness—you've preached on it; so have I. But have our sermons done much good? At a recent pastors' conference, several men shared their frustration about the casual attitude some believers have in serving the church. Every congregation can boast of a few dependable, joyful volunteers. Unfortunately, they are sometimes the exception rather than the rule.

The casually committed are those who habitually arrive late to every meeting. Some of them must even plan to be late. I'm sure they haven't heard the invocation of a morning service for years.

Then there are those who never let anyone know when they will be absent. Sunday school teachers, ushers, and committee workers simply don't show up for their assigned responsibilities. Consequently, someone has to scurry around looking for a harried replacement.

We're all acquainted with those who accept responsibilities but don't follow through. Jane promises to offer Donna a ride; John will see if Bill needs further counsel; Peter vows to write an important letter; Frank assures us he will be at the next committee meeting. But nothing happens—not this week or the next five.

Our congregations are also populated by those who justify their negligence with flimsy excuses. "We had company," someone will say. "The weather turned cold [or hot or windy or humid, depending on your location]," others say.

Such performances would not be tolerated in the secular world. Many believers who would never be late on Monday morning shirk their Sunday duties without a twinge of conscience. Of course, we can't threaten to fire them.

An Army of Volunteers

"Remember, these are all volunteers," someone once said to me. "You can't fire people who don't get paid. When you've got a volunteer army, you take what you can get."

So we continue with latecomers, promise breakers, and procrastinators. And our volunteer army limps along. Many of us can appreciate this parody of the hymn "Onward Christian Soldiers":

> Like a mighty turtle,
> Moves the church of God;
> Brothers, we are treading
> Where we've always trod.

In a recent *Atlantic Monthly* article, James Fallows bemoans the deterioration of the U.S. Army since the draft was abandoned. He quotes an essay published in 1980 by William Hauser, a retired colonel.

Hauser claims there are four elements sustaining the "will to fight." To learn *submission*, a soldier must repeat disagreeable tasks. To counter *fear*, he must know and trust his comrades. That will encourage him to fight alongside them instead of running in the wrong direction. To evoke *loyalty*, the Army requires that the men sleep, work, and eat together. They will eventually gain a sense of responsibility for one another's welfare. Finally, the army attempts to develop a sense of *pride* that will remind a man that others depend on him and value his contribution to the unit's safety and success. Thus he fights, hoping that he will not be brought home in a body bag.

Each of those qualities, however, has diminished with the volunteer force. Recruitment is now based largely on self-interest rather than on service to our nation. As a result, those who enlist are only casually committed. They are more interested in retirement benefits than in whether they are really prepared to fight.

Sound familiar? I think it's time we challenged the notion that the church is a volunteer army. Since when did God give us the option of enlisting? Does He discuss terms of commitment with us? Should faithfulness be expected only of those who get paid for their work?

Do we have the right to expect less on Sunday morning than we do on Monday morning?

An Army Under Orders

Let's remind ourselves of some facts. First, we didn't choose Christ; He chose us. Jesus said, "You did not choose Me, but I chose you, and appointed you, that you should go and bear fruit" (John 15:16 NASB). As Commander in Chief, He has a role for each of us to play. We are, as Peter Marshall pointed out, "sealed under orders."

Our Commander decides how and where the battles should be fought. Paul learned submission and obedience by becoming Christ's bondslave. We can't ignore the divine call without becoming an outright deserter.

Second, faithfulness in small details promotes greater responsibility. "He who is faithful in a very little thing is faithful also in much; and he who is unrighteous in a very little thing is unrighteous also in much" (Luke 16:10 NASB).

As pastors, we wouldn't think of being late for a morning worship service. After all, it's a public event. But is it any less important to be on time for Sunday school or a counseling appointment? In the eyes of men, yes; in the eyes of God, no.

When it comes to seeking obedience from their children, parents care little whether they are working on minor or major tasks. It's the child's attitude of obedience that counts. Our heavenly Father shares the same sentiments. When we are unfaithful in "small" matters, we insult our Commander in Chief. He doesn't overlook apparently insignificant details. Even a cup of cold water offered in Christ's name merits reward.

Third, our motivation must be to please the Lord, not men. Paul wrote to Timothy, "No soldier in active service entangles himself in the affairs of everyday life, so that he may please the one who enlisted him as a soldier" (2 Tim. 2:4 NASB).

In Napoleon's army, men endured physical pain, illness, or even the sacrifice of an arm or leg just for an approving nod from their leader. Nothing will purify our motives like deciding to be obedient to Jesus, regardless of whether we are recognized in this world.

When washing the disciples' feet or preaching the Sermon on the Mount, Christ had the same motivation. He said, "I always do the things that are pleasing to [My Father]" (John 8:29 NASB). He wasn't playing the game of life for the benefit of His contemporaries. He did not consider Himself merely a volunteer but a humble servant compelled to do the Father's will.

Even the ungodly are faithful when they're getting paid. Christians, however, should be distinguished by their positive attitudes toward minor, unrewarded tasks. They should have the faith to believe that they will be rewarded in another world. After all, is it not our view of eternity that separates us from the values of this temporal world?

How can we, like Gideon, distinguish between the committed worker and the one who is along for the ride? We might want to grant an honorable discharge to anyone within the church who is shirking his or her responsibilities. It is better, though, for people to recognize their own deficiencies and dismiss themselves from active service.

Begin by establishing written performance standards for church positions. Those could include attendance, follow-through in responsibilities, and an outline of acceptable performance. Then share the guidelines with committees and board members. Let it be known that church leaders expect faithfulness. Let it also be known that the same leaders set an example of faithfulness to others.

Don't be afraid to let someone go. If you need to, leave a position vacant. That is a better option than filling it with another nonperformer. Look and wait for a qualified, reliable replacement. And pray. Then pray again.

Pastors, we need to display faithfulness in our own responsibilities. God will eventually provide a core of dedicated soldiers, willing to endure hardship for the cause of Christ. Increasing the number of dependable, qualified, and deeply committed believers starts with us.

A volunteer army will never do. Only one conscripted by a higher calling will have the determination to finish the task.

• 7 •

Church Splits

When Are They Worth the Cost?

I'm weary of hearing about church splits over trivial issues. In one church, a few men wanted their pastor to enforce a dress code and to conduct the services according to their liking. He didn't fully accommodate them. Because they thought their authority was slighted, small matters were magnified. Soon, everything the pastor did was wrong. His detractors scrutinized his sermons to find hidden meanings directed toward them.

The pastor resigned. He probably had the support of 90 percent of the congregation, but he grew tired of the hassle. He was not a fighter. He left an effective ministry because of a few disgruntled members. Just recently another pastor friend of mine did the same thing. Some of the leadership wanted his church to be a clone of a larger church in the same area. He could not take the constant comparisons, which he deemed to be unfair.

How long has it been since you heard that a church was divided because of the Virgin Birth or salvation by faith in Christ alone? Most of the strife I hear about concerns budgets, music, or leadership philosophy. Often, the real issue is who's in charge.

These resignations caused me to reflect on this question: What should a church member do if he or she wants to voice a legitimate complaint? Most of the people are not on a church board, yet they have deep feelings about the ministry of the church. If we are wise, we will find ways by which we can forestall some of these disagreements.

What Usually Happens?

Unfortunately, many church members take one of two courses of action when they have a complaint. The first course is to share criticism with others in order to drum up support. The tongue is the greatest cause for division within the church. "And the tongue is a fire, the very world of iniquity; the tongue is set among our members as that which defiles the entire body, and sets on fire the course of our life, and is set on fire by hell" (James 3:6 NASB).

To use our tongues to rally support for our viewpoints is to spread the fires of hell within the church. Sometimes the church is already polarized over an issue before the elders or the pastor even know about the problem. Certainly, there is a time to speak, but that time does not come as frequently as some people think it does.

An equally disastrous procedure is to bring up the matter in a church business meeting. Often, this is done to score points publicly even when no attempt has been made to resolve the issue privately. Any matter that can be dealt with between one or two members or that could be cared for through other legitimate channels should never be mentioned for public discussion.

I know a pastor who was humiliated in a church business meeting; he had to endure totally unexpected personal criticisms. Surely Satan must rejoice in church meetings where everyone feels he has the freedom to air his favorite gripe.

We must instruct our congregations on the need for unity, but at the same time we should allow for dialogue regarding disagreements. If not, resentment and misunderstanding will only build. People must feel that their complaints have been heard.

What Can Be Done?

First, *we ourselves must set an example of submission*. Paul wrote, "Be subject to one another in the fear of Christ" (Eph. 5:21 NASB). I wince when I hear a pastor teach his congregation to submit to authority when he believes he is an exception to the rule. "I'm accountable to God alone" sounds pious, but it can be poisonous.

The New Testament teaches that a congregation is to have a plurality of godly leaders with no one person assuming the role of dictator. Though some congregations are polite enough to tolerate authoritarianism, others chafe under the strain. Individuals know that their input is worthless because the pastor receives his instruction privately from God.

Or at times a pastor might be defensive, unwilling to accept criticism. He might listen politely, but in his heart he is convinced that whatever is said is untrue. We all find it difficult to see ourselves objectively; some pastors find it impossible. Every comment is deflected, unable to penetrate the mind or the heart.

Don't be surprised, then, when believers feel frustrated in their attempts to get their points across. If the pastor is a law unto himself, why cannot they be? Like pastor, like people.

No doubt many churches have split because God wanted to bring the pastor and the congregation to a place of mutual submission. But when the pastor isn't responsive to the authority of his board, the congregation often rejects the authority of the pastor as well. Meanwhile, the gap between the pastor and the board widens.

As church leaders, we must set an example of humility. We cannot exercise authority unless we ourselves are under authority. That does not mean that we back down over every issue; certainly, there are times when we must defend ourselves. But how, when, and why are important.

Second, *we must teach that Matthew 18:15–16 applies to all kinds of disagreements.* "And if your brother sins, go and reprove him in private; if he listens to you, you have won your brother. But if he does not listen to you, take one or two more with you, so that by the mouth of two or three witnesses every fact may be confirmed."

The believer is responsible to go directly to the person against whom he has a grievance. If the issue involves specific sin, then there is an obligation to go to the person even if he is a church leader. But Paul warned, "Do not receive an accusation against an elder except on the basis of two or three witnesses" (1 Tim. 5:19 NASB).

If the issue remains unresolved, then others—particularly other members of the church board—must become involved. And the elder or pastor must defer to their authority.

But what about opposition to a building program, the pastor's salary, or the length of his sermons? To discuss such disagreements with members of the congregation sows seeds of discord that grieve the heart of God. Here also, members should go directly to the person responsible, even if it means a trip to the pastor's office or writing him a signed letter.

At this point, our attitude as pastors is critical. If we ignore what is said or if we dismiss the criticism without learning from it, we may be encouraging the concerned member to try another approach—to recruit other members to his position through gossip.

I've found that an honest discussion clears the air and can cement a relationship, even if the disagreement persists. There's something gratifying about having someone else try earnestly to see your point of view, even if he remains unconvinced. What is difficult is when a parishioner thinks he has not even been heard.

That doesn't mean we have to agree with everything that is said to us. But I've often found that there may be more truth to criticism than we are willing to admit. It's easy to listen politely but then dismiss what has been said without thoughtful consideration and prayer.

In my opinion, if a church member takes a matter of concern to a member of the board, that is as far as he or she should go in their criticisms of the pastor. Even if the board fails in their responsibility, members do not have a biblical mandate to begin petitions, write letters, and use the telephone to drum up support for their cause. The New Testament pattern is that a church be led by a plurality of godly leaders. If you cannot agree with the action of the board, you might want to think about worshiping elsewhere.

Of course, I don't mean to stifle profitable discussion among church members about improving the ministry or talking about matters in preparation for a church business meeting. We should expect our people to discuss various ministries within the church. But once a decision is made, there must be submission to the will of those in authority.

Waiting for God

In a day when people demand their rights, it's difficult for a congregation to submit to church leaders and wait for God to work His will even in controversial decisions. Sometimes a member of the congregation might have an idea that is correct, but the timing is wrong. We forget that God works among His people despite diversity of opinion and imperfections of church leaders.

That fact applies to those of us who are on a church board as well. I've had to submit to the will of leaders even on those occasions when I may have had a difference of opinion. God is honored when we are willing to set aside disagreements over non-biblical issues for the unity and harmony of the body.

Only heaven will reveal the damage done to the body of Christ by members of the congregation who feel called to correct all the faults of the church or to campaign for their pet grievances. We have too many people who believe that their spiritual gift is that of criticism.

I fear for those who are determined to force the resignation of a man of God by petty criticisms. I fear for those who have divided a congregation because of intransigence over a building program or the proposed budget.

Yes, there are times when a church split is justified, perhaps even necessary. But let's be sure that it's over a clear biblical issue and not just a preference we hold dear.

Paul wrote, "If any man destroys the temple of God, God will destroy him, for the temple of God is holy, and that is what you are" (1 Cor. 3:17 NASB). The word *temple* refers to the congregation of believers. God says He will destroy the one who destroys the work of the church. Often, He grants that person a hard and bitter heart, or He may use other means of discipline.

Dr. Paul Brand says that white blood cells, the armed forces of the body, guard against invaders. When the body's been cut, these cells abruptly stop their aimless wandering and home in from all different directions on the scene of the battle. As if they have a sense of smell, they hurry through tissue via the most direct route. When they arrive, many of them give their lives to kill the bacteria. They subject themselves to the good of the larger organism that determines their duties. If a cell should lose its loyalty and cling to its own life, it shares the benefits of the body but sets up a rival organism called cancer.

Our churches are filled with parasites who benefit from the ministry but who refuse to submit themselves to the leader of the organism. As a result, the body is cancerous, weak, and unprepared for battle. Sometimes, so much energy is spent in resolving internal conflict that there is no time to confront the world with Jesus Christ.

If we're guilty of dividing the body, we'd better repent. When we disagree with church leaders, we should talk to God rather than to our friends. He is able to direct His own church in His own time and in His own way. To destroy the temple of God is to toy with the wrath of God.

• 8 •

Politics

Where Should We Draw the Line?

Some preachers have jumped into the political arena with both feet, causing us to rethink our stand on political involvement. Christians by the hundreds of thousands are becoming politically active. The religious right is a force that cannot be ignored.

There are good arguments in favor of political activism. Americans are entitled to work through the political process to effect change. Why should evangelicals sell out to radical feminists, gay liberationists, and abortionists? We have an agenda of our own and a right to be heard. Perhaps the ballot box does speak louder than words.

What better way to get our message across than to organize and vote the humanists out of office? Why not elect those who would enact laws that reflect a more biblical approach to morality? In a democracy, political power talks.

Then there is the precedent set by liberal religious organizations such as the World Council of Churches, which uses political clout to accomplish social and economic change. Why can't we do the same?

Evangelicals, often marginalized as an embarrassing anachronism in American history, have finally tasted political power. With the rise of the religious right, liberal politicians have had to take stock of their positions. After all, some people think that Christians, if well organized, can "throw the bums out."

I agree that we can be grateful for every Christian in politics; we ought to support organizations that attempt to educate the religious constituency about the issues being debated in Washington. Christians ought to make their influence felt in local and national elections and to speak up for what they believe. Often, we've lost crucial battles by default.

Yet, I am troubled because I believe that we are being tempted to fight the battle in a way that undermines the very message we want the world to hear. Ask the average person what Christians believe, and he will give you a long agenda: they are opposed to abortion, hate gays, and want television programs censored. He will also probably say that they want to impose their agenda on everyone.

Regardless of whether such a characterization is fair, we are stuck with it. And perhaps the reason is because we have fought too many battles under the Christian banner; we have needlessly confused the issues and have often done so with bigotry, anger, and a victim mentality. We have often not represented Christ with clarity and charity.

I am troubled when I see ministers speak out on matters that would be better left to politicians. As a minister, I have no right to endorse a political candidate, even if he happens to be a Christian who holds a biblical worldview. Speaking as a private citizen is one thing, but to use the pulpit as a platform for political endorsement is another. We must remember that we have a responsibility to speak to all political parties; we must stand for truth in all walks of life, and we dare not confuse the Cross with partisan politics.

But there are other dangers as well.

The Dangers of Political Involvement

As was already indicated, biblical and political issues tend to be mixed together as one lump. If we label all of these issues "Christian," we can easily be misunderstood. Indeed, the message of the Cross can be severely compromised when it is encumbered by a host of agendas.

Abortion is a biblical issue, we can all unite in opposition to the arbitrary killing of human life. But what about tax breaks for families and term limits for congressmen? These and a half-dozen other issues have been supported under the Christian banner. They are worthy issues, perhaps, but such legislation can be supported by many non-Christians, too. The problem is that people no longer think of Christ when they think of Christianity; it is a political agenda that comes to mind.

Second, I fear that political reformation could subtly substitute for spiritual transformation. Of course, we all favor laws that reflect biblical morality. But even such progress falls far short of the real answer to our national decay. Ultimately, it is only the gospel of Christ that can stem the tide of moral decadence.

Suppose that prayer is restored in the public schools. In our society, such prayer would be based on the lowest common denominator of all religions. Christ's name would not be mentioned, hardly a credit to the One whose sacrifice is the only means of reconciling our nation to God. We would be forcing unbelieving teachers and students to recite a prayer with their mouths, though they resent it in their hearts. Most countries in Europe still have prayer in schools, but that has not kept the church strong, nor has it prevented moral and spiritual stagnation. Might we do better to restore prayer back to our churches instead?

Suppose that teaching creationism in our public schools was mandatory. That would hardly make our public schools Christian. Whatever lip service such laws would achieve, it would fall short of the change of heart God desires.

Civil religion can help bring about a moral reformation. But at the same time, it gives a false sense of security. We may honor God with our lips, but our hearts are far from Him. We know that the law cannot save an individual; neither can it save a country. As ministers, we must teach our people never to settle for less than the radical transformation that the gospel can bring.

Third, what if we simply don't have the political power to bring about reform? And when we openly join with those who explicitly deny the gospel in our effort to turn America back to God, are we not thereby leaning on a broken reed? The issues that unite us with other religions cannot possibly be the primary mission of the church.

Yes, we might win some battles and make a few reforms. But our gains are dependent on the ballot box. In a democratic political process, one reaction will always spawn another. Someone once said that "the art of politics is the art of destroying your enemies." To fight moral issues with political muscle is a high-risk venture that fluctuates each passing year. Fighting spiritual battles with carnal weapons is even more sure to fail.

Christ was largely silent about political matters. He never encouraged a revolution against Rome. Paul did not speak out against slavery lest Christianity be charged with causing political upheaval. Instead, he taught slaves to "regard their own masters as worthy of all honor so that the name of God and our doctrine may not be spoken against" (1 Tim. 6:1 NASB). Admittedly, in those days slavery was so interwoven with the fabric of society that overthrowing the practice would have been impossible. Indeed, in later centuries Christianity was the force that battled slavery. But the point is that Paul did not want to identify with external political and social changes that might detract from the purity of the gospel.

Of course, I agree that our day is different. We are encouraged to be involved in the political process. But we must choose our battles carefully lest the Cross of Christ be linked with many political causes. We must gain consensus with all those inclined to agree with us for political ends, but the message of the gospel must often be shielded from such associations.

Our Response

What should be our response in the face of the moral and spiritual decline of our nation?

First, we must admit that the true church is defenseless in the world. We are strangers and pilgrims who cannot afford to pin our hopes on the fortunes of the erratic political process. God alone is our defender.

Fortunately, our strength does not depend on a political majority. The fortunes of a nation often depend on a godly minority, as in the case of Gideon. If God does not take up our cause and fight in our behalf, we shall eventually be destroyed. We must seek His face, humbly asking that He would, even at this late hour, grant us mercy.

Second, we must understand the exalted role the church plays in the political affairs of this world. The bride of Christ holds back the coming judgment of God. The world, if I might humbly suggest, has no idea how much it owes the church. As for God, the church is number one on His agenda. Everything He does in this world is somehow related to the body of Christ; thus, everything shall someday be summed up in Him (Eph. 1:10).

Therefore, our spiritual condition as a church determines in a large measure God's blessing or judgment on our nation. Too often we have blamed the humanists for the moral decay around us without realizing that God may be judging us through them. It was God's prophet Jonah, not the pagan sailors, who caused the storm on the Mediterranean.

If we are able to turn our nation back to God, it most likely should be attributed to a godly remnant's intercessory prayer for spiritual revival. The righteousness that exalts a nation is the fruit of repentance. God certainly does not owe us a revival, but if we cry out to Him, He might yet show us mercy.

Of course, prayer must be combined with action. Parents must become involved in their school systems, we must stand against the infiltration of pornography into our homes and schools, and we must most assuredly fight against abortion. But we must fight like Christ, because at the end of the day, people must see Jesus. Our attitude is as important as the issue we are addressing.

So, as ministers we must address the moral issues of our time with courage and clarity. Our positions on abortion and homosexual perspectives must be knowledgeably analyzed and critiqued. Whenever the laws of the state conflict with clear biblical convictions, we must obey God rather than men, even if it means going to jail.

We must not be intimidated by those who wish to silence the mouths of ministers under the guise of separation of church and state. But we must also remember that our message is not a political agenda but the full biblical mandate of submission to the will of God.

But—and this is important—we must not be angry and bigoted in our criticisms. Moreover, we must remember that our primary responsibility is to share the good news of God's love and forgiveness. We must be agents of healing and not division, of understanding and not distortion. In short, we must represent Christ, living His values and message. We must keep the Cross at the forefront of our minds, our hearts, and our ministries.

To fulfill such a calling, we cannot be wedded publicly to any political party. Of course, we vote, but as ministers we don't tell our congregation how they should vote. In our fallen world, even born-again candidates can disappoint us. Each party has its own peculiar blend of good and evil. We must condemn evil wherever it is found, without any indebtedness to a party or a candidate.

The revivals of John Wesley and George Whitefield resulted in great social changes. God brought them about by the miracle of the new birth. He prefers to work from the inside out. What political power could never do, the conviction and the power of the Holy Spirit accomplished.

I believe it's time for us as individuals and churches to seek the Lord with repentant hearts. If we look to Washington, we will be disappointed. We can only submit ourselves unreservedly to the will of God and become personal and corporate witnesses to His power in our decadent society.

If our problems were political, a political solution would be all that was needed. But if they are spiritual, they must be addressed from that vantage point. If we, as God's people, repent, He may yet restore the years that the locusts have eaten. For in God we have the greatest power that could ever be unleashed. Politics is the art of achieving the possible, but faith is the art of achieving the impossible.

This nation needs to experience the impossible.

• 9 •

Envy

How Should We Live in the Shadow of Success?

A fable tells how Satan's emissaries were trying to tempt a holy man who lived in the Libyan desert. Try as they might, the demons could not get the man to sin. The seductions of the flesh and the onslaught of doubts and fears left him unmoved.

Angered by their failure, Satan stepped forward. "Your methods are too crude," he said. "Just watch." He whispered in the holy man's ear, "Your brother has just been made Bishop of Alexandria."

Instantly, a malignant scowl clouded the holy man's face.

"Envy," Satan said to his cohorts, "is our final weapon for those who seek holiness."

Making Comparisons

As pastors, we struggle with the same enticements as the people in our congregations. But because our ministries are public, our most powerful temptation may be envy. We all know how much it hurts to be compared with a pastor who is more successful.

"You're OK, but you're no Swindoll," a parishioner tells us with a touch of finality. Or a board member asks, "Why aren't we growing like Willow Creek's congregation?"

But such comments are passing, and we can handle them with a bit of good humor. It's more difficult when your congregation prefers your assistant pastor's preaching—or when the church next door is bursting at the seams while yours is slowly declining. Then it's easy to become critical and defensive. We say we have "a ministry of depth, not a numbers racket." Or we accuse the congregation of liking the assistant's preaching better because he "tickles their ears."

Our fallen nature loathes to be cast in bad light. It's difficult to rejoice with those who are more successful. At times, we even have quiet satisfaction when we learn about others' failures; by comparison we think we are doing better.

What aggravates the problem is that God's blessings seem so inconsistent. We see a church with phenomenal growth even though its pastor is a dull preacher who does little to inspire his congregation. At the same time, another church with an excellent preacher and good public relations skills may decline in membership.

Some pastors' theology is weak, their methods of fundraising are suspect, and their personal lives are in shambles, yet they are blessed with growth and money. Meanwhile, other pastors with integrity and faithfulness can't raise enough money to paint the church. No wonder a missionary once said to me, "Have you ever noticed how often God puts His hand on the wrong person?"

It's hard not to wonder why; it's hard not to envy.

The Strength of the Poison

Envy will cripple any pastor and his ministry. First, it erodes faith. Jesus asked the Pharisees, who were men pleasers, "How can you believe, when you receive glory from one another, and you do not seek the glory that is from the one and only God?" (John 5:44 NASB). With their eyes on one another, they were unable to focus their eyes on God. The envious are in no position to please God. They are not free to believe wholeheartedly in Christ.

Second, envy produces isolationism. A pastor who fears the success of others will withdraw from fellowship and cooperation with other churches. He may say his reason for separation is the need for doctrinal purity. At times, important doctrinal matters are at stake and separatism is necessary. But if our hidden motives were exposed, much of our separation is rooted in the fear of allowing our congregations to be blessed outside the walls of our own little kingdom.

Although the Pharisees said they were crucifying Christ for doctrinal reasons, that was not the *real* reason they condemned Christ. Pilate discerned their underlying motive: "For he knew that because of envy they had delivered Him up" (Matt. 27:18 NASB). Envy was the motive; theology was the smoke screen.

Paul had a similar experience in Pisidian Antioch, where his preaching drew large crowds. "But when the Jews saw the crowds, they were filled with jealousy, and began contradicting the things spoken by Paul, and were blaspheming" (Acts 13:45 NASB). Once again, theology was the excuse for antagonism, but the motivation was less noble.

Writing to the Philippians, Paul discerned that some people were preaching Christ out of envy and strife, hoping to make him look bad. Yet, he rejoiced that Christ was preached, even though their motives were sinful (Phil. 1:12–18).

An envious person may fear unfavorable comparison so much that he works behind the scenes to sabotage a colleague's ministry. If he operates carefully, his hidden motive may never come to light. This, of course, makes the judgment seat of Christ all the more important, for God shall expose the motives of men's hearts.

King Saul was not as careful to hide his jealousy. He was so angered by the comparison in the cheers of the crowd, "Saul has slain his thousands, And David his ten thousands" (1 Sam. 18:7), that he became obsessed with killing his young rival. God's response was to send a demon to trouble him, evidently so he would be goaded into repentance. Instead, Saul eventually committed suicide.

Once envy has found a home in the human heart, it resists eviction. Even death may seem more attractive than conceding success to someone who is younger and less qualified. Don't ever underestimate the depths to which we are able to sink in order to make ourselves look good.

Neutralizing the Poison

How do we overcome this deceitful monster? We must treat envy for the sin it is. It is rebellion against God's providential leading in the lives of His children. An envious person is saying God has no right to bless someone else more than himself.

Jesus told a parable about a landowner who agreed to pay a denarius a day to workers who arrived early. Others who came later in the day didn't haggle about their wages but were willing to trust the landowner's fairness.

At the end of the day, those who came last were the first to be paid. Each received a denarius. Those who had worked since morning assumed they'd be paid more, but they were shocked when they, too, received one denarius (Matt. 20:1–12).

Unfair.

Imagine an employer paying those who arrive at 3:00 P.M. the same as those who show up on time. But Jesus gave the story a surprising twist: it was fair because the first workers got what they'd agreed on. If the landowner wanted to pay the latecomers that much, too, he was at liberty to do so.

Speaking for the landowner, who represents God, Jesus said, "Is it not lawful for me to do what I wish with what is my own? Or is your eye envious because I am generous?" (v. 15). God can do what He wishes with His own. He can be more generous with others, and we have no right to complain. Envy is rebellion against His sovereign rights.

Envy is also a sin against God's goodness. Whatever we have, be it little or much, it is a gift of God. When Jesus Christ eclipsed John the Baptist's ministry and, therefore, his cousin in the flesh was tempted to envy, he rightly replied, "A man can receive nothing, unless it has been given him from heaven" (John 3:27 NASB). Envy is based on the assumption that our abilities and gifts are something we're entitled to have.

Envy is a sin that lashes out against God's goodness and sovereignty. It's the pot telling the potter how to make other vessels. Francis Schaeffer said there is no such thing as small people and big people, only consecrated people and unconsecrated people. One pastor said, "When I finally accepted the fact that God did not want me to be well known, I began to experience His blessing."

Paul taught that it was God who determined where we would fit within the body of Christ. "But one and the same Spirit works all these things, distributing to each one individually *just as He wills*" (1 Cor. 12:11 NASB, emphasis added). To be dissatisfied with our gift is to be dissatisfied with our God.

Comparisons of ministries or preachers are almost always sinful. We must not be like the disciples who asked, "Who will be the greatest in the kingdom of heaven?" The fact is, we don't know. We can easily see that a skyscraper is taller than a small apartment building, but if we compare both buildings against the height of a distant star, there's not much difference between them. Likewise, the differences among us fade into oblivion when we compare ourselves with Christ.

God wants to give us humble satisfaction with our place in His vineyard. Having any place in the vineyard affirms His mercy and grace. To envy those who are given greater blessing is to imbibe a spirit of thanklessness and rebellion.

Moses was a Spirit-filled man, but God multiplied his ministry in the lives of seventy elders who were given the gift of prophecy. Two of those elders, Eldad and Medad, were particularly gifted and prophesied in the camp. When a young man came running to Moses and told him the news, Joshua said, "Moses, my lord, restrain them."

But Moses said to him, "Are you jealous for my sake? Would that all the Lord's people were prophets, that the Lord would put His Spirit upon them!" (Num. 11:28–29 NASB).

You can't destroy a man who rejoices in the success of others. He has a proper perspective of himself and his God. He can rejoice in those who are more successful. He's thankful for even the small opportunities to serve because he hasn't lost the wonder of the Father's care. And a genuine smile breaks forth when you tell him that his brother has been appointed Bishop of Alexandria.

· 10 ·

Burnout

Can Wet Wood Still Be Ignited?

A church janitor was heard to say, "The blower still works, but the fire has gone out." He was discussing a problem with the furnace, but the parishioner who overheard him thought he was speaking about the pastor.

One definition of burnout is "a syndrome of emotional exhaustion, depersonalization, and reduced personal accomplishment that can occur among individuals who do 'people work' of some kind." Its symptoms include increased fatigue, tiredness even after a good night's sleep, loss of interest in one's work, and a pessimistic, critical spirit often accompanied by withdrawal, depression, and a feeling of futility.

According to Archibald D. Hart, dean of the graduate school of psychology at Fuller Theological Seminary, however, burnout may be beneficial as a warning that something has gone wrong. It may intervene and take you out of a harmful environment when you're on the road to stressful destruction.

"It instantly slows you down and produces a state of lethargy and disengagement," Hart says. "The system 'gives out' before it 'blows up.'"

Whereas stress is characterized by overinvolvement, burnout is characterized by withdrawal and a loss of meaning and hope. Regardless of what the person does, the rewards seem too small to bother. It can lead to depression.

59

Causes of Burnout

One study indicated that one-third of the pastors surveyed had considered leaving the ministry because of burnout. Although burnout can occur in all professions, ministers are particularly vulnerable. One reason may be the conflict of roles.

We are expected to be good preachers, counselors, and organizers; know something about publicity; and have the fine art of loving people and showing it in our relationships. When these responsibilities are not accompanied by rewards, the pushes and pulls of those expectations can lead to a sense of futility and despair. Because people come to the pastor to *get* rather than to *give*, his emotional resources can easily become depleted.

Second, the pastor is often alone in his struggles. Though the members of the church can speak freely to him about their problems, he is not free to reciprocate. As J. Grant Swank Jr. says, "Pastors wonder who is going to pull the supports out from under them if they open up, if they are honest about the tensions of the pastorate. Consequently, in too many cases it is very hard for the minister to discover a partner in ministry other than the spouse."[1]

If the pastor's marriage is falling apart or if his children are an embarrassment, he feels trapped and unable to extricate himself from his emotional lows. Soon, he wonders how he can be of help to others when he himself has such a strong sense of failure.

All of us have feelings of inadequacy. And we are not helped when we are compared with the television preachers who are able to draw large crowds and money. Though our faults are well known to our congregations, the people hear of only the successes of radio and television preachers.

If we preach one poor sermon, everyone knows it; if we get indignant at a board meeting, word gets around. Soon, we think we are unappreciated. If we are particularly sensitive to criticism, we will try to overachieve to please everyone. If we don't receive adequate emotional and spiritual compensation for our efforts, we will be left wondering if it's all worthwhile.

Dr. David Congo, associated with H. Norman Wright's Family Counseling Clinic in Santa Ana, California, says the ministry can be represented by either a "rat race" or a "relay race." Both require a great deal of energy, but a rat race has no clear sense of purpose. A relay race, however, has direction, a prescribed course, cooperation, and team spirit. The pastor in a rat race often feels like a victim controlled by his situation. It's hard to say whether that is the cause of burnout or its result, but there's a direct relationship in either case.

Congo lists four personality types linked to burnout:

- those with a high need for approval
- the workaholic
- the unassertive, passive victim
- those with a "messiah complex"[2]

All of us are tempted to give beyond our own spiritual and emotional resources to be thought of as successful. The result may be our feeling fulfilled. Or it may do the opposite—lead to inner anger and disillusionment.

If a pastor feels unappreciated, his response may be to "cop out." He absorbs many hurts, each of which diminishes his self-esteem, which, in turn, contributes to an attitude of "Why should I care about you, because you don't care about me?" At that point, either the fire goes out or it is stoked with anger and becomes the fire that destroys rather than the fire that cleanses.

The simple fact is that many pastors have unresolved anger that they are unwilling to admit. This anger is often cloaked with phrases such as "righteous indignation" or "ministerial earnestness," but it is there nevertheless. Often, they are angry because as children they felt disconnected from their parents, or perhaps they are now resentful because the ministry has been hard and thankless. As was already mentioned, the rewards for their efforts are simply not worth the cost.

Cures for Burnout

What is the cure? The usual advice follows these lines: exercise regularly, get proper rest, take a vacation, and reorganize your priorities. Those suggestions would undoubtedly contribute to recovery, but often the root goes deeper.

Who of us hasn't taken time to relax, only to discover we can't because of a nagging sense of guilt or failure? What about the anxiety we feel as we anticipate the next board meeting, when our new proposal will be discussed? And how can we enjoy our vacation if we suspect a member of the board might undermine our leadership while we're away?

There is a surer path.

The first part of the answer to burnout is to be controlled from within rather than from without. We must be satisfied with doing the will of God rather than being overly dependent on the opinions of men. That may require getting away from it all for a week's retreat or even taking a leave of absence to get it all together. But it is in that quiet, inner world that we meet God and that the answer will eventually be found. Remember, burnout is something we do to ourselves and only secondarily something that the ministry does to us.

In *Ordering Your Private World*, Gordon MacDonald describes the difference between a person who is driven (such as King Saul) and a person who is called (such as John the Baptist). A driven person is gratified only by accomplishments and its symbols. He often possesses a volcanic anger that erupts anytime he senses opposition or disloyalty. When he cannot achieve his goals in public ministry, he becomes disillusioned because his private life is left empty and wanting.

John realized that the crowds did not belong to him; he ministered as the Lord saw fit. He didn't need the exhilaration that comes through public affirmation, nor did he see himself out of focus. He might have been tempted to think of himself as a great preacher, but he directed the crowds to Christ: "He must increase, but I must decrease" (v. 30).

John's contentment was not built on his career; he could find stability in his private, inner world. Pastors who neglect their inner world soon find themselves unable to cope with the weight of the external demands placed upon them.

Burnout may be a reminder to develop our inner world. Spending time in quietness before the Lord and asking His guidance in those areas of neglect and failure could be just the experience we need. Perhaps those of us who say yes to too many invitations will discover we weren't called to save the world. We don't have to live up to the expectations of our congregations; we can be content serving in faithfulness within the limitations of our gifts and aptitudes.

In 1749, Jonathan Edwards chose to break with the tradition of the day and insist that only those who gave evidence of conversion should be allowed to participate in Communion. Though he wrote a book to defend his views, few read it. Instead, disgruntled members took up the cause and garnered enough support to oppose Edwards. The members of his church openly reproached him, accusing him of being more concerned about himself than the good of the church. They held meetings in his absence, and discord was sown far and wide.

Finally, on June 19, 1750, a council, consisting of many churches, met and recommended that the relationship between Edwards and his church be dissolved. When the church itself voted, many of Edwards' supporters stayed away. In the final tally, 230 members voted for his dismissal; about 29 people voted for him to stay. The deed was done.

How did Edwards accept this harsh and unfair decision? A close friend who observed him, wrote:

> That faithful witness received the shock, unshaken. I never saw the least symptoms of displeasure in his countenance the whole week but *he appeared like a man of God, whose happiness was out of the reach of his enemies* and whose treasure was not only a future but a present good, overbalancing all imaginable ills of life, even to the astonishment of many who could not be at rest without his dismission.[3] (emphasis added)

Of course it hurt. Indeed, Edwards felt betrayed by his friends and lonely in being "separated from the people between whom and me there once was the greatest union." Yet he also saw in this the providence of God. God would use him to do missionary work among the Indians and to write books that would benefit future generations.

Years later, one of the dissenters confessed that the real reason behind opposition to Edwards was pride. "I now see that I was very much influenced by vast pride, self-sufficiency, ambition, and vanity." But it was too late.

My point is that Edwards could accept unfair treatment in the ministry because *his happiness in God was beyond the reach of his enemies*. Here was a man who learned what Martin Lloyd-Jones would say many years later: "Don't let your happiness depend on preaching, for the day will come when you can no longer preach. Find your happiness in God who will be with us to the end."

The second part of the answer to burnout is to confide in close friends. Every pastor should have several people, perhaps outside his congregation, with whom he can be honest about his struggles. We all need the acceptance and confidentiality of friends who will listen carefully and pray fervently.

During days when we're unsteady emotionally, everything is distorted. We desperately need the perspective of those who have maintained their emotional equilibrium. Blessed is the pastor who can be open with at least a few friends during his emotional blackouts.

James B. Scott experienced burnout and resigned from his church. He wrote, "The most difficult part of the death of a dream was the feeling of loss and fear of not knowing if anything would ever come along to replace the loss." But eventually he realized that the ministry was in God's hands, not his. He continued, "Brokenness and healing has, by the power of God, produced unexpected results in my life. Strange how the pain of brokenness can miraculously bring about fullness and a tenacity of power and resources unknown previously."[4]

Many of us need once again to experience the inner power of God. There, in His presence, we must find meaning and tranquillity within rather than being sustained by approval from without. God wants us to find our joy coming from Him rather than from the unpredictable, often conflicting attitudes of men.

Sometimes, we may not be able to pinpoint the cause of burnout. Even so, we must interpret it as a reminder from God that our inner life needs special attention. "In quietness and in confidence shall be your strength" (Isa. 30:15 KJV). C. S. Lewis says the Lord shouts to us in our pains, but, I might add, He also speaks to us in our emotional doldrums.

Jesus demonstrated an inner satisfaction that enabled Him to cope with the stresses of His ministry. When a huge crowd gathered to hear Him, He disappointed them by going to another town and leaving them waiting (Mark 1:37–38). When He learned that Lazarus was sick, He stayed away two extra days, knowing that the will of God was being accomplished despite the disappointment of His friends Martha and Mary (John 11:6).

Christ never seemed to be in a hurry because He cared only about pleasing the Father. We must learn from Him the importance of playing the game for the coach, not for the fickle applause of the fans.

Burnout may mean that fresh coals must be offered on the altar of the heart. The God of Elijah is able to ignite even wet wood if it is laid out before Him in submission and anticipation.

Burnout need never be permanent if we are willing to wait for God to rekindle the flame.

• 11 •

The Church and the World

Who Is Influencing Whom?

Recent Gallup polls have uncovered conflicting trends in our society: religion is on the upswing, but so is crime and immorality. George Gallup calls it "a giant paradox that religion is showing clear signs of revival even as the country is ridden with rising crime and other problems regarded as antithetical to religious piety."

Addressing a national seminar of Southern Baptist leaders, Gallup said, "We find there is very little difference in ethical behavior between churchgoers and those who are not active religiously. The levels of lying, cheating, and stealing are remarkably similar in both groups."

Eight out of ten Americans consider themselves Christians, Gallup said, yet only about half of them could identify the person who gave the Sermon on the Mount, and fewer still could recall five of the Ten Commandments. Only two of ten said they would be willing to suffer for their faith. Many Christian university students have adopted a "silent contract," kindly refusing to share their faith to fit in with the politically correct policies of the university. Thus, the desire to graduate is more important to them than representing Christ and taking the rap for it. Unlike the early church, few Christians think it a badge of honor to suffer for the suffering Savior.

What an indictment of American Christianity to have religion up while morality is down. Let's not excuse ourselves just because we suspect that the majority of those interviewed were not born-again believers.

Within evangelicalism is a distressing drift toward accepting a Christianity that does not demand a life-changing walk with God.

Thanks to our limited knowledge of church history, many evangelicals don't realize that the church has always been an island of righteousness in a sea of paganism. The early Christians did not have the benefit of a sympathetic culture or government; they expected persecution and got it. But, as a result, they "turned their world upside down." We are proving that it is difficult to rear saints who are willing to suffer when we have become accustomed to an affluent culture.

Religion à la Carte

Like the nominally religious person, we choose what we will believe and how we will act without much concern for what the Bible teaches. F. H. Henry wrote, "Millions of Protestants, many evangelicals among them, choose and change their churches as they do their airline—for convenience of travel, comfort, and economy." For us, as well as for the world, it's religion à la carte.

What can account for this? Since evangelicalism became popular a few decades ago, many people have felt free to identify with it at no personal cost. The stigma of Christianity is gone, but so is its power.

Within the evangelical camp is a growing trend toward accommodation—selecting what we like from the Bible and leaving the rest. We've been so caught up in the spirit of our age that we change colors like a chameleon to blend in with the latest worldly hue.

When gay rights activists argue that homosexuality is but an "alternate sexual preference," we find evangelicals writing books agreeing that the Bible doesn't condemn homosexuality. They say the Old Testament passages are a part of the law that doesn't apply today and that Paul was condemning only those who turned to homosexuality, not those who grew up that way.

When the feminists press their demands for equality, some preachers "restudy" the New Testament and discover that Paul didn't really mean what he wrote. They conclude that the husband is not the head of the wife and that women have the right to be ordained. Even more frightening is one evangelical's conclusion that Paul's view of women was just plain wrong.

When a socialistic mood sweeps the country, we have Christians who advocate the application of a Marxist theory for the redistribution of wealth. And when the peace movement gained momentum, some evangelicals jumped on that bandwagon, too.

I agree that we must examine our understanding of the Bible in relation to modern issues. But if we accommodate Scripture to whatever wind is blowing, we will become so absorbed by our culture that we will have nothing to say to it. In our zeal to be relevant, we will have lost our prophetic voice.

I'm reminded of the boy who bought a canary and put it in the same cage as a sparrow, hoping the sparrow would learn to sing. After three days, he gave up in disgust. The sparrow didn't sound like the canary; instead, the canary sounded just like the sparrow.

In *The Great Evangelical Disaster*, Francis Schaeffer says, "Here is the great evangelical disaster—the failure of the evangelical world to stand for truth as truth. . . . The evangelical church has accommodated to the world spirit of the age."[1]

However much we fault German theologian Rudolf Bultmann for rejecting the parts of the Bible that did not suit his fancy, we do the same when it comes to practicing biblical truth. Our actions show that we believe that scriptural authority rests with us and not with the text.

What is the result of this accommodation that picks and chooses from a religious smorgasbord? Society is being overrun by the cults, inundated with pornography, and destroyed by abortion on demand.

There are almost as many divorces within the church as outside of it. Sexual perversions of every kind are found within the church community, too. As Gallup suggests, the ethical behavior of those who attend church and those who do not is remarkably similar.

The new philosophy that "God wants you to be rich, happy, and healthy" has appealed to a generation that is quick to accept the benefits of Christianity without its painful obedience. Like a child standing by a slot machine hoping he can win the jackpot with a single coin, many churchgoers expect maximum return from minimum commitment. When they are not healed or don't get a promotion, they take their quarter and go elsewhere.

Our Response

How should we respond to such an attitude? Perhaps we have to begin by returning to the gospel as found in the New Testament. Many of us are weary of "decisional regeneration" whereby we pronounce people saved because they have walked an aisle or filled out a decision card. We forget the words of Christ, "Every plant which My heavenly Father did not plant shall be rooted up" (Matt. 15:13 NASB).

I'm not saying that we should add stipulations to the free offer of the gospel, but that we must not think that people are regenerated because they tell us they are or because they met one of our requirements. The difference between believers and unbelievers will become more clear when we realize that only those who are called by God will come to Him; only when salvation is again considered as a work of God's sovereign grace will we appreciate its implications and transforming power.

We must teach believers that the Christian life has both privileges and responsibilities. Taking up our cross means just that: a willingness to suffer because we belong to Christ.

Specifically, we must expose the sin of the "me first" cult of individualism that has infected the church. We've read about the woman from a small Oklahoma congregation who took three elders to court for exercising church discipline against her. She objected to the idea of confessing her sin to the church. After winning the suit and receiving a financial settlement that was greater than the congregation's budget for six years, she declared, "I'm not saying I wasn't guilty. I was. But it was none of their business."

In this instance, submission to church leadership (Heb. 13:17) and the clear teaching that we should not take fellow believers to court (1 Cor. 6:1–8) were set aside in favor of personal interests. Her attorney remarked, "He was a single man. She was a single lady. And this is America." In other words, although obedience to church leaders may be laudable biblically, it is contrary to the American way of life.

How different this is from the spirit of Jesus, who pleased not Himself but made Himself of no reputation and was obedient to death (Rom. 15:3; Phil. 2:7–8). He did it for us, but more important, He did it for God.

We must also learn that selective obedience nullifies the authority of God. We've all been tempted to neglect church discipline for fear of criticism, a charge of inconsistency, or possibly a church split. But does our well-intended negligence further the work of Christ?

Under the guise of being relevant, loving, and broad-minded, we weaken the impact of the gospel. Little wonder that a member of a large evangelical church could tell me, "I can't remember the last time we've had someone saved."

As pastors, let's remember that we're not the ones who determine what we should preach, who can be remarried in our church, or what the structure of the home should be. It's not up to us to decide whether we should be selective in the television programs we watch, how much we should give, or whether we should witness to our neighbors. We are bondslaves of Jesus Christ, obligated to search Scripture to find an answer to the question, "Lord, what wilt thou have me to do?" (Acts 9:6 KJV).

George Gallup is optimistic. He believes that if properly nurtured, the new awareness of religion in America could bring more genuine converts into the church. But I fear that it won't happen as long as the distinction between the church and the world remains blurred. We've come a long way from the early church, when fear fell upon the multitudes and "none of the rest dared to associate with them" (Acts 5:13 NASB).

The millions who take their religion à la carte will someday discover they've had the wrong menu. Only those who pay the price of obedience can enjoy the nourishment of the bread from heaven.

It's not the people who claim to be Christians who will affect our country; it's those who accept the cost and live the Christian life.

• 12 •

Counseling

Must We Be Experts in Psychology?

Is a pastor without psychological training qualified to counsel his flock, or must he limit himself to spiritual counseling and refer the more difficult cases to professionals?

Many Bible school graduates think they have to get a doctorate in psychology at a state university so they can become a counselor. They think they have to combine psychological training with their Bible school knowledge for maximum effectiveness. But psychologists and theologians dispute the extent to which psychological studies can successfully integrate with the Bible.

Personally, I am wary about attempts at integration. I find no biblical support to distinguish a spiritual problem from a psychological problem. At root, man's psychological problems, unless they are the result of physical or chemical causes, are spiritual—and where could we find a better analysis of man's need along with a supernatural remedy than in the Scriptures? Peter writes that our Lord's divine power has granted us "everything pertaining to life and godliness, through the true knowledge of Him who called us by His own glory and excellence" (2 Peter 1:3 NASB).

Paul writes, "For in Him all the fullness of Deity dwells in bodily form, and in Him you have been made complete, and He is the head over all rule and authority" (Col. 2:9–10). That leaves little room for using the techniques of secular psychology to help Christians achieve emotional and spiritual wholeness.

I am well aware that this matter of integration is more complicated than it appears on the surface. It is easy to say that we should use only the Bible and turn a deaf ear from everything psychology would teach us. But, thanks to common grace, even those who do not believe the Bible have occasionally hit upon biblical truths. So psychology may have some value in helping us understand man's predicament; it might provide some fodder for analysis. But its limitations and potential for deception must be understood.

Larry Crabb, in his book *Effective Biblical Counseling*, advocates that we "spoil the Egyptians"—we should use the insights, principles, and techniques of psychology that are consistent with Scripture to help us become more effective. I appreciate his desire to test the presuppositions of secular theories so that we would accept only what is biblical.[1]

Interestingly, in more recent writings, Crabb has concluded that professional counselors often do not achieve the results attributed to them. He believes that what broken people really need is the love and support of the church, the body of Christ. When our physical body has a wound, it has the power to heal itself; similarly, a healthy church has the power to provide healing for its broken members.

Crabb says there must also be the humble recognition that some members of the body will never be healed until they arrive in heaven. Indeed, our first priority should never be having our emotional needs met, but rather worshiping God. Thus, philosophies of counseling often are wrongheaded; we must return to the conviction that our desire for God must supersede our desire to be "fixed." In Crabb's words, "Our agenda is to fix the world until it can properly take care of us. God's agenda is to bring all things together in Christ until every knee bows before Him."

And that, ultimately, is why we must be biblical in our counseling. While secular theories might alleviate someone's pain and while purely psychological insights might enable the hurting to cope, when all is said and done, it is their relationship with God that really matters. A biblical counselor will always see beyond time to eternity.

Counseling is best described as accelerated discipleship. It is helping people apply God's solution their problems; it is a redirection of their lives to that which will matter for all of eternity.

A Biblical Approach

It's unfortunate that the expression "biblical counseling" has a negative connotation. Some people think it means that the antidote to every problem is just information, and that the relationship between the counselor and the counselee is therefore mechanistic and impersonal. Others see it as a simple philosophy that simply seeks to uncover hidden sins, and if these are confessed and forsaken all will be well.

A thoroughly biblical approach rejects such a simplistic notion. Paul stressed the personal dimension in exhortation and encouragement. He was a father to those who needed discipline and a mother to those who needed tender care (1 Thess. 2:7).

A familiar story from the Old Testament illustrates the point that often only godly insight can uncover the root cause of a problem and prescribe a cure. In Joshua 7, Israel lost thirty-six men when trying to conquer Ai. What would a secular analyst say about that ignominious defeat? That the army used the wrong strategy? That the weapons were outdated? That too few men were sent to the battle zone?

Incredibly, military matters had nothing to do with Israel's defeat. God said the reason was that a man had stolen some items and had hidden them in his tent (Josh. 7:10–12). One man's sin indicted others. God established a cause-effect relationship that defies scientific analysis. Secular man often fails to uncover the true nature of a problem because the cause may lie entirely outside his investigation. Spiritual causes are discovered only by those with scriptural insight into the ways of God and His dealings with men.

If I had been telling the story of Achan, I would have said, "Achan sinned." But God's commentary says, "The sons of Israel acted unfaithfully" (Josh. 7:1 NASB). Israel was a spiritual commonwealth bound together by a covenant.

A similar relationship exists between members of a family. "I, the Lord your God, am a jealous God, visiting the iniquity of the fathers on the children, on the third and the fourth generations of those who hate Me" (Exod. 20:5 NASB). When Ham acted indecently, his son Canaan was cursed (Gen. 9:25). Demons may harass a family line; hence, a child may be afflicted (Mark 9:20–21). In such cases, the influence of the parents and grandparents must be broken. Perhaps that is why the people of Israel confessed the sins of their fathers (Neh. 9:2).

Conversely, blessings may often be attributed to godly influences. The Lord shows "lovingkindness to thousands, to those who love Me and keep My commandments" (Exod. 20:6 NASB). Solomon was spared judgment because of his father David's sake (1 Kings 11:12). Laban was blessed because of Jacob (Gen. 30:27). And an unbelieving marriage partner is set apart for spiritual privileges because of a believing spouse (1 Cor. 7:14).

Concerning the body of Christ, Paul wrote, "If one member suffers, all the members suffer with it; if one member is honored, all the members rejoice with it" (1 Cor. 12:26 NASB). Here again we see that our lives are interrelated. We must recognize that one part of the body cannot suffer without the whole being affected. But, thankfully, it is also true that the more healthy the body, the more likely it is able to bring healing to its ailing members.

This solidarity helps us understand sin's consequences and cure more clearly. We will have a better understanding of how healing takes place.

A reflective knowledge of the Scriptures along with a compassionate heart can, under the guidance of the Spirit, be used to uncover the root cause of problems that elude a purely psychological approach. And what is important to remember is that there is not one right prescription for every problem.

The Body Healing Itself

When a fellow believer falls into sin, part of the responsibility may be ours. If one member is spiritually cold, he lowers the temperature of everyone around him. If I stumble, I might bring you down with me. We are united in our failures.

Spiritual power is unleashed when the church diffuses its strength throughout the whole body. Believers overcome depression, forgive abusive parents, and develop wholesome self-images when the body provides love and acceptance. Fractured personalities can be put back together within the context of people who see another's needs as being their own.

No one counsels with a sense of detachment when he realizes that failure is a shared experience. When a family breaks up, we all hurt. My first response to a believer's defeat should be to search my own heart.

Such an understanding of Scripture does not absolve individuals of responsibility. We are not programmed by the performances of others. God has tempered parental influence with personal responsibility (Ezek. 18:20).

The church family owes a huge debt to God because of our disobedience; we bear the burden of our sins both corporately and individually. The warriors who went to capture Ai would have had a greater concern for Achan's spiritual life if they had remembered that his actions were bound up with theirs.

Personal sin is also interrelated. The works of the flesh come in clusters. We cannot tolerate sin in one part of our life and be experiencing victory in another. If we close one room of our life to God, darkness settles over the whole house.

One man who struggled with pornography could not overcome his secret sin until he made restoration for items he had stolen many years ago. Another man overcame cigarette smoking after he asked his parents to forgive him for the rebellion of his youth, accepting responsibility for the days when he had begun the habit against their wishes.

In marriage counseling, I've sometimes asked a couple if they had premarital sex. "What difference does that make?" they retort. But if they have, they've planted seeds that have borne bitter fruit. They've forgotten that you never reap in the same season that you sow.

Sin sprouts roots in any number of unpredictable directions. If covetousness can lead to the defeat of an army, might not cheating on one's income tax lead to excessive anger or even immorality? James says, "A double minded man is unstable in all his ways" (James 1:8 KJV).

This knowledge of sin's effects ought to influence our counseling. We must see failure in its larger context and take time for spiritual inventory.

How might we have failed our brothers and sisters in Christ? What hidden sins within a family or church might have provided the climate for marital strife, moral sin, or emotional turbulence? I must ask God to search my heart and then seek His wisdom to identify the cause of personal and corporate defeat.

I believe that if Joshua had come to God before he sent men to Ai, the Lord would have revealed Achan's secret sin, and Israel would have been spared defeat. But Joshua acted hastily. Even on a later

occasion, he got into trouble by not seeking the counsel of the Lord
(Josh. 9).

When unconfessed sin is found, it must be judged. Achan and his
family were stoned and then burned (Josh. 7:25). A heap of stones
was left in the Valley of Achor as a memorial of that shameful event,
and "the Lord turned from the fierceness of His anger" (v. 26 NASB).

But often God does judge us as individuals and as churches because we have been unwilling to make a thorough housecleaning of
our lives. The Holy Spirit is willing to search our hearts when we
become honest (Ps. 139:23–24).

Achor means "trouble," an apparent reference to the severe judgment that Achan and his family received there. But hundreds of years
later, the prophet Hosea said that the Valley of Achor will be a door of
hope (Hos. 2:15). Hidden sin becomes a place of judgment; when sin
is confessed and forsaken, however, that place becomes a door of hope.
Once sin was put away, Joshua and his men defeated Ai, apparently
without the loss of a single soldier. When sin is judged, blessing flows.

Every pastor must be comfortable with his own philosophy of counseling, but I suspect that we'd all be more successful if we sought
God's wisdom in uncovering the causes of spiritual failure. God wants
to build a monument of victory in the valley of defeat, and He's given
us the tools to help Him.

Let no one say that my theory of counseling is simply to hunt for
hidden sin. In some instances, the cause may be sin in general; no
specific sin needs to be confessed.

I've learned several very important lessons in counseling. First,
we cannot expect to have the same approach to every problem. Sometimes, we must try to uncover sin; at other times, we must simply
give love and support. An abused child, for example, needs unconditional love and acceptance. His emotional problems likely will not be
helped by trying to uncover hidden sins, though forgiveness toward
his parents will become necessary at some point.

I feel sorry for counselors who think that everyone needs the same
approach, the same analysis, and the same truth. Each person is
different; each needs an individualized approach. Not everyone suffers from rejection. Not everyone who is depressed is struggling with
anger. Not everyone is helped by telling them that they just must
"obey God" and all will be well.

Second, though my counseling experiences are limited, I have seen the best results through persistent, believing prayer. I spend a good chunk of time praying for my counselee as well as having him or her pray according to my direction. I am a firm believer in the promise that God not only gives us wisdom but also pours healing into the lives of all who earnestly seek Him. "He heals the broken-hearted, and binds up their wounds" (Ps. 147:3 NASB).

We don't need to be experts in psychology to be effective counselors. We just need to be scripturally sound and emotionally sensitive to enter into the needs of our people. Our faith is not in ourselves but in the "Wonderful Counselor" who will hear our prayers as we call upon Him.

• 13 •

Worship

Can It Happen in a Structured Service?

As a new bride, a woman in a remote village dreamed about the security and happiness her marriage would bring. Perhaps her expectations were unrealistic. Maybe she was too preoccupied with her own ambitions to recognize the first signs of tension in her marriage.

But the tensions mushroomed. Eventually she and her husband agreed they could no longer live together. The decision was agonizing but from all appearances necessary. They were divorced.

Time heals all wounds, or at least lessens the pain. After the woman had pulled herself together emotionally, she met a man who seemed to have all the qualities her first husband lacked. This marriage would be a success, she thought.

When her second marriage showed signs of strain, the woman dared not let herself think it would end like the first. Yet, the foundations of that relationship began to crumble. Before long, the woman experienced a second divorce.

. Some women would have buried their frustrations in a career. They would have relocated in another city, gone back to school, or learned a skill. But this woman could not. Her family believed not only that a woman's place is at home but also that she is to be obedient to the whims of her husband. Furthermore, in her locality, no jobs were available to women. All she knew—all she *could* know—were house-hold chores, the drudgery of routine.

Her decision to marry the third time was easier to make. By that time, the woman was bitter at God and disgruntled with men. If her marriage didn't work, another divorce would rescue her from the bonds of meaningless vows. Predictably, she experienced a third divorce. Then a fourth and a fifth.

When she met another man, she decided not to bother with the formality of a wedding. They just lived together under common law.

And then she met Jesus Christ, who offered her living water. He also invited her to worship the Most High God. "Our fathers worshiped in this mountain," she offered (John 4:20 NASB). "Woman, believe Me," Christ replied, "an hour is coming when neither in this mountain, nor in Jerusalem, shall you worship the Father. . . . But an hour is coming, and now is, when the true worshipers shall worship the Father in spirit and truth; for such people the Father seeks to be His worshipers" (John 4:21, 23 NASB). Christ extended an invitation for her to become a worshiper, and through her, the invitation is given to us all.

The Essence of Worship

"To worship," said William Temple, Archbishop of Canterbury from 1942 to 1944, "is to quicken the conscience by the holiness of God, to feed the mind with the truth of God, to purge the imagination by the beauty of God, to open the heart to the love of God, and to devote the will to the purpose of God."[1]

The woman at the well considered worship a matter of outward conformity. But Christ taught that it was a matter of spirit and truth. The Jews worshiped in Jerusalem, the Samaritans on Mount Gerizim. From that time, worship would not be confined to geography. It was no longer a matter of being in the temple or on the right hilltop.

How often we assume that we must be in church to worship. We are told that the church building is "God's house," but that can be misleading. In the Old Testament, God dwelt in the temple; His glory settled within the holy of holies. But God was displeased with the temple worship in Jerusalem. He is equally unimpressed with our cathedral worship today.

Today the holy of holies resides in the body of every believer. Worship can take place anywhere; we are always in God's presence, and He is available for our adoration. Worship isn't just listening to a sermon, appreciating choir music, or joining to sing hymns. In fact, it isn't even necessarily prayer, for prayer sometimes comes from an unbroken, unyielded heart. Worship is not an external activity precipitated by the right environment. To worship in spirit is to draw near to God with an undivided heart. We must come in full agreement without hiding anything or disregarding His will.

Augustine spoke of those who have tried unsuccessfully to find God. "They were probably inflated by their pride of learning and so were misled into seeking Him by throwing out their chests rather than beating upon their breasts."

In worship, our hunger for God is both satisfied and increased. In His presence, we desire "all the fullness of God" and we want to be done with sin, we want the church purified, and we long for the return of Christ. We are even homesick for heaven.

Leading Others to Worship

How can we as pastors help our people worship? First, we must stress that worship demands preparation. People cannot worship in church if they have not met the Lord before arriving at the door. The sixty minutes before Sunday school and church is, for many Christians, the most unholy hour of the week. Eating, dressing, and scurrying around the house to finish those last-minute tasks and then driving to church out-of-sorts with one another is not conducive to a prepared heart. What we do *before* the service will determine what happens *within* the service.

The form of worship is not as important as the spiritual condition of the human heart. John MacArthur Jr. wrote in *The Ultimate Priority*, "If our corporate worship isn't the expression of our individual worshiping lives, it is unacceptable. If you think you can live any way you want and then go to church on Sunday morning and turn on worship with the saints, you're wrong."[2]

David said, "Unite my heart to fear Thy name" (Ps. 86:11 NASB). Our congregations must also come to God single-mindedly, in full agreement. We dare not think worship takes place automatically because we are all in the same place.

Second, we must worship in truth. Worship is not just an emotional exercise but a response of the heart built on truth about God. "The Lord is near to all who call upon Him, To all who call upon Him in truth" (Ps. 145:18 NASB). Worship that is not based on God's Word is but an emotional encounter with oneself.

Do you remember what happened when Nehemiah asked Ezra to read the scrolls of Scripture? "Then Ezra blessed the Lord the great God. And all the people answered, 'Amen, amen!' while lifting up their hands; then they bowed low and worshiped the Lord with their faces to the ground" (Neh. 8:6 NASB). The truth of God in their minds led the Israelites to bow their knees in worship.

In his book *Between Two Worlds*, John Stott says, "Word and worship belong indissolubly to each other. All worship is an intelligent and loving response to the revelation of God, because it is the adoration of His name. Therefore, acceptable worship is impossible without preaching. For preaching is making known the name of the Lord, and worship is praising the name of the Lord made known."[3]

There can be no worship without obedience to truth. That's why worship often involves sacrifice. It's not just praising God but praising Him through our instant response to His requests. When Abraham was asked to sacrifice Isaac, he said to his young men, "Stay here with the donkey, and I and the lad will go yonder; and we will worship and return to you" (Gen. 22:5 NASB). Abraham expected to slay his son; yet, he called that worship. Worship is wanting God more than the life of a son. And we cannot worship in church unless we have made some hard choices for God during the week. To speak of worship without surrender is like expecting an airplane to fly with one wing.

The people in Isaiah's day were not condemned because they sang the wrong songs. God did not judge them because they prayed unorthodox prayers. The nation even brought sacrifices. But they lacked surrendered hearts. Christ, quoting Isaiah, said,

"You hypocrites, rightly did Isaiah prophesy of you, saying,
'This people honors Me with their lips,
But their heart is far away from Me.
But in vain do they worship Me,
Teaching as their doctrines the precepts of men.'"
(Matt. 15:7–9 NASB)

Talk is cheap. It's obedience to truth that really matters. That's why worship is always costly. It means we come before God with a signed blank check.

Finally, Christ said that worship is a matter of priority. "Such people the Father seeks to be His worshipers" (John 4:23 NASB). At first glance, that statement seems odd. Would not all people, especially Christians, want to worship the Father? Would it not be natural for us, the creatures, to want to meet our Creator? Yet, it's Almighty God who does the seeking. My guess is that relatively few people respond.

How can we entice our people to take God up on His offer? For one thing, we must be worshipers ourselves. If we don't schedule time to worship God with meaning, we can't expect our congregations to do it either. Ann Ortlund wrote, "A congregation doesn't become broken because the minister tells them to. They get broken when he gets broken."

Second, we must concentrate on sharing with our people the glories of who God is. We should let them know that the Christian life is more than seeking freedom from sin.

Christians must also long to draw closer to God. If we are quenching our thirst at forbidden fountains, we have no reason to expect God to be satisfying. If we are not nourished by the bread from heaven, we will satiate ourselves with crumbs from the world. Once we have become addicted to the world's nourishment, our appetite for God is spoiled.

How can this apply to next Sunday morning? Pastors are not actors performing on stage for a crowd of staid bystanders. Rather, the whole congregation must participate while God, our audience, watches to see how well we do. He's monitoring us to find those whose hearts are perfect toward Him.

Let's begin by asking: How can we lift our congregations into God's presence and leave them there to cry, praise, and enjoy? Do we emphasize that they are actually on stage before God? Is there planned spontaneity, where the Lord is free to do something not listed in the bulletin?

God gave the privilege of worship to an immoral woman. Regardless of her past failures, worship was an exciting possibility. He now extends the same invitation to us. RSVP.

• 14 •

Public Invitations

Are We Being Misunderstood?

"Those who want to accept Christ as Savior, please leave your seats and come and stand at the front of the platform."

Most of us have heard invitations like that ever since we were children. And if we were shy, we might conclude that we simply cannot be saved.

In some churches, abandoning the invitation would be considered the first step toward liberalism. Even those who think that "coming forward" has no biblical support still practice regular public invitations and would never dream of changing them.

In the minds of many, having people come forward proves that the pastor is evangelistic and that God is at work. Regardless of what happens in the counseling room, the fact that there has been an outward sign gives the congregation the feeling that the church is on the move.

But this past summer, as I sat on a park bench and heard a young preacher urge people to come forward to receive Christ, I realized once again our urgent need to rethink our method of giving invitations. No matter how accustomed to them we may be, we must subject our practice to vigorous biblical scrutiny.

Charles Finney was among the first evangelists to call people forward during a service. He defended the practice by saying it served the same purpose as baptism in the days of the apostles. But he was putting the cart before the horse; baptism is a sign that one has been converted, not a prerequisite for conversion. Ever since Finney's time, public invitations have generated similar misunderstandings.

In some churches, walking forward and "coming to Christ" are linked to the point that people are led to believe one action can't happen without the other. To come forward is to "come to Jesus."

What happens when we link these two separate acts? Basically, it perpetuates the notion that walking before a crowd has some special merit in the conversion process. Those who are afraid to go forward may actually think they cannot be saved.

When I was ten years old, I was too embarrassed to walk in front of several hundred people. So I suffered through those invitations in which we sang all the stanzas of a hymn half a dozen times. Meanwhile, I was thinking, "If I have to go forward in front of all these people, I'll just have to go to hell."

More recently, I attended a meeting where the evangelist said, "Come, run to Christ!" A couple got up and ran forward, and he said, "See this couple! Others of you should get up and *run* to Christ!" I felt sorry for people with physical disabilities who wouldn't even be able to "walk to Christ," much less *run*! Yes, there are people who think they can be saved only when they go forward in a meeting and register their "decision" for Christ.

Perhaps there is a reason why a major denomination in the United States disclosed that, in a specified year, they had recorded 294,784 "decisions for Christ." But they could find only 14,337 in fellowship. Yet, the process of recording these great numbers continues without anyone asking what has gone wrong.

D. L. Moody, bless him, refused to count the number of decisions because he knew that many of them were not genuinely converted. Our numbers and God's numbers are just not one and the same. Perhaps not even close.

Misconceptions About Invitations

Although evangelists privately admit that a person can be saved without going forward, many of them do not want the word to get around. Saying, "Why don't you leave your seat and come to receive Christ?" is carefully calculated to urge people to respond physically to their appeal.

One evangelist obscures the issues even more by saying he wants to make it hard for people to respond to Christ. He derides this generation's "easy believism"; he wants to make faith tough. For him, the place to begin is by walking forward in front of the whole congregation. Taking Christ's invitation to discipleship as an invitation to salvation, he insists that people walk forward publicly to be saved.

Another preacher says he wants to give people an opportunity to "demonstrate" for Jesus Christ: "People are demonstrating for everything today; why don't you get out of your seat and demonstrate for Christ?" He thought he was making it difficult to become a Christian, but actually he was making it easy. There is nothing repulsive to the flesh about demonstrating for a worthy cause. Little wonder that when a counselor asked a young man why he had come forward his unhesitating reply was, "Because the world's in a mess, and I want to help."

Yes, it is difficult to become a Christian. But the difficulty is in acknowledging our sin and helplessness—precisely what proud hearts are unwilling to do. It's hard to admit that we must cast ourselves on the mercy of God in Jesus Christ. The difficulty is with the blindness of the human heart and an unwillingness to see our own condition before God.

Many people who pray to be saved are unchanged simply because they have not understood the seriousness of their condition and why their trust must be transferred to Christ alone. They consider "receiving Christ" as one more good thing to do, like attending mass or praying the Lord's Prayer. They are glad to recite a prayer but quite unwilling to acknowledge their utter helplessness in God's holy presence.

Making it appear as if walking forward is the hard part and necessary for salvation contributes to people's confusion about the gospel. It mixes faith and works and gives the impression that being willing to come forward is somehow related to being willing to "come to Christ" a phrase that means different things to different people.

I cringed when I heard a person who attends a church that gives such invitations say, "I want to be saved, but I'll have to wait until next Sunday." This popular misconception about invitations not only adds the requirement of works to the gospel but also puts assurance on a wrong foundation. Many people today think they are saved because they have gone forward to "receive Christ."

Somehow, the natural man thinks that if he hasn't performed a saving act, he has at least contributed to it by walking forward. Because of his heart's blindness and deception, he thinks he must do the best he can to repair his relationship with God. And afterward he prides himself in having had the courage to do so.

I've often heard a Christian who should know better say, "Wasn't it great to see three people saved this morning?" Because three people went forward during the invitation, he assumed that regeneration had taken place. But someone can go forward, pray an appropriate prayer, and still leave unconverted.

Yet, this style of invitation is sometimes defended because it makes good psychology: people should make some kind of response to "nail down" their decision. That phrase sounds reasonable, but it breeds confusion. Those who haven't gone forward may think they cannot be saved, and those who have gone forward think they are saved because of their courageous act of walking in front of several hundred people.

Dr. Lewis Sperry Chafer, founder of Dallas Theological Seminary, frequently gave public invitations in the early years of his ministry. But he eventually concluded that they obscured the issues of the gospel. He said, "Careful students of evangelism have noticed that where the necessity of public action as a part of conversion has been most emphasized there has been a corresponding increase in the God-dishonoring record of so-called 'backsliding'; and this is natural."[1]

The reason is obvious. Unconverted people think they are saved simply because they came forward. They feel better after they have done something.

In the New Testament, some people believed on Christ while He was teaching. Let's not think that the Holy Spirit converts people only when they respond to a public invitation. I'm glad I discovered that I could be saved in my own home, on my knees in a sparse farm living room. Let us make it our supreme task to urge men and women to believe in our mighty, omnipresent Christ.

I realize, however, that many have received Christ as Savior when they responded to an altar call. Some even say that deciding to walk forward was a test of their sincerity in surrendering to the Holy Spirit's conviction. But we should never give the impression that the new birth and walking forward are inseparably linked.

A Balanced Approach

God's part in salvation is to convict the sinner, draw him, and grant him the gift of repentance. All man can do is respond to what God is doing and cast himself upon God's mercy that he might be saved. To associate that step closely with the act of coming forward in a meeting is to dilute the purity of the gospel and to focus on the wrong issue.

It's not whether a man is willing to walk in front of other people that is important to God. It's whether he is willing to acknowledge his sin and receive the mercy that God extends to him through the Cross.

As Chafer said, "The one necessary step—the acceptance of Christ as Savior—can be performed only in the secret of the heart itself, by a personal choice and action of the will. This is a dealing with Christ alone, and as the time of this decision is the most critical moment in a human life, reason demands that it should be guarded from every distracting and confusing condition."[2]

Giving a public invitation to the unconverted has also led to the embarrassment of large numbers of apparent converts coming forward and then failing to show spiritual fruit in their lives. We could be spared this questioning of the power of the gospel if we waited for the fruit of repentance, rather than counting converts based on the outward sign of walking forward.

Of course, the need to give an invitation is urgent; but it must always be an invitation to come to Christ, not to the evangelist or to the front of the platform. Whenever possible—publicly or privately—we should urge men and women to repentance and faith. We must not let them think that they can add to the work that Christ has already done.

After all I have said, you might be surprised to hear me say that there is a place for invitations, as long as they are not directly associated with accepting Christ as Savior. It is appropriate to give Christians an opportunity to confess Christ or to invite people to receive spiritual counsel.

Paul wrote, "If you confess with your mouth Jesus as Lord, and believe in your heart that God raised Him from the dead, you shall be saved; for with the heart man believes, resulting in righteousness, and with the mouth he confesses, resulting in salvation" (Rom. 10:9–10 NASB).

But that passage cannot be interpreted to mean that regeneration comes about by a public confession. Such an understanding would disagree with scores of other passages. Verse 9 must be interpreted in the light of verse 10. How is a right standing gained before God? "For with the heart man believeth unto righteousness" (v. 10 KJV). It is in the heart that the will exercised by the Holy Spirit responds to the saving work of Christ. The confession "unto salvation" is a result of having received the gift of righteousness. Thus, the believer testifies with his mouth to what God has wrought in his heart.

So we could invite new converts to share their decision with the pastor, a counselor, or the whole congregation. In effect, this "confession" could be a testimony of God's saving grace. It also would be the opportunity to receive further counsel. With such invitations God is well pleased.

We could also make an effort to separate the physical response from the spiritual act of conversion. At Moody Church, I invite people to the front so they can discuss a spiritual need with a member of the pastoral staff or a counselor, providing an opportunity to pray, ask questions, and receive counsel—whether one is saved or unsaved.

Let's not associate the act of walking forward with "coming to Christ," and let's not be afraid to tell people that they can be saved where they are seated—or wherever they might find themselves next week—to tell them that they should go home and seek God, preferably on their knees, that they might come to the assurance of faith. They don't have to wait until next Sunday.

If, after considering this matter, you still believe that you must give an invitation that urges the unconverted to come forward, I beg you to be honest, clear, and simple. You and I have heard evangelists say, "Just raise your hand," and the sinner thinks that that act is the end of the matter. But then, suddenly, he is told to "come forward," which he never intended to do. In extreme cases, I have actually been present when preachers have pointed out those who have raised their hands. One even said, "The man with the blue shirt . . ." That kind of gimmickry is surely unworthy of the gospel. Let us not be surprised when some people who have been embarrassed leave the church and never return.

Yes, let us urge people to come to Christ—not to the preacher, the platform, or even a counselor—but to the invisible Christ. Only a clear invitation is worthy of a clear gospel.

• 15 •

God's Judgment

How Can We Recognize It Today?

At a recent meeting of religious leaders, one respected observer of the American political scene remarked, "We've lost the abortion battle in Washington. Now there's no turning back . . . ; we are sliding toward the judgment of God."

I'm not qualified to say that the fight against abortion is dead politically, nor can I put a timetable on God's judgment. But we cannot escape the consequences of killing four thousand unborn babies every day.

Of course, America is inflicted with many other ills: violent crime, divorce, teen suicide, and a sharp increase in illegitimate births. As William J. Bennet has pointed out, no matter how much the government spends on pathologies, the situation is only becoming worse. "Many of the most serious social and behavioral problems we now face (particularly among our young)," he states, "are remarkably resistant to government cures."

It's popular to blame the Supreme Court, the humanists, and the radical feminists. To be sure, they have contributed to the liberalization of America. But if God is using them to judge us, might not the responsibility more properly be laid at the feet of those who know the living God but who have failed to influence society?

If we were few in number, we could more easily evade censure. But there are tens of thousands of evangelical pastors in America who lead several million born-again believers. Yet, we're losing one battle after another. Perhaps the church doesn't suffer for the sins of the world as much as the world suffers for the sins of the church.

Because of our cowardly silence in the midst of abortion, pornography, and the erosion of our religious liberties, and because of our acceptance of compromise within the church, the salt has lost its savor and the light flickers. In our desperation, we look for solutions to stem the tide; we want to have someone rise up and fight our battles for us.

Perhaps the answer we seek is close at hand, but we have been confused regarding our agenda. We have failed to be the church at a time when our nation needs to see righteous examples of leadership and hope. We are indeed under God's judgment as a nation, but perhaps we are unaware of it. The matter is worthy of careful thought.

Where Have We Failed?

First, we have neglected the unconverted. We give our lives to an evangelical subculture that is known to many only by the caricatures of the media. Unfortunately, the message that means most to us is often lost simply because we have been unwilling to share the gospel backed by a credible lifestyle.

If each Christian family actively witnessed and discipled those who come to Christ (we expect much more from our missionaries), our impact among the unconverted would be phenomenal. Yet we are told that 95 percent of all Christians have never given a clear witness to an unsaved neighbor. However much we may talk about the power of the gospel, we are apparently afraid to share it. At root is our reluctance to believe that the gospel is actually "the power of God unto salvation" (Rom. 1:16 KJV).

Second, we have retreated behind what Francis Schaeffer calls "false pietism" in regard to social issues. We have eschewed anything that necessitates sacrificial involvement. We've neglected to "do good unto all men, especially unto them who are of the household of faith" (Gal. 6:10 KJV). As long as we live well, can choose our friends, and are assured a comfortable retirement, we don't care too much about newspaper headlines. What matters is that our personal peace and affluence not be disrupted.

Of course, we may preach an occasional sermon against abortion, but are we willing to help teenage girls who are pregnant? We may condemn injustice, but are we willing to use our own finances and influences to help those who have been treated unfairly? Talk is cheap. It's easy to say the right words and then hope that someone else will fight our battles.

Also, we have accepted the world's values in entertainment, leisure, and success. We have lost our ability to critique society. Since the church is so often indistinguishable from the world, the unconverted have no model of righteousness.

Every Christian couple that divorces causes others to question the power of God. When a church splits over trivial matters, it says to the community that God cannot bring restoration and forgiveness to His people. When fathers neglect to lead their families in prayer and Bible instruction, they subtly give the impression that God's counsel is optional! And when we are willing to rationalize sensuality, selfishness, and greed, we are, in effect, admitting that Christ is unable to free us from sin. As a result, we have nothing to say to this generation.

In desperation, we have turned to politics, believing that if only we had the right leaders we would turn this nation around. We have forgotten that if there is any good news it will never come from Washington but rather from the people of God who can point others to Christ.

What Form Will God's Judgment Take?

During the cold war era, we often imagined that judgment would come in the form of war with Russia. We expected a nuclear holocaust that would wipe us off the map. We thought we ourselves might be enslaved to Communism during the days when its leaders assured us that they would rule the world.

Today, some people think that the judgment will come in a famine, an earthquake, or killer tornadoes. Yes, these are the judgment of God, given by Him to remind us that we all must die and that it is a fearful thing to fall into God's hands. Although these judgments fall on the just and the unjust, they are a picture of God's future judgment. The earth is corrupt, and more corruption will follow.

Yet, there is another form of judgment more closely tied to the cause-effect relationships of sin. After God warned the Israelites of famines, wars, and boils, He predicted that the final judgment would be captivity. "Your sons and your daughters shall be given to another people, while your eyes shall look on and yearn for them continually; but there shall be nothing you can do" (Deut. 28:32 NASB). The severest judgment was the scattering of Israel's families.

Though in a different way, the same thing is happening to us today. One-half of all children born this year will, at some time, live with only one parent. As our homes continue to break up, depression, hatred, and child abuse result. Such consequences of disobedience will escalate.

Or perhaps God's judgment will include intensifying emotional disorders. He told the Israelites that their disobedience would bring "despair of soul" (Deut. 28:65 NASB). Unresolved guilt surfaces under different labels—anger, insensitivity, depression. With millions of women having abortions and an equal or even greater number of men guilty of sexual immorality, future generations will find mental illness on the increase. We can expect our nation to rot from within.

What Can We Do?

The only hope for America can be found in the church. The body of Christ still wields awesome power. If we are brought to our knees, and if we are willing to pay the price of obedience, God may begin to give us spiritual victories that could stem abortion, infanticide, and drug abuse. Perhaps, in His grace, He might even be pleased to send us a spiritual awakening.

When Mordecai told Esther that she should go before the king to intercede for the Jews, she hesitated, fearing for her own life. But Mordecai replied, "Do not imagine that you in the king's palace can escape any more than all the Jews. . . . And who knows whether you have not attained royalty for such a time as this?" (Esther 4:13–14 NASB).

Esther had to be willing to lay her life on the line before deliverance would come. She couldn't feel content because of her own supposed security. In the end, it wasn't the rooms of an opulent palace but only God who could save her. So she risked her life, saying, "If I perish, I perish" (v. 16). Only at such cost did God bring deliverance. Though Esther and the Jews were a minority, that mattered little when God took up their cause.

Our political options in fighting matters such as abortion, the expansion of homosexual rights and the disintegration of TV entertainment appear to be limited, but that is not a cause for discouragement. What the Supreme Court thinks is meaningless when God fights on behalf of His people.

Perhaps God is trying to teach us that we cannot depend on human agencies to turn this nation back to Him. We must wait before Him until He gives us the grace to weep for our nation and its leaders. We must repent of our comfortable relationship with the world. We must grieve not so much for ungodly men who make unjust laws but for the people of God who are spiritually paralyzed and unable to witness to Christ's power in every sphere of life.

God is willing to meet us, but, even at this late hour, I'm not sure that we are ready to pay the price.

If we are as desperate as we profess to be, I propose that we as pastors

- lead our congregations by example in witnessing, community involvement, and teaching
- spend one day a week in prayer and fasting for ourselves, our churches, and our nation
- stand with our families in their desire to represent Christ in their schools and their vocations
- refuse to buy into the present culture of sensuality, individualism, and greed
- teach our people how to defend their faith in our pluralistic world

Our time is short. Our political and legal options are beginning to close. We are on the way down. Only God can save us now.

A Kinder, Gentler Theology

Is It Biblical or Cultural?

Listen to some evangelicals and you'll be led to believe that man does not exist for God's benefit but that God exists for man's benefit. Man tells God when he wants to be saved, how rich he'd like to become, and even his own version of theology.

The clay is giving the Potter instructions.

We've been seeing trends in this direction for some time. Many evangelicals have left the Reformation doctrines of total depravity, the bondage of the human will, and man's need for sovereign grace. A general commitment to Christ substitutes for repentance, and emotional feelings replace worship.

I agree with Joe Bayly, who wrote, "In our 'let's give God a hand' (applaud, everyone) Christian culture, we have lost a sense of wonder, of awe, of approaching an Almighty God when we pray. Even our worship is narcissistic."

A spirit of accommodation permeates the evangelical pulpits of our land. Sometimes obvious, sometimes subtle, but always dangerous, much preaching today is shaped by the culture of our times. The Bible is bent to accommodate culture rather than to change it.

A New Theology

I don't know when these trends received their greatest impetus, but I know that Robert Schuller articulated a man-centered approach to evangelical theology in his book *Self-Esteem—The New Reformation.* Although it was appropriate for Calvin and Luther to think

95

theocentrically, because in their day everyone was in the church, Schuller says times have changed: "What we need is a theology of salvation that begins and ends with a recognition of every person's hunger for glory."[1]

Sin, traditionally thought to be against God, is now defined as against man: "any act or thought that robs myself or another human being of his or her self-esteem."[2]

The differences between the sixteenth-century Reformation and this new reformation are obvious. Gone is the idea that a knowledge of God is one's highest goal; a knowledge of ourselves and of our need for self-respect is now the first item on the theological agenda. God is not so much a judge who has been offended as He is a servant who is waiting to affirm our dignity. We come to Him on the basis of our self-worth rather than the blood of Christ.

How, then, shall we present this gospel? Schuller says that Christ never called anyone a sinner. "The Gospel message is not only faulty, but potentially dangerous if it has to put a person down before it attempts to lift him up,"[3] he says. In effect, we stand before God to be exalted, not to be abased.

This reformation, then, is basically a call to a new preoccupation with ourselves rather than with God. But, unfortunately, as man is lifted up, God is dethroned.

Let's not think, however, that Schuller's book is an isolated case of Christian humanism. The fact that some so-called evangelicals accept this new reformation is proof enough that man-centered theology has permeated high places. I'm afraid that all of us have been affected.

The outworking of such a view of theology can be seen in how some ministers have accepted Evangelical Feminism in which great erudition is used to set aside the clear biblical teaching concerning male leadership in our homes and churches. There is little doubt that many arguments for egalitarianism are much more dependent on the spirit of our age than on Scripture.

Radical Armenianism, with its emphasis on free will and the unbiblical notion that not even God knows the future (hence, not even He knows who are the elect!), is little more than an accommodation to the man-centered theology of the age. One minister in an evangelical denomination, true to the Armenianism of the day, read John 3:16 from his pulpit this way: "God so loved the world that He *bet* His only begotten Son that whosoever believeth in Him should not perish . . ." (emphasis added). He said that Christ might have died and without saving anyone; God just took a risk and had no idea whether anyone would believe.

It's regrettable that the church leadership did not rise up to censure him. I would like to think that even older Armenians would have agreed that he was preaching heresy. But there is a new wind blowing, and many evangelicals are setting their sails to catch the breeze. God is being refashioned, made into our own image.

The Consequences

What are the consequences of such thinking? First, theology itself becomes relative. To a greater or lesser extent, theology itself is based on the opinion poll. Men such as Schuller know that people want to hear something positive, so they give it to them. A pastor in one of America's largest and most innovative churches says that he cannot preach on holiness because no one is interested. To reach the unchurched, all messages must conform to this basic dictum: Help them see the immediate benefit Christianity can be to them.

Can you imagine Isaiah asking the people of Judah what they'd like to hear before he prepared his sermon? Or Christ tailoring His message to suit the Pharisees' hunger for personal glory?

It's easy to recognize the extremes, but we as pastors also ought to plead guilty to preaching what is popular rather than what is true. We sometimes skirt church discipline, the biblical standards for church leadership, and the Scriptures' denunciation of materialism for fear of rocking the ecclesiastical boat. Why alienate those who pay your salary? A bugle call is an unwelcome irritation to those at ease in Zion.

Many pastors who would die for the doctrine of the infallibility of Scripture never preach on the doctrine of hell. Indeed, many pastors who profess allegiance to the Scriptures no longer believe in eternal punishment but have adopted the theory of annihilation; they believe that the unconverted will be thrown into the flames and consumed. Apparently, this kinder, gentler punishment is not based on a careful rethinking of Scripture but on our natural abhorrence of the doctrine of hell.

How easy it is to exchange "Thus saith the Lord" for "Thus saith psychology," or "Thus saith the church board," or even "Thus saith society." Pastors are called by God to stand apart from society, to preach the Word of God regardless of whether it's what people want to hear. God's absolute justice, mercy, and love, along with Christ's substitutionary atonement, can never be compromised to accommodate current psychology. We can't criticize the world's relativism if we have a relativism of our own. Good preaching brings together the turbulent predicament of man and the unchangeable grace of God.

Second, man-centered theology leads to incomplete repentance. What is the basis on which we approach God, our inherent value as persons, or Christ's sacrifice on the cross?

For the Christian humanist, man's sin is not so much an offense to God as it is an offense to man. Because we are valuable unconditionally, God is waiting to accept us. The assumption is that He owes us something; we do not come as undeserving but as deserving sinners.

How different is the teaching of the Bible. Yes, we have dignity as persons; but, because we are corrupt, God owes us nothing. If we get what we deserve, we'll be in hell forever. So we come in humility, recognizing that whatever God gives us is a gift—an undeserved favor. And the basis of our coming is the blood of Christ, not our value as persons.

I've found that incomplete repentance often leads to resentment against God. The logic is obvious: If He exists for my benefit, what happens when my "hunger for glory" remains unsatisfied? Why does God not come to my aid to help me become the fulfilled human being I desire to be?

Humans are notorious for insisting on their "rights." If we don't see ourselves as undeserving sinners, we'll be upset when God doesn't do what we think He ought. Ultimately, those who are willing to bow under God's sovereignty are those who are satisfied.

Initially, Job felt that God owed him blessings. He believed that if he served God faithfully, blessings ought to follow. When tragedy came, his wife suggested, "Curse God and die!" (Job 2:9 NASB). She thought that God owed her happiness. If He did not come through for them, so be it.

But at the end of the book, Job came to full repentance. God owed him nothing—not even an explanation for his suffering. When he saw God, he abhorred himself and said, "I repent in dust and ashes" (Job 42:6 NASB).

No one repents unless he sees himself as undeserving. If I am worthy of God's blessing, grace is diminished. It's His acceptance of us despite our corruption that magnifies His grace. We are not doing our parishioners a favor by exalting them at the expense of God.

Third, our watered down theology dilutes our impact in society. We all know about the resurgence of evangelicalism in the last twenty years, but our influence is not being widely felt. As I have mentioned elsewhere in this book, religion is up, but morality is down.

Recently, I heard a report that the TV viewing habits of Christians and non-Christians are practically indistinguishable. New attempts to rate TV programs and provide incentives for better viewing content have largely failed. In our desire to be heard by the world, we have lost our motivation to be separate from it. Our witness for Christ has a hollow ring.

Might not our impotency be traced to an exaggerated view of man's ability to the detriment of God's sovereignty? One reason Jonathan Edwards and George Whitefield had such widespread influence is because they insisted that the human heart is in a state of total corruption apart from the gracious intervention of God.

Such preaching confronted men and women with their needs. Sinners cried to God for mercy that they might not be consumed by His wrath. Conversion was not a decision made leisurely, but people sought God "to make [their] calling and election sure" (2 Peter 1:10 KJV).

Someone has said that the marks of a strong church are wet eyes, bent knees, and a broken heart. We'll never be powerful until we let God be God and jealously guard His honor.

Our Responsibility

How can we stem the drift toward a man-centered approach to theology? We would be wise to set aside the new reformation and return to the old one. Let's not shrink from preaching the unpopular doctrines of Paul—the total depravity of man and the spiritual deadness of the unconverted. Of course, we should preach in love and without self-righteous judgmentalism. But truth is truth, and half-truths often do the same damage as error.

Please don't interpret this position to mean that we must angrily denounce sin from a pedestal of self-righteousness. Far too many angry pastors vent their hostility by railing against sin as if they themselves do not participate in the pollution of the human race. We must preach biblical messages but in a spirit of personal repentance and humility.

We should not blush to admit with Luther and Calvin that repentance is a gift of God, granted to those who cast themselves on His mercy. The worship of God is man's highest calling. Indeed, creation exists for His good pleasure. This traditional emphasis leads us to self-understanding. Far from stripping us of dignity, such exaltation of God would help us to see ourselves as He sees us.

King Nebuchadnezzar saw himself as Christian humanists would recommend today: he had self-confidence, esteem, and, apparently, an integrated personality. He was a positive thinker whose great plans were realized. "Is this not Babylon the great, which I myself have built as a royal residence by the might of my power and for the glory of my majesty?" he asked (Dan. 4:30 NASB). His hunger for glory was satisfied.

God's response was to smite him with insanity. Nebuchadnezzar lived with the beasts of the field and ate grass like the cattle. His hair grew like eagles' feathers and his nails like birds' claws. That experience delivered him from a distorted view of himself. When he finally saw himself as he was before God, his sanity and position as king were restored.

He then blessed God and offered this praise:

For His dominion is an everlasting dominion,
And His kingdom endures from generation to generation.
And all the inhabitants of the earth are accounted as nothing,
But He does according to His will in the host of heaven
And among the inhabitants of earth;
And no one can ward off His hand
or say to Him, "What hast Thou done?"
(Dan. 4:34–35 NASB)

Thereafter, God blessed him, because he knew that he was the clay and God was the Potter. Nebuchadnezzar understood that God came first in theology. In our slide toward narcissistic preoccupation with ourselves rather than God, this is a truth we need to reaffirm.

• 17 •

Priorities

How Can I Get My Act Together?

No pastor wants to climb the ladder of success only to discover that his ladder was leaning against the wrong wall!

We all want to end with the satisfaction of knowing that we have done not just good things but the best things. In serving Christ, Martha did what was *beneficial*, but Jesus pointed out that she had neglected the one thing that was *needful*. Despite her good intentions, she had a problem with priorities.

Success is a series of right choices. Each day we stand at a fork in the road. When we say yes to one activity, we must say no to another. A night out with the family means we disappoint the hospital patient who thinks a visit from the pastor is overdue. Saying yes to a luncheon means less time for study.

"Effective leadership," Ted Engstrom says, "is the willingness to sacrifice for the sake of predetermined objectives." We've got to know what we want to achieve and then go for it with single-minded determination. As D. L. Moody said, "This one thing do . . . , not these forty things I dabble in."

But what should our priorities be? How should our time be spent when there is an endless array of good things from which we must choose? The thought that we are going to have to give an account to Christ "for the deeds done in the body, whether good or bad," should sober us and help us get our priorities straight.

Each pastor has to determine the specifics for himself. There is no one right answer to the question of how much time to spend each week in counseling versus visitation. Those matters will be determined by your gifts, the size of your church, and the expectations of your congregation.

But principles exist that should guide us regardless of our specific job descriptions. The following list of priorities helps me sort out the many options that confront all of us in ministry.

Praying Is More Important Than Preaching

When I say that "praying is more important than preaching," I don't mean we must give more time to prayer than to study—though there might be times when that would be profitable. What I mean is that we must guard our time for prayer even more closely than our time for study. When we're forced to choose, prayer should get top priority.

That was true of Christ, who spent a large part of His ministry in prayer. One day, His miracles so astonished the crowd that the whole city gathered at the door. It was a pastor's dream; people were everywhere. The next morning, He arose early and went to a secluded place to pray. Peter and some of the other disciples interrupted Him, saying, "Everyone is looking for You" (Mark 1:37 NASB).

What would we have done? We'd have returned to Capernaum to meet the expectations of the crowd. But Christ said to His disciples, "Let us go somewhere else—to the nearby villages—so I can preach there also. That is why I have come" (v. 38 NIV).

Because He had other responsibilities, He left the multitude disappointed. He refused to let the crowd dictate His schedule. Prayer in the morning hours was more important than ministry.

Jesus taught that men ought always to pray and not to faint, implying that we will do one or the other. Though a man of God may be naturally gifted, he must develop through travail in prayer. E. M. Bounds was right when he said, "Prayer that carries heaven by storm and moves God by a restless advocacy makes the pulpit a throne and its deliverances like the decrees of destiny."

Though we ought to spend much time preparing our minds for preaching, great men of the past have often spent the same amount of time in prayer, preparing their souls. Prayer, it is said, is not the preparation for the work, *it is* the work.

If your prayer life is mediocre or inconsistent, your first priority is to set aside time for this exercise. It doesn't have to be in the morning, but I've learned that if I do not spend time with God before 9:00 in the morning, I might not pray for the rest of the day. You might want to begin with fifteen minutes or half an hour. But whatever you do, make it such a priority that only an emergency would make you miss your appointment with God in prayer.

Preaching Is More Important Than Administration

Many pastors spend so much time running the church that they have little time for study and reflection. The temptation is to spend most of our time in our "comfort zones." The one who enjoys study often ignores administration; the one who thrives on administration tends to neglect study. Blessed is the church whose pastor has both gifts.

Committees are necessary. Even more important is vision and the ability to move the congregation toward the goals of the church. But when push comes to shove, it's the ministry of the Word that gives us our greatest impact. A church can usually put up with weak administration if it has effective preaching. But there's nothing quite as pathetic as people coming to a church and returning home without spiritual food.

One way to carve more time out of a busy day is to exercise the art of delegation. Ask yourself what you are doing that someone else could do; be generous in giving away all the responsibilities you reasonably can. Doing so will save you several hours per week. Have we forgotten that no one person has all the gifts, that the Lord has places for others in the body? Or are we so desirous to maintain control that we will let nothing go from our hands? Perhaps our desire for control is best left at the foot of the cross.

The wise pastor will concentrate on his strengths and delegate other responsibilities. Personally, I prefer to say no to invitations to serve on other boards, committees, and meetings to which I am invited. Since my primary gifts are preaching and writing, I want to use them to the best of my ability.

Join me in making this resolution: that *we make preaching our one big business.*

The Family Is More Important Than the Congregation

The importance of the family has been stressed so often that it scarcely needs to be mentioned. But many of us still have not gotten the message. As pastors, we receive our affirmation from the congregation; our successes or failures are known by many people, not by just a handful in an office. As a result, we feel vulnerable to the pressure of public opinion. This explains the strong temptation to meet the expectations of our congregations above the needs of our wives and children.

The pastor often feels as if he has many bosses. But keeping all of them happy will drive him to ignore the feelings of those he loves dearly—those who will, at least for a time, put up with neglect.

To reinforce our conviction that the family is more important than the congregation, each of us ought to make some hard, deliberate choices in our families' favor. We should take our wives and children out for ice cream rather than attend a finance committee meeting— at least once! Spend an evening on a family project rather than attend the meeting of the Sunday school council.

As I look back over my years of ministry, I wish I had been more relaxed, more spontaneous with my wife and children. I've tried to cut down on outside speaking engagements for the benefit of my family and the church. But often it's those small daily decisions that really reveal whether we value our families above those who pay our salaries.

Start today by making some tough choices in favor of your family. Let's not be easily seduced by the wide spread notion that "quality time" will make up for the quantity. There has to be a balance, of course, but usually it is our families who come up short.

Faithfulness Is More Important Than Competition

It's easy to get discouraged in the ministry when we compare ourselves with others. Members of our congregation compare us with television preachers or the superchurch pastor who is in his third building program.

Stories of successful ministries are legion. If we focus on them, we will soon be dissatisfied with our acre in the Lord's vineyard. We know we have overcome a spirit of comparison when we are able to rejoice in the success of those who are more gifted than we are. When we are content with our little part in the total work of God on earth, we will have a sense of satisfaction and fulfillment.

A legend states that one day Christ asked each of His disciples to pick up a stone and carry it. Then, after a few days, He turned the stones into bread. Those who had chosen larger stones were glad they did. When Christ asked them to choose stones again, all the disciples chose heavy ones. But after many days, Christ had them simply throw the stones into the river. The disciples were bewildered, wondering at the purposelessness of it all. But Christ said to them, "For whom do you carry the stones?"

If we carry the stones for Christ, what He does with them will not make any difference. The issue is not whether our stones become bread but whether our Master is pleased. Faithfulness, not success as generally defined, is what He seeks.

Love Is More Important Than Ability

Obviously, we cannot function without gifts that qualify us for the demands of the ministry. We must know the Word and be able to communicate it. And we must have skills in leadership and working with people.

Yet, surprisingly, Paul gave those essentials a lesser place than the quality of our love. Speaking with impressive ability, exercising the gift of prophecy, having the faith to move mountains, and even giving all possessions to the poor—all these actions, without love, are folly (1 Cor. 13:1–3).

Of course, love in itself would not qualify us to shepherd a congregation. But Paul would tell us we ought to concentrate on love first. When faced with a choice, we ought to develop the ability to love rather than the ability to minister.

Even the best Bible teaching does not change lives if it's not filtered through a personality filled with love. When we preach against sin harshly, we seldom motivate the congregation to godliness. But when we preach with brokenness and love, the Holy Spirit melts hardened hearts. We cannot say it often enough: *Without love, we are nothing.*

For many of us, more than half of our ministry is over. We will never pass this way again. If our priorities are misplaced, now is the time to get our house in order. Before we know it, our ministries will be over.

Look over your week's schedule and ask what you would change if you lived it according to God's priorities. When a famous sculptor was asked how he made an elephant, he answered, "I take a block of marble and cut out everything that doesn't look like elephant."

Take that block of time and cut out everything that isn't a top priority. List your activities based on comparative worth. By deliberately choosing to give more time to those things God thinks are important, we will probably find that we are accomplishing as much as ever. When we seek first the kingdom of God and His righteousness, our productivity does not cease. Only when we have done what is essential do we give God an opportunity to add to our ministries other matters that formerly were our primary concern.

If our priorities aren't straight, our ministries won't be either.

• 18 •

Failure

Why Does It Sometimes Happen?

Recently, I spoke to a discouraged pastor. His deacons were not supporting him, the congregation was apathetic, and his wife was complaining about his salary.

He was searching for an honorable exit, a way to resign with dignity. He planned to apply as a salesman with a firm that he had worked with before seminary.

Regardless of whether he had been called to the ministry, he felt as if he had given it his best but in return was greeted with one discouraging experience after another.

What Constitutes Failure?

Was that pastor a failure? The answer depends on one's perspective.

There are at least two kinds of failure. We can fail in the eyes of men. That hurts our egos. Those of us in public ministries are observed by many people; there's no such thing as resigning "quietly." And unless we move to larger churches, we're often viewed as failures.

Of course, it's possible to fail in the eyes of men and succeed in the eyes of God. The prophet Isaiah was called to be a failure (Isa. 6). If you measured his ministry by statistics, he would not win the Most Outstanding Prophet award.

But the reverse is also possible: we can succeed in the eyes of men and yet fail in the sight of God. In this second kind of failure, we may tell ourselves that our success is for the glory of God, but the hidden motive may still be self-aggrandizement.

This leads to a question: Is it possible to be called by God and yet fail in our calling? Yes. That's what happened to the disciples in Luke 9.

The Failure of the Disciples

Peter, James, and John had just come down from the Mount of Transfiguration with the Lord Jesus Christ. A crowd of people had gathered to watch the disciples free a boy from demonic enslavement.

The boy's father ran toward Christ, shouting, "Teacher, I beg You to look at my son, for he is my only boy, and behold, a spirit seizes him, and he suddenly screams, and it throws him into a convulsion with foaming at the mouth, and as it mauls him, it scarcely leaves him. And I begged Your disciples to cast it out, and they could not" (Luke 9:38–40 NASB).

And they could not! There you have failure in the ministry. As any preacher knows, it's tough to get a crowd; when you've got one, you'd like to be at your best. But though the disciples wanted to see God glorified, they couldn't perform the miracle. The crowd was about to leave disappointed.

Let's give the disciples credit for trying. Some pastors would never even attempt to cast out a demon. At least the disciples exposed themselves to the possibility of failure. They did not back off.

Yet they failed. Did they go beyond their calling? Were they attempting a task that was beyond their ability and depth? No. Earlier, Christ had called the Twelve, and He "gave them power and authority over *all* the demons" (Luke 9:1 NASB, emphasis added). They should have been able to cast out this disobedient demon.

Were they out of the will of God? No, they were exactly where God wanted them. But sometimes, while doing the will of God, we experience some of the greatest difficulties we have ever experienced. We can fail at the very task to which God calls us.

On an earlier occasion, the disciples were asked to go across the Sea of Galilee and meet Christ on the other side. Yet, even as they obeyed, they encountered one of the greatest storms on the lake. Yes, the will of God is often fraught with difficulty and danger; it is often the very place we experience the most resistance.

But now, as the disciples stood at the base of this mountain trying to cast out a demon, their call seemed ineffective, their commission

wasn't successful, and their authority didn't work. Why? Three reasons come from the text.

Reasons for Their Failure

First, they lacked *faith*. Christ answers them, "O unbelieving and
perverted generation, how long shall I be with you, and put up with
you?" (v. 41).

Christ calls them unbelieving. Whatever the cause, they didn't
have faith for this particular miracle.

We as pastors can identify. Almost every problem in the congregation eventually comes to our attention. We see divorce, moral failure,
and personality conflicts. Under the weight of such discouragements,
it's easy to entertain doubt.

"If Christ's power is so great, why doesn't He heal this marriage?
Why doesn't He . . . ?" At that point, we're on the verge of being spiritually paralyzed, unable to fulfill our calling. Without faith, we are
powerless.

We know how discouraging it can be when nothing goes as planned,
when our family is being attacked by Satan, and when church members
turn against us. When our confidence in God is eroded, we are vulnerable to failure. Christ called His disciples an "unbelieving generation."

Second, they lacked *discipline*. In the parallel passage in Matthew 17,
the disciples asked Christ why they could not cast out the demon,
and He replied, "Because of the littleness of your faith; for truly I say
to you, if you have faith as a mustard seed, you shall say to this
mountain, 'Move from here to there,' and it shall move; and nothing
shall be impossible to you" (Matt. 17:20 NASB). Then Christ added,
"But this kind does not go out except by prayer and fasting" (v. 21).

Prayer and fasting! The disciples' authority was not automatic.
Just because they had cast out demons in the past did not mean they
could count on such authority in the future. Their calling would have
to be renewed by fervent prayer and fasting.

Maybe they were too busy for a time of spiritual refreshment. They
may have begun to live off their own success stories and to think
they were too busy for the basics.

We're not very adept at fasting. Warren Wiersbe says, "Call a feast
and everyone is there. Call a fast and nobody shows." Without discipline, our ability to function spiritually is jeopardized.

There is a story about a man who was chopping trees, flailing away, the sweat running down his brow. A friend stopped by and asked whether he had sharpened his ax. The answer: "No, I have to get these trees down by noon, so I don't have time to sharpen my ax." But of course, we all know that the ten minutes needed to sharpen his ax would have been well spent. Similarly, the spiritual disciplines are the means by which we are refreshed, our ax is sharpened.

Third, they lacked *humility*. They asked a question we hear repeatedly in our day: "Who is the greatest in the kingdom of heaven?" (Luke 9:46). Who has the greatest church, the greatest Sunday school? Who is the greatest preacher, the greatest author?

Those questions reveal a carnal sense of comparison. On a dark night, we can argue about which star is the brightest, but when the sun comes out it makes no difference—all stars fade in its brightness.

Paul said that those who "compare themselves with themselves" are "without understanding" (2 Cor. 10:12). We don't know who the greatest preacher is. That's for God to judge. When we stop comparing ourselves with ourselves and compare ourselves with Christ, we find that there isn't much difference between us.

The disciples' pride led to a spirit of criticism also. They tried to prevent someone else from casting out demons in the name of Christ "because he does not follow along with us" (Luke 9:49 NASB). This person was successful in the very ministry in which they had failed. Like us, they tended to be suspicious of those who were succeeding at a task in which they were floundering.

God often uses people who don't agree with me. My pride has occasionally prevented me from rejoicing in the success of those who don't belong to my denomination or who differ from my theology. When we are humble, we will rejoice in the success of others and we will give God the credit for whatever little success we might have.

Do you remember the story in the book of Acts when the sons of Sceva tried to cast out a demon in the name of Jesus? They had watched Paul deliver people in the name of Jesus, so these young men thought they could do the same. They thought the name of Jesus was a good luck charm that could be used whenever they wished. But they were in for a surprise.

"And the evil spirit answered and said to them, 'I recognize Jesus, and I know about Paul, but who are you?' And the man, in whom was the evil spirit, leaped on them and subdued both of them and over-powered them, so that they fled out of that house naked and wounded" (Acts 19:15–16 NASB).

The lesson? We cannot take our authority for granted. There is more to winning against Satan than simply using the name of Jesus. Without devotion and discipline, we will discover that we cannot do ministry.

Reasons for Our Failure

Today, people still gather to see a display of Christ's power. They want to see drug addicts converted and marriages saved. They want to hear songs sung with joy and the Word preached with power. But unless we have faith, discipline, and humility, we will not be able to fulfill our calling.

We'll say to this mountain, "Be cast into the sea," or we will command the demon, "Be gone in Jesus' name." Neither will budge, and the crowds will leave disappointed. We know we were called, but our authority has evaporated. We've failed in God's work.

Maybe my pastor friend who is planning to become a salesman wasn't called to be a pastor. Or maybe he's in the wrong church. Then again, he might be in the will of God but passing through a desert experience. He just needs someone to encourage him, to let him know that he is appreciated. Or perhaps he has taken his calling for granted and has begun to live off substitutes. It may be that he has lost his authority, not his calling. That's why the mountains aren't moving and the demons refuse to leave.

I've learned that when I cannot exercise my authority to minister, God is calling me back to the basics. Faith, discipline, and humility can restore us to the place of blessing. Even commissioned disciples fail when they take their calling for granted.

• 19 •

The Fallen

How Can We Reach Out and Restore?

A seminary professor once told his students that they should become familiar with a vocation other than preaching because a certain percentage of them would eventually fall into immorality and have to leave the ministry. Although we might cringe at such advice, the professor was probably right.

A few months ago when I heard that a friend had to resign because of adultery, my reaction was, "He's the last person I'd expect that to happen to." But, unfortunately, the last is often the first.

The High Price of Sin

Recently, I asked some evangelical leaders whether a man who had fallen into sexual immorality should be restored to the pastorate. They said it's possible but highly unlikely. According to 1 Timothy 3:2, an elder is to be "blameless" (KJV) or "above reproach" (NASB). It's difficult to regain the public trust and to rebuild a reputation destroyed on the rocks of infidelity.

Many people believe, however, that Paul's standards in that passage refer to the *present* spiritual condition of an elder. For example, he is to be "free from the love of money" (v. 3), but that doesn't rule out the possibility that he did love money even after he was converted. There is growth in the Christian life; there is change and transformation.

These qualities refer to a man who has moved on spiritually and put his past life of sin behind him. At first glance, it seems reasonable that if a man falls into sexual sin, repents, and submits himself to the discipline of his church, he could once again be "blameless," because he has dealt with his sin biblically.

With that in mind, I asked the same leaders if their church or denomination would ever call as a pastor a man who had fallen but over time had demonstrated the fruits of repentance. Again, they answered no, unless many years had elapsed and the matter was long forgotten. Some of them knew of cases, however, in which a man was restored to an effective pulpit ministry, but his congregation did not know about his past.

My informal survey, however, was conducted several years before some rather high-profile pastors who had fallen into sexual sin were restored. I suspect that if the same questions were asked today, many leaders would be more open to the possibility of restoration to ministry. I can rejoice in such restoration, but I am also concerned that the high standards for ministry are being eroded. What does such restoration to the pulpit say to young men who are tempted to find fulfillment outside of their own marriage bond? Knowing that the mind can rationalize any sin that the heart wants to do, it is easy for a minister to think, "Look at so-and-so. He sinned and yet was restored. That's not so bad."

Marshall Shelley writes, "On the one hand, pastors are full-fledged members of the human race. They sin daily. On the other hand, pastors labor in a profession in which character is critical. They're called to lead and teach and model not some technical skill, but a life. When pastors fall, they can wound many believers."[1]

Yes, it is impossible for a pastor to stumble without causing others to be hindered in the race of life. Some will be emboldened to sin; others will lose confidence that sexual purity can be preserved.

An argument could be made that we are inconsistent in our standards. While sexual sin has routinely required stepping down from the ministry, sins of the spirit have been overlooked. The apostle John defined three root sins: pride, covetousness, and lust (1 John 2:16). Yet, I have never known of a pastor who had to resign because of pride or the love of money.

Martin Luther wrote, "God frequently permits a man to fall into or remain in grievous sin so that he may be put to shame in his own eyes and in the eyes of all men. Otherwise, he could not have kept himself free of this great vice of vain honor and a famous name if he had remained constant in his great gifts and virtues."[2] Yes, often pride lies at the root of other sins, even sexual immorality.

But regardless of how offensive pride is to God, sexual sin is in a class by itself. Paul wrote, "Flee immorality. Every other sin that a man commits is outside the body, but the immoral man sins against his own body" (1 Cor. 6:18 NASB).

Sexuality is such an intimate part of our lives, we cannot fail in it without guilt and shame. In adultery, there is also the constant reminder of the consequences of sin in someone else's life. What is more, the marriage relationship is to mirror Christ and His church. When a pastor shatters the intimate bond of marriage, we should think that he forfeited his right to the pulpit.

Sexual sin is usually accompanied by other sins. A person who commits adultery breaks at least five of the Ten Commandments. He puts his desires above God, steals, covets, bears false witness, and breaks the explicit commandment "You shall not commit adultery" (Exod. 20:14 NASB).

John Armstrong, in his helpful book *Can Fallen Pastors Be Restored?* writes, "Thus when we commit sexual sins we transgress directly against God's ordered plan for creation and His awesome holiness. We aggressively attack His holy name, His holy character and His holy law."[3] The breaking of a marriage vow, the violation of another person in an intimate unholy union, and the destroying of the picture of trust between Christ and the Church—this is a serious matter indeed.

Because of the shame of sexual sin, there is an overwhelming tendency to commit other sins to cover the deed. If someone had told King David he would get a man drunk and eventually have him murdered, he wouldn't have believed it. Yet, sexual sin made him a liar, a thief, and a murderer.

One denominational leader who had investigated a number of instances of alleged infidelity said he was surprised at how often pastors would lie, even invoking God's name, in covering their sin. Yet, we shouldn't be surprised. If a man can violate one of God's clearest commandments, other sins come easily.

A person who falls into this sin also tends to develop a pattern of infidelity. One pastor's wife complained that her husband was unfaithful not only in their first church but also in each successive pastorate. He kept believing he could get by because no one was willing to blow the whistle.

Sexual sin is a serious offense. Nevertheless, too often we force a man to the sidelines because of a single immoral act that we refuse to forgive and forget. Some former pastors have genuinely repented and have accepted the discipline of the church. Even if they cannot be restored to the pastorate, they could be used effectively in related ministries.

The Possibility of Restoration

In Galatians 6:1, Paul answers the questions we might have about restoration: "Brethren, even if a man is caught in any trespass, you who are spiritual, restore such a one in a spirit of gentleness; looking to yourselves, lest you too be tempted" (NASB).

What does it mean to restore one who has fallen? The Greek word *katartizo* was also used to refer to setting a broken bone. Unfortunately, many bones in the body of Christ have remained out of joint and have never been restored.

In a typical case of a pastor who commits grievous sin, he resigns almost immediately, has nowhere to go, and is forced to leave the area. Often, his salary is cut off with no provision made for his future. Because of his shame, he does not seek the fellowship of his friends. They feel awkward about approaching him, so a curtain of silence falls around him and his family.

The minister's wife is usually much more deeply wounded than she can ever tell. Committed as she is to Christ and the church, she must say all the right words, that yes, she forgives her husband, and yes, she will make the marriage work. But it might take years for the trust to be rebuilt and the joy to return to their relationship. She has to live with the painful reality that her husband violated their personal covenant and shared sexual intimacy with someone else. No wonder the restoration of their marriage takes time. This is a process that cannot be hurried along.

The couple feels ostracized, but their friends see their hasty exit as evidence that they are really not willing to be restored or repentant. The friends feel too uncomfortable to visit the wounded couple, not knowing what kind of a response they will receive or what they will say. Thus, the friendships that are so desperately needed often do not develop.

One evening, I had dinner with two friends, both of whom had to leave the ministry because of sexual sin. I asked one of them how many people had come to minister to him and how frequently his friends stopped by to pray with him. I was shocked to hear him reply, "I receive no visits; no one comes by to pray with us." That was the response even though members of the church lived close by. If we do not shoot our wounded, we most assuredly leave them bleeding along the side of the road.

Paul identified who should take the initiative: "you who are spiritual." When someone falls into sin, the difference between carnal Christians and spiritual Christians becomes clear. Under the guise of holiness, carnal believers will be critical, always demanding the maximum penalty.

One denominational leader told me that when a brother falls, some people almost show delight rather than sorrow and remorse. The self-righteous believer uses the opportunity for self-exaltation, seeming to enjoy picking on a brother who has been wounded. No matter how many sins are in his own life, a self-righteous man will see a pastor's moral failure as one more reason either to justify his own indiscretions or to make himself feel a tad more righteous.

A group of pastors sat discussing the news that a fellow minister had resigned amid rumors of sexual unfaithfulness. Yet, when one of them asked whether anyone had contacted him, they were reduced to silence. No one had.

The truly spiritual believer will be grieved and ask how his comrade can be restored. It's not the fallen brother who should do the restoring; the initiative should come from sensitive, spiritual Christians. They will be willing to risk reaching out despite the possibility of being misunderstood and accused of being "soft on sin."

Finally, how should restoration be done? Paul said, ". . . in the spirit of meekness" (Gal. 6:1 KJV). If a person has a broken bone, he doesn't want it pushed into place with a crowbar. It needs to be set with gentleness. There is no room for condemnation or self-righteousness. We must be aware that we could commit the same sin.

If the brother acknowledges his sin and repents, then fellowship can be restored. That's the first step in the long healing process.

But there is a difference between restoration to the body of Christ and restoration to ministry. Certainly, such a one will be able to serve the Lord again, though perhaps in a different capacity. We cannot predict what God might yet do through the life of a repentant, restored sinner. Sometimes the bird with the broken wing does soar again.

Let's not concede the whole tournament just because the devil has won a game.

• 20 •

The Church

What Is Christ's Blueprint?

Whenever I'm asked, "Where is your church?" I'm tempted to answer, "On Sunday, it's at 1609 N. LaSalle Street in Chicago, but during the week, it is scattered throughout the entire Chicago area!"

The word *church* is never used in the New Testament to refer to a building but rather to the people of God, those who are "called out" by God to form the body of Christ. It refers to saints on earth as well as saints in heaven. Those churches on hilltops with cemeteries around them are communicating a powerful theological lesson: the saints militant and the saints triumphant are all part of the same family. That's why the cemetery surrounds the church—you have to walk past the alumni association before you get to the undergraduates!

I think it was Reinhold Niebuhr who wrote that the church reminded him of Noah's ark—you couldn't take the stench within if it wasn't for the storm without! Whatever we may say about the church, this much is certain: it represents the highest priority on God's agenda and is His blueprint for completing His plans on earth. When Christ predicted the formation of the church, He highlighted certain features to which we must return again and again if we don't want to waste our time taking costly detours. His words are familiar: "And I also say to you that you are Peter, and upon this rock I will build My church; and the gates of Hades will not overpower it" (Matt. 16:18 NASB).

If we understand the features of the church, we will be able to serve with freedom and joy. What do we learn about the church in this statement?

119

Christ Owns the Church

"I will build My church." Believers were purchased at high cost; understandably, we are God's property. If the value of an object is determined by the price paid for it, then we are valuable indeed. We are not purchased with silver and gold but with the costly blood of Christ. The cross of Christ is an everlasting testimony to how much believers are actually worth to God! Of course, we are not valuable in and of ourselves; we are valuable because He chose to love us. In choosing to die for us, our Lord affirmed that we are infinitely precious to Him.

The implications for our ministry are obvious. God's people do not exist for their own benefit but for *His* benefit. In our interpersonal relationships, we must remember that we are dealing with God's property, His people redeemed for His own purposes. That's why church leaders are exhorted to humility and not to dictatorial leadership: "Therefore, I exhort the elders among you, as your fellow-elder . . . , shepherd the flock of God among you, not under compulsion, but voluntarily, according to the will of God; and not for sordid gain, but with eagerness; nor yet as lording it over those allotted to your charge, but proving to be examples to the flock" (1 Peter 5:1–3 NASB).

There's no place for manipulation or coercion within the church. Certainly, church leaders have to exercise authority as the Scriptures teach but not with the hidden motive of making their ministries appear successful. All fund-raising techniques and building programs must be examined closely; hidden motives must continually come under the scrutiny of God's microscope. Why? Because we are dealing with His people, His handiwork.

Furthermore, we are accountable to one another. The leader who says, "I am accountable only to God," speaks arrogantly and ignorantly. He forgets that God expects mutual submission and servanthood from every member of the body. All believers belong to the same family and have privileges and responsibilities.

Whenever I use carnal methods to accomplish worthy goals, I have forgotten who owns the church; whenever I am envious of those who are more successful than I am or whenever I use the church to exalt my abilities or to give the appearance of success, I have forgotten who owns the church.

What a relief to realize that the people in my congregation are God's property! Aren't you glad that those who stubbornly refuse to see your viewpoint don't belong to you? Like Moses, we must tell God from time to time, "Remember, these are Your people!"

If you have never given your congregation to God, do so right now. You will find a new freedom to serve when you recognize God as the rightful owner of His people.

Now, for a second feature of the church.

Christ Builds the Church

"I will build My church," Christ said. In all of our discipleship and evangelism, we must realize that we cannot do Christ's work for Him. Before He left, He gave instructions to the disciples to "make disciples of all nations" just as He had done while He was on earth. Now we are His representatives, standing in for Him during this period of His physical absence from earth. He did not make disciples en masse, nor can we!

Several years ago, I attended a joint session of the National Religious Broadcasters and the National Association of Evangelicals in Washington, D.C. Hundreds of displays exhibited the latest in technology, all used to spread the gospel around the world. After walking through acres of equipment, I began to wonder how the early church ever made it!

They, of course, made disciples the hard way, one person pouring his life into another in "on-the-job" training. Since those believers could not rely on the mass media, they felt an obligation to witness with their own lives and lips to everyone who crossed their paths. That's how the church was built, and that's how Christ intends that it be built today. We can be grateful for the Christian mass media, but there is no shortcut to building the church.

The stones for Solomon's temple were cut in a distant quarry and then brought into the temple area and assembled without the noise of a hammer. In Ephesians, Paul says that God is building a habitation, and believers are the stones. He chooses those whom He will save and brings them into a relationship with both one another and Himself. He fits us into the building as it pleases Him. He is building a place in which He Himself will dwell (Eph. 2:20–22).

Building the church is not left up to us, though we participate in the process. Our responsibility is to find how Christ did it and then reproduce His methods. Recognizing that He is the primary builder gives us hope and courage in the building process.

Today, much is written about church growth methodology and how to make a church more appealing to "seekers." Certainly, there is much we can learn from those who have been successful in seeing a church go from a few hundred to many thousands. The problem is that the success is often explained in terms of this particular method or that particular approach. Isn't it time that we saw churches grow with no explanation except that Christ has sovereignly chosen to build His church?

How refreshing it is to find a church whose only explanation is prayer, worship, and sensitivity to the leading of the Holy Spirit! Of course, I do not mean that we should expect a church to grow without training in evangelism, missions, and disciple making. He uses us to do His work. We have to plan, strategize, and determine what God wants us to do. Paul says that "we labor together with Christ." But in the end, our people should be convinced that what they have seen is the hand of the Almighty.

Christ is often robbed of the credit He so richly deserves whenever we try to find human explanations for a divine enterprise. Let us learn what we can from the experts, but let us never point to methods as an explanation for success. We must intentionally depend on Him for the growth of the church and make sure that He gets the praise when it happens.

One further implication: If a particular church is not growing numerically, it might not always be the fault of Christ's human instruments. Churches in hostile countries have sometimes been diminished through persecution and cultural conflicts. Even in our own country, there are times when the church itself is not at fault if it is not growing numerically. I say that not to excuse sloth and lack of vision, but simply to affirm that the growth of the church ultimately rests with Christ and not with us. And yet there is more.

Christ Preserves the Church
"The gates of Hades will not overpower it," Christ said (Matt. 16:18 NASB). This expression probably refers to His impending death. The

same description is used by Hezekiah in Isaiah 38:10 to refer to his own death. What Christ seems to be saying is this: Although the gates of Hades will close behind Me, they are powerless to keep Me within their grasp. The advance of the church will not be halted by such apparent setbacks. The church is indestructible.

That ought to take some of the pressure off our schedules! We can be involved in building the church with a sense of trust, believing that God's ultimate purposes will be accomplished. When the believers in Rome saw the unbelief of Israel as frustrating the purpose of God, Paul assured them, "But it is not as though the word of God has failed. For they are not all Israel who are descended from Israel" (Rom. 9:6 NASB).

The imagery is that of a ship that has not drifted from its intended destination. Paul is saying that the word of God is not "off course." God's purposes are on schedule; His work in the world continues, and it will be accomplished.

Paul writes in Ephesians 2:20–22, "Having been built upon the foundation of the apostles and prophets, Christ Jesus Himself being the corner stone, in whom the whole building, being fitted together is growing into a holy temple in the Lord; in whom you also are being built together into a dwelling of God in the Spirit" (NASB).

Notice the three passive verbs that Paul uses to show that the church is both built and preserved by God. We, "having been built," are also "being fitted" and again are "being built together into a dwelling of God in the Spirit." Believers are being acted upon by God, who is in the process of doing His work on earth. Like the stones referred to earlier, God is using His chisel and hammer to ready the church for His own purposes.

What an encouragement! To be involved with Christ in the building of the church is a no-risk venture. Eventual success is guaranteed. Peter Marshall said, "It is better to fail in a cause that will eventually succeed than to succeed in a cause that will eventually fail." Think about the implications: though we may fail in many ways, we are embarked upon an enterprise that has God's highest priority, and eventual success is inevitable. The gates of Hades will not prevail against it.

Christ Empowers the Church

To Peter Christ said, "I will give you the keys of the kingdom of heaven; and whatever you shall bind on earth shall have been bound in heaven, and whatever you shall loose on earth shall have been loosed in heaven" (Matt. 16:19 NASB). Later, Christ gave the same authority to all the apostles.

Here, Christ is giving the apostles power to carry out their assignment. It's unthinkable that He would give the disciples a blueprint and not give them the ability to carry it out. If I send my child to the store to get some groceries, I must give her the money to buy the items. Whether the list is long or short, whether it is costly or cheap, she must look to me for the resources to pay. Christ must give resources to those who would work with Him in building the church. Because all authority has been given to Him, He can say to us, "Go ye therefore."

The church is God's number one priority in the world. It displays His wisdom, both now and in the ages to come, "in order that the manifold wisdom of God might now be made known through the church to the rulers and the authorities in the heavenly places. This was in accordance with the eternal purpose which He carried out in Jesus Christ our Lord" (Eph. 3:10–11 NASB).

Christ has not left us alone. He resides in us and works with us in the building of His church. When Augustine was told that Rome had been sacked, he reportedly said, "Whatever men build, men will destroy . . . , so let's get on with building the kingdom of God."

Since whatever men build, men will destroy, let us get on with the business of building the church, for our Lord has promised that the gates of Hades cannot prevail against it. No risk is entailed. We have His promise of eternal success.

Notes

Chapter 1

1. Garry Friesen, *Decision Making and the Will of God* (Portland, Oreg.: Multnomah, 1981).
2. J. Oswald Sanders, *Spiritual Leadership* (Chicago: Moody Press, 1994), 18.
3. John Jowett, *The Preacher: His Life and Work* (Grand Rapids: Baker, 1968), 21.
4. Ibid., 12.

Chapter 3

1. Bruce Stabbert, *The Team Concept* (Tacoma, Wash.: Hegg Brothers, 1982).

Chapter 4

1. Marshall Shelley, *Well-Intentioned Dragons* (Carol Stream, Ill.: Christianity Today, 1985), 110.
2. Ibid., 107.
3. Ibid., 133.

Chapter 5

1. John Owen, *Sin and Temptation* (Portland, Oreg.: Multnomah, 1983), xviii.

Chapter 10

1. J. Grant Swank Jr., "Who Counsels Pastors When They Have Problems?" *Christianity Today,* 25 November 1983, 58.
2. David Congo, *Theology News and Notes* (March 1984): 8.

3. Iain Murray, *Jonathon Edwards* (Scotland: Banner of Truth Trust, 1987), 327.
4. James B. Scott, *Theology News and Notes* (March 1984): 15.

Chapter 11
1. Francis Schaeffer, *The Great Evangelical Disaster* (Westchester, Ill.: Crossway, 1984), 37.

Chapter 12
1. Lawrence Crabb, *Effective Biblical Counseling* (Grand Rapids: Zondervan, 1977), 47.

Chapter 13
1. William Temple, quoted in John MacArthur, *The Ultimate Priority* (Chicago: Moody Press, 1983), 147.
2. Ibid., 104.
3. John Stott, *Between Two Worlds* (Grand Rapids: Eerdmans, 1982), 82–83.

Chapter 14
1. Lewis Sperry Chafer, *True Evangelism* (Grand Rapids: Zondervan, 1919), 15.
2. Ibid., 14–15.

Chapter 16
1. Robert Schuller, *Self-Esteem—The New Reformation* (Dallas: Word, 1982), 26–27.
2. Ibid., 14.
3. Ibid., 127.

Chapter 19
1. Marshall Shelley, quoted in John Armstrong, *Can Fallen Pastors Be Restored?* (Chicago: Moody Press, 1995), 17.
2. James Atkinson, *Luther's Works: The Christian in Society I*, vol. 44 (Philadelphia: Fortress, 1966), 45.
3. Armstrong, op. cit., 51.

Also by Erwin Lutzer

The Doctrines That Divide

A Fresh Look at the Historic Doctrines That Separate Christians

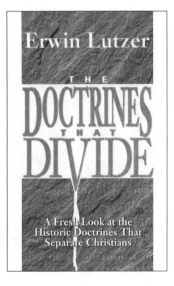

ISBN 0-8254-3165-4   256 pp.

Lutzer examines various controversies that exist within the broad sprectrum of Christianity, presenting the historical background of the issue and the biblical understanding of the doctrine.

The Doctrines That Divide provides a non-combative look at "hot button" issues in the church, which include

- infant baptism
- the deity and humanity of Christ
- the sacraments
- the worship of Mary
- predestination or free will
- justification by faith or works
- the canon of Scripture
- eternal security
- the sovereignty of God

"I recommend this book highly. The writer is a patient, persuasive pastor and never resorts to name-calling or condemnation. . . . buy this book!"

—Harold Lindsell

Lessons in Leadership
by Randal Roberts, general editor

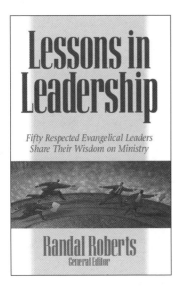

Dear Friend,

Now, you have no doubt heard the old adage that a pastor needs "the mind of a scholar, the heart of a child, and the skin of a rhinoceros," and there is a certain amount of truth therein. But I prefer to think of the pastor as a person called to be a servant of God, a proclaimer of truth, and a lover of people. And there's a bittersweetness to all three. . . .

Wherever I go, the people of this fellowship to whom I've devoted many years of my life smile at me, their hands reach out to me . . . [And] in some strange way they let me know that I belong in their midst and they in some indefinable manner belong in my life. No one told me that being a pastor would be like this.

ISBN 0-8254-3630-3   288 pp.

Sincerely,
Stuart Briscoe

This and forty-nine other letters offer insightful counsel for pastors or seminary students from today's Christian leaders, pastors, and professors, including

- Bill Bright
- Jill Briscoe
- Ted Engstrom
- Kenneth O. Gangel

- Carl F. H. Henry
- Walter C. Kaiser Jr.
- Jay Kesler
- Woodrow Kroll

- Aubrey Malphurs
- Luis Palau
- Earl D. Radmacher
- Moishe Rosen

kregel
PUBLICATIONS

Grand Rapids, MI 49501

Connections

The Threads
That Strengthen
Families

JEAN ILLSLEY CLARKE

1949-1999
HAZELDEN

HAZELDEN®

INFORMATION & EDUCATIONAL SERVICES

Hazelden
Center City, Minnesota 55012-0176

1-800-328-0094
1-651-213-4590 (Fax)
www.hazelden.org

The epigraph to chapter 13 is reprinted with the permission of The
Peters, Fraser and Dunlop Group. The quotation is reprinted from
Cautionary Verses (London: Random House UK Ltd.).

Library of Congress Cataloging-in-Publication Data
Clarke, Jean Illsley.
    Connections : the threads that strengthen families / Jean Illsley
    Clarke.
        p.   cm.
    Includes bibliographical references and index.
    ISBN 1-56838-342-8
    1. Parent and child.   2. Parenting.   3. Communication in the
    family.   I. Title.
    HQ755.85.C577   1999
    306.874—dc21   99-35167
                                                              CIP

03 02 01 00 99   6 5 4 3 2 1

Author's Note
The stories in this book are true. Names and situations have been
changed to protect the privacy of those who shared them. Some cases
are a composite of events. My sincere thanks to all of you who gave
me permission to use your stories.

Cover design by David Spohn
Interior design by Will Powers
Typesetting by Stanton Publication Services, Inc.

To all of you who are connected with me
and have taught me about connections.

Contents

Contents

Preface

Being connected is one of the
most important human experiences.
—ELIZABETH SHIPPEE

The Need for Connection

From time to connection

Connection is the issue. When I wrote "Time-In: To Discipline Is to Teach" I focused on time.[1] I was wrong. During the writing of *Time-In: When Time-Out Doesn't Work,* I got it![2] The issue is connection, the result of time spent with others in a way that builds strong, supportive, positive relationships. I read the research that shows that young children are responsive to parents' requests because of the relationship they have with the adults, not because of certain discipline practices or punishment.[3] Cooperation comes from connection.

I have been following the research on resilient children, those children who grow up in adverse circumstances and still function well.[4] It seems that resilient children always have at least one adult who believes in them and cares about them—one adult with whom the children have a positive connection.

Many families' connections are currently at risk as family members become overscheduled in activities outside of the home, as cultural pressures urge us to put everything from work to play ahead of family,[5] and as government policies often remain indifferent or hostile to the needs of children and families.[6]

As I thought more about it, I noticed connections, and more often lack of them, in many places. This book is an exploration of connection. My editor, Domenica Di Piazza, and I have rearranged it several times. Sometimes it has felt like the old saying *Writing a book is like scrubbing an elephant: There's no good place to begin or end, and it's hard to keep track of what you've already covered.* But, that doesn't really matter as long as you get the elephant clean, so feel free to read it in any order that fits for you. I hope it will stimulate and support you to do your own thinking about connections, to value the ones you have, and to create the ones you need.

Looking in a new way

A friend, Sheri, on reading the first draft of this manuscript, started to look at things in a new way and made an important discovery.[7]

> Dear Jean,
> My input is specific to the very beginning, because that is as far as I got. Not because I wasn't interested in going further, but because the message about connections was so powerful, I didn't want to go any further. It grabbed my attention and sent me on a trip down memory lane.
>
> For those of us who have never felt like we "belonged" or were "connected," the message is that life is about being connected. While that may sound simplistic, for those of us who don't "belong" or aren't "connected," the word at least offers a glimpse of what we are looking for. If you know what you're looking for, you have a better chance of discovering it.
>
> I have done many years of therapy and been involved with support groups for some time, but the concept of connectedness never made it to my consciousness. That is not to say that it wasn't presented—I'm just saying I didn't get it if it was presented.
>
> For me, thinking about connectedness is different from thinking about getting rid of old messages and behaviors. It's different from thinking about communication patterns. It's about how you get "close to" others. I have this image in my head of feathery strings that attach me to others—feathery strings that are connected, but not confining—they have some elasticity so that I can move closer or further away without breaking the connection. Being connected is part of belonging, the third level of Maslow's hierarchy of needs—it certainly is a primal instinct for adolescents.[8]

Sheri speaks of herself, but her message reflects the lack of connection that is common in America today. The need to be connected is deep in each one of us. In fact, the need to belong is so strong in some children and teenagers that they will commit tragic crimes in order to be accepted by a gang if they believe they do not belong anywhere else.

What Is Connection, Anyway?

True connection is a state of being in relationship. It may be close or distant, constant or infrequent, but it is held by a thread of real caring and it enhances the lives of everyone involved. It is a set of attitudes: mental, emotional, and physical. It is congruence between commitment and action. It allows for disagreement, but not for exploitation. Connection is not the same as being combined or blended with people or with misusing others. It is a balance between giving and taking. It grows out of and it breeds empathy. We may have an association or even a bond with someone who has treated us badly, but for the purpose of this book, let us use the word *connection* to indicate a positive, health-giving experience. It is a thing of the spirit. It is essential to helping children grow, because children learn about relationships in relationships, not in isolation. To be connected is our birthright. We are born of the closest physical connection between man and woman, hopefully a loving one. We started with possibly the most dramatic connection of our lives.[9] Listen to the wise one, the storyteller:[10]

> Once upon a time, a fateful time as long ago as you are old, an awesome event occurred. The most agile, determined sperm made his way through a pack of thousands. All were rushing and thrashing about. All were striving for the same goal. He resolutely pushed and shoved and propelled himself up the long passageway, thrusting himself beyond the others! The welcoming ova waited and when he resolutely burrowed his way into her pocky wall, she shut the others out to let this union grow. And become you. You come of a reaching out, and an acceptance. The essence of connection.

Why, then, should we not expect to be connected with ourselves and with others throughout our lives? Should this not be the pattern of our lifelong development? Jean Baker Miller and Irene Pierce Stiver say it well in *The Healing Connection*:

> In our view, the goal of development is not forming a separated self or finding gratification, but something else altogether—the ability to

participate actively in relationships that foster the well-being of everyone involved. Our fundamental notions of who we are are not formed in the process of separation from others, but within the mutual interplay of relationships with others. In short, the goal is not for the individual to grow out of relationships, but to grow into them. As the relationships grow, so grows the individual. Participating in growth-fostering relationships is both the source and the goal of development.[11]

But, for some, this does not seem to be easy. In many parts of the world groups of people are at war because they want to separate or they don't trust each other or they want to dominate. At the individual level, some of us have trouble staying connected with our friends or lovers, or even our children. Men and women may express these growth-fostering relationships differently and that can lead to misunderstandings.[12] Or we are not sure how to teach our children to be respectfully connected with us. Some of us have become confused about what connection means.

'Tis-Tisn't'

Listen to Laura: "Is this connection? Yes, it is. Well, I thought it was. But now it feels more like submersion. That's it. I'm a submarine, edging along the murky bottom of my relatives' unmet needs, of my children's incessant, self-centered demands, of my partner's unreasonable expectations. I am unappreciated and unfulfilled. I'm connected, all right. I'm bound in the chains of roles and expectations, of unmet promises and guilt. I'd like to disconnect."

Some of us have been disappointed or wounded so many times that we have forsaken being truly connected with anyone. We have said, *Enough. No more trying to be connected with people!* We have convinced ourselves that we are better off being loners. We have chosen work or play or food or violence or gambling or computers or the bottle or the needle instead.

Since drugs are often used to deaden the pain resulting from lack of connection, the use of the word *connection* to identify the supplier of illegal drugs or a transaction involving them is understandable. It is an unfortunate use of the word because true connection is central to drug abuse prevention.[13] When we have become bewitched by our substitute connection, others call us obsessed. In our search for substitute connections, we can even forget how to be connected with ourselves. We no longer know what we need. We no longer trust our own inner voice, the wisdom within ourselves.

When that happens, we need to remember that chains that bind are not about connection. True connection is meeting, not submerging. It is enhancing, not engulfing. It is fulfilling, not frustrating. There can be deep discomfort in connection when sadness comes from loss and when our anger is deep because we care so much. But if what seemed to be connection carries the pain of coercion, it is time to disengage, to step back, to start looking in a new way, to reclaim our hopes and dreams, and to make room for new connections. We need to reclaim our birthright, to become truly reconnected. We need to look at things in a new way; we can begin by reclaiming the promise of a better future.

The Promise

There is a promise that things can be better. The promise comes from Pandora's box.[14] Remember the Greek myth about the beautiful young maiden Pandora? The story goes that each of the gods on Mount Olympus put something harmful into a box and secured it with a rope tied with an impregnable knot. Zeus gave the box to the human maiden Pandora and forbade her to open it, ever. Pandora agreed, but her curiosity got the better of her, and one day she succeeded in undoing the impenetrable knot. When she lifted the lid, all manner of evil and hateful creatures burst out—hate, envy, greed, disconnection, alienation, illness, despair, and all the other evils, including death, famine, pestilence, and war. Horrified, Pandora slammed shut the lid of the box. Too late. Then she heard a soft call. She felt a longing, a yearning, and she cautiously lifted the lid again, just a little, and looked in. There was one creature left. Hope fluttered from the box. Small, bright, shiny hope.

The New Way

Hope promises that there is always something we can do to make things better. Sometimes courageous, physical actions are necessary. Sometimes we need to invoke golden patience. Sometimes we gather up the daring and ingenuity to look at things in a new way. This book is about hope. It is about connecting, not about giving up or just letting go. Letting go often leaves bumpy residue and ragged edges that chafe, annoy, and fester when we least want them because, since traces of all of our experiences remain in us, it is difficult to "let go" completely.

This book is about looking at things in a different way. It is about examining old attitudes toward closeness and distance, toward belonging or being controlled, toward time and energy, toward parenting and discipline, toward shame and guilt, toward grief and grieving, toward kith and kin, and even toward ourselves.

This book is about transforming and not letting old hurts or imaginings or outworn beliefs get in the way of our claiming our birthright, our ability to connect and to teach our children how to build healthy connections. It is especially about looking at time in a new way, about exploring a new idea called *time-in*.

It is said that there is nothing new under the sun. That may be true, but as you encounter the not-new ideas in this book, you may decide to look at them in a new way.

Acknowledgments

I thank all those directly and distantly connected with me who helped me on the time-in journey, including the people who read the manuscript before the publication of *Time-In: When Time-Out Doesn't Work*.

The people who read the manuscript for this book on connections offered many challenges and valuable additions. Thank you Ann Woodbeck, Phyllis Sweet, Amy Stone, Gary Rowland, Todd Pointer, Russell Osnes, Dana McDermott Murphy, Sue Murray, Maggie Lawrence, Shirley Knox, Sandy Keiser, Laurie Kanyer, Karen Ihnen, Eveline Goodall, Sheri Goldsmith, Mary Gautschi, Nate Eppley, Connie Dawson, Susan Legender Clarke, Joan Comeau, Jennifer Clarke, Joan Casey, and Suzanne Begin.

Among the many people who helped me think are Joan Laurie, George Kohlrieser, and Tony White. I appreciate them and all of my teachers of Transactional Analysis upon which theory this book is based.

The many people who contributed their valuable ideas and their stories include Amy Johnson, Sandy Keiser, Kaye Centers, Millicent Adams Dosh, Laurie Hamilton, Don and Sue Murray, Bob Elliott, Russell Osnes, Sally Hill, Kaara Ettesvold, Mary Claire Kalamafoni, Kath Hammerseng, and of course our children, Marc, Jennifer, and Wade, son-in-law Gary, and daughter-in-law Amy, and our granddaughters, Addie, Gressa, Freya, and Disa.

I give special thanks to the wise stepparents and stepchildren who read the chapters on blended families and added forceful words.

I am grateful to Kathy Shibley and Sue Johnson for dispelling my doubts and telling me how to write this book, and Connie Dawson and Jennifer Clarke for nudging me to complete it.

I am grateful to my husband, Dick, who, on a three-day ramble with me, helped clarify the theory underlying the relationship be-tween connection and boundaries.

I recognize the consistent encouragement of Athalie Terry and Ann Treleven-Carl whose daily patience and support helped this book take physical form.

Introduction
Why a Book about Connection?

Why, indeed? Why a book about connection?

Because to be connected is our birthright.

Because connection is the goose that laid the golden egg.

Because feeling connected lets children know that they belong.

Because a sense of connection gives parents direction and families stability.

Because it is what lets generations learn from and give wisdom to each other.

Because connectedness helps balance the spiritual and the physical parts of life.

Because lack of connection can lead to depression or addiction.

Because technology that helps us connect can also help us disconnect.

Because being truly connected is deeply satisfying.

Because children need to learn the life skills of connection, and the easiest place to learn those skills is in the family.

Because independence is not the goal of maturity; independence is a stepping stone to the larger goal, the grown-up connection of interdependence.

Because being truly connected means being able to listen to the wise one within oneself.

Because connectedness lets us build healthy communities.

Because people in many parts of the world are fighting because they aren't connected and they want to dominate.

Because the willingness to be truly connected brings a fountain of inexplicable riches into one's life and family.[1]

SECTION I

Time-In:
Ways to Connect

Chapter 1

Time-In, Time-With, Time-Out: Looking at Time in a New Way

Time is, twenty-four hours a day, every day.
—THE OLD STORYTELLER

Time

Listen to Fred: "I work; I fix the house; I buy insurance; I spend some time with my family. Sure, I play a little golf, but it seems as if I hardly have time to eat and sleep, let alone connect. Doesn't connecting take time?"

Connecting does take time. But time is there—twenty-four hours a day. Everyone has it. The same amount. Connecting is about *taking* time, and it is about *how you interact* with people while you are doing all the things you do.

Besides taking time, connecting takes energy. But it probably takes less energy than avoiding people, harboring grudges, or planning how to sabotage, put down, or get even with someone. It also takes less energy than worrying, bullying, feeling lonely, or playing psychological games.

Time-In

Time-in is the term we will use to indicate that we are deliberately building connection. It includes connecting by **attending, asking, acting,** or **amending.** Connecting involves spending time-in instead of time-out or time-with or time avoiding. Sometimes we all need time-out, time to withdraw, calm ourselves, and think. Time-out is wonderful when it is correctly used.[1]

Time-with is the time we spend in activities with others, and it can build connection, but it may not. We can be with a family member watching TV, or walking or riding, or even eating dinner with no more intimacy than we would have with the stranger sitting next to us on the bus. In fact, time-with activities can cause distance rather than connection if one person perceives that his needs are not being met or if another feels that she is being patronized, ridiculed, or ignored. Those experiences weaken connection.

Time-in is time spent guiding, loving, supporting, and respecting people. It not only builds other people and helps them connect with their own goodness, but it also frequently prevents problems. It frees up time for productivity and fun, and it builds connection.

The Myth of Quality Time

Some years ago, when parents became concerned because they were gone from their children too much, the term *quality time* became popular.[2] To some parents it meant take your children fishing. To others it meant reading to your children. To others it meant to get on their children's level and ask what they need. To some it was a reminder to ask, *How did your day go?* as if the day had legs or wheels and could go wherever it chose to take the child, rather than asking, *What did you do today?* which implies that the child is responsible for his actions.[3] Some parents used short bursts of quality time as a way to relieve guilt about not being with a child.

Yet quality time, at the convenience of the parent, can't create true connection because of its up-down nature. It treats the child as an object to be acted upon, not as an equal human being to relate with. It's impossible to have *quality* time that builds connection without having *quantity* time, enough time together for the life-connecting events to take place.

There is another hazard to quality time if the parent views it only as fun time. The research on overindulgence by this author and Dr. David Bredehoft revealed that adults who had been overindulged as children often identified lack of doing household chores as more of a pain-producing form of overindulgence than of having too many clothes or toys.[4] Teaching children how to do chores, overseeing them, and introducing standards takes quantities of time. In practice, quality time was usually identified as fun time or pleasant time rather than the real time it takes to teach, guide, agree, and disagree.

Children may not view chores as fun, but doing household chores, learning how to be a contributing member of the family, is a crucial way to learn life skills and to build connections.

Using Time Our Way

Think about how your family uses time and about how your culture approaches it. Some groups, especially some Western cultures and the Japanese, use time in a linear way: do one thing at a time, follow a plan, take deadlines and schedules seriously. This is called *monochronic* time use. In Latin America, Mediterranean countries, and the Middle East, for example, *polychronic* use of time is common. Here people do many things simultaneously, don't need an agenda, and don't value being "on time." In these cultures, relatives and friends are more important than preserving a schedule.[5]

Neither way is better; people using both ways can live good lives and get things done, but when adults from the two systems come together, they have to do some major adjusting to connect with each other. Children are natural polychronic time users, so if you live in a monochronic culture, teaching your children how to use time monochronically is one of your tasks and may be one of your frustrations. Most children respond best if this is done gradually from toddlerhood onward.

Time-in can be used in either a monochronic or polychronic setting. Time-in is a specific set of ways to foster a positive relationship. Using it with children teaches responsibility and respect for self and others. It builds connection even when children are being disciplined. We will apply it to discipline in chapter 7. First let's learn about the four puzzle pieces of time-in.

The Four Puzzle Pieces of Time-In

Think of connecting as a puzzle to be solved, not by you alone but by you and the other person. It is the puzzle of what to offer and how to respond. The four puzzle pieces of time-in offer alternative starting places. You may already be using all four; however, time-in can be a new way of thinking about them and of combining them. Sometimes one puzzle piece is all you need. Other times you need all four.

The four puzzle pieces are

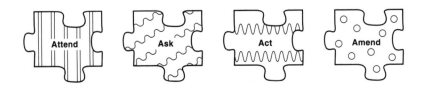

Let us look at a brief overview of the four pieces before each is addressed at length in chapters 2–5.

The **attend** puzzle piece is being aware, paying attention, listening and hearing. It has two levels: The overarching level means gathering the necessary information to know how and when to **ask** or **act** or **make amends**. The other level involves specific ways of attending to everything from routine events like spilled milk to something as traumatic as a broken heart. Teaching children to attend to the results of their actions—to the broken vase, the hurt feelings—is central to helping them become responsible for their behavior.

The **ask** puzzle piece builds connection if you are genuinely interested, withhold criticism, and are respectful of the other person's response to your question. The inquiry may be as benign as, *Did you enjoy the movie?* Or as discomforting as, *Can you tell me what happened right before the accident?*

The **act** puzzle piece means moving your body, doing something in behalf of the other person's enjoyment, enlightenment, or protection. Acting can offer support or confrontation. It can be as simple as holding someone's hand or as complex as supporting someone through a long illness.

The **amend** puzzle piece, or restitution, not only builds connection, but is also crucial to maintaining a strong connection with another person. Any long-term relationship will, at some time, include mistakes, something forgotten, something ignored. These happenings rupture the bridge of trust and, if not repaired, will fray the line of connection. The need to make good may be for a little thing like borrowing a shirt without asking or for a big thing like harming a reputation.

No Best Puzzle Piece

All four puzzle pieces are equally important. If you have a preference for one of these four, you may be missing connections with people who prefer one of the other three. Unlike a jigsaw puzzle, these four A's do not have to be joined in a specific pattern. They can be combined in any order or linked in any direction. They can be used singly or in combination.

*When Lena heard that her sister Josie had lost her best friend, Lena **asked**, "Will you tell me about it?" Lena listened attentively (**attended**) while Josie recounted the story. Lena knew that telling the story helps resolve grief. It wasn't necessary for Lena to take any other **action** and there was nothing to make **amends** for. Earlier in her life, Lena had been uncomfortable with grief and had avoided people who had experienced losses because she didn't know what to say. Then she felt guilty because she hadn't done the right thing. Understanding the potency of each of the puzzle pieces helped Lena choose a way to connect with Josie when Josie needed support.*

Time Enough

If you think you do not have enough time with your family, take a close look at your priorities. Chances are your family values are sound, but you get busy because you want to provide a fine lifestyle for your children and you want to give them lots of opportunities. However, if your work and community activities and your children's lessons, games, clubs, and social events have replaced chores with chauffeuring time, and family together time with juggling schedules, you may want to think again. William Doherty's fine book *The Intentional Family* offers solid help for people who have sacrificed family rituals and family hang-out-together time to the cultural hurry up.[6] Doherty observes that many American families are overscheduled outside of the family and underscheduled within the family. Like the white rabbit in *Alice in Wonderland*, we have no time to say hello, good-bye, and too little time for what goes in between.

Instead of looking for ways to cram more activities into each day, we can try turning ourselves upside down and looking at time in a whole different way. Some of us have to reclaim our time, the twenty-four hours every day that is ours, and be in charge of it. And some of us have to limit our children's out-of-home involvements so we can have time-in to reconnect. Fifty years from now the quality of our children's lives will depend much more on their ability to connect than on the number of sports they played in school. The benefits of teaching children how to connect are well worth the time, on the personal, the family, and the global level. Take the time you need to be with your children.

> *Forget the past and live the present hour.*
> —*Sarah Knowles Bolton,* The Last Word

You can use the "Time-With Chart" on page 9 to help you think about ways you want to connect with your children. Following is a partial list of ways adults have *time-with* children. To help clarify your thinking about time-with, quality time, time-out, and time-in, identify the ways you think time is used during each of these time-with activities. Add more activities of your own. You may check more than one box for each activity.

For example, the times when Fred is driving the carpool is high quality time when he and the children are sharing riddles and laughing together. It is time-out for Fred when the riders are talking among themselves and Fred's mind is elsewhere. It is time-in when he is **attending** carefully to the children's conversation to learn about his son's peers. It would be time-in if the boys were quarreling and Fred **acted** by stopping the car and announcing that he would start the car again as soon as the quarrel was stopped. It could be time-in if Fred were to **ask** the boys why they think having rules makes the soccer game more fun.

Check each box to indicate how the time-with is being used. If it could be time-in and isn't, place a star in the last column and think whether you could start with an **ask**.

Time-With Chart

Time-With	Quality Time	Time-Out no connection	Time-In with connection	Could be Time-In?
drive carpool				
chat with				
sing to/with				
play with				
sit close to				
read to/with				
listen to				
do a household task with				
do an errand with				
go for a walk with				
do a sport with				
read a map with				
solve a problem with				
look up data with				
clean a drawer with				
do the laundry with				
build a shelf with (even two-year-olds can find the long screws and stick them in the holes)				
build a sand castle with				
color beside each other				
color the same picture with				
bake a cake with				
look for bugs with				
eat popcorn with				
create a mystery story with				
play a board game with				
go for a bike ride with				
plan a picnic with				
play musical instruments with				
fish with				
watch TV with				

Chapter 2

Attend

Pay attention to what you are paying attention to.
—MARILYN DE LONG

The **attend** puzzle piece is the glue of connection. When we attend, we strengthen belonging because we accurately notice and are aware of what is needed or is going on. It is not hovering or controlling, but being aware. It is the little and big things we do to reassure people that we are aware of their existence, their accomplishments, and their needs. Remember that ignoring, shunning, and isolating can strain even well-formed connections and are sometimes used as severe forms of punishment.[1] The art of attending is an important puzzle piece because if we have neglected to attend, we could **ask** or **act** in ways that cause distance instead of enhancing connectedness. Attending is also a very important part of catching problems when they are small, before they cause a serious rift in connections.

The Four Pillars of Attending

The level platform of attendance rests on four pillars. They are *noticing, being present, empathizing,* and *looking after.*

Noticing

The **attend** puzzle piece builds connection when we take time and energy to be alert, to notice and be responsive. Someone said, *Noticing is like watching animals at the zoo, but not getting in the cage.*

As Josh rushed into the house, Mom noticed that he was unusually excited or agitated.

   "Hi, Josh, what's up?" Mom asked.

   "Nuttin'," replied Josh.

   "Okay, I'm here to listen if you want to talk," said Mom, reassuringly.

Mom noticed Josh's mood and offered her help, but she didn't jump into the cage and get so involved with her own agenda that she ceased to notice Josh.

   Parents also notice a child's accomplishments and behavior, and they report what they see and how they feel. To the toddler, *You crawled behind the sofa! I am glad you found that little hiding place.* To the teenager, *I'm delighted you found a summer job early this spring! I know that took some organization and ingenuity on your part.* To the new driver, *I'm pleased that you are observing the speed limit. I'm concerned about how wide you take corners. Slow down a bit and keep the car in your own lane.* To the young adult, *I like your new apartment. I see you have figured out what to look for.* Noticing in this way builds self-esteem and is far more helpful than, *You are a good boy* or, *Good job* or, *You are a bad driver.*

   We notice changes in behavior.

When their teenager started sleeping more than usual, Mom and Dad agreed they would have to determine if Lamar was in a sudden growth spurt or if something else was going on.

We notice messages not spoken. When a friend or co-worker seeks us out, we attend to the overt request and notice whether there is also a need for approval or a connection behind the person's request. We respond, *I'm glad you asked me. We haven't talked for a while. Anything special going on?*

   Sometimes, by being aware of our intuition, our inner wisdom, we notice that we have not heard from a friend in quite a while, so we call. If the friend is experiencing hard times, our reaching out can be very important. Noticing helps maintain the connection.

   We notice the effect of family rituals. We may notice that the daily bedtime ritual is not regular enough to help the toddler get to bed, or that a yearly holiday ritual has become too rigid and causes resentment. Then we take action to create a ritual that helps build connection.

   We notice whether the family activities are reinforcing family values and morals. If we go out to dinner to be together and then give the children coins to play video games, we are defeating the purpose of the outing. If we take the children with us when we deliver food to the foodshelf distribution center, or if we join the children in picking up roadside litter, we reinforce the family value of extending ourselves to others.

Being present

Our physical presence is important to the connection process. To attend, for example—to *apply the mind* to a person or situation—one must be with that person and be alert for new information.

When we cannot be physically present, we listen to the story later.

Having Dad attend soccer games is important to Steven. When Dad is going to be out of town, he lets Steven know ahead of time and drops in on a practice. Dad listens to Steven's full account of every missed game.

Also, unless we are vigilant, we may view things through the filter of our own experience, not through the perceptions of the other person. Attending means using our eyes, our ears, and our intuition to help us be aware. It often means using the 20/80 rule—talk no more than 20 percent of the time, just enough to encourage and show understanding. Listen for the other 80 percent. We use our eyes and our ears when we are physically present.

Madeline quietly mentions that her friend's parents are getting a divorce. Mom stops what she is doing and gives Madeline her full attention. Mom watches, listens, comforts, and asks gentle questions as she attempts to discern what this means for Madeline.

The telephone is an extension of physical presence.

When Adele's sister Phyllis was hospitalized in a distant city, Adele called daily to give moral support and to tell funny stories. Phyllis felt cared for and connected.

John and Evan have a longtime friendship. They seldom see each other, but when they talk on the phone, each gives undivided attention to the conversation. They feel each other's presence.

E-mail is presence if it takes into account what is going on with the other person.

Jane used e-mail to make sure all family members agreed to the date and place of an anniversary celebration.

Simply having your body present is not enough. An emotional, intellectual, and spiritual posture of openness is also important. Martin Buber's concept of the *I-Thou* helps some people better understand this need for openness. In his book he says:

> Those who experience do not participate in the world. For the experience is "in them" and not between them and the world . . . the world as experience belongs to the basic word I-It. The basic word I-You establishes the world of relation.[2]

To think about I-You versus I-It may sound easy, but Buber's I-Thou concept is more complex and demanding than it seems at first glance. It is a challenge for some of us to set our egos aside enough to be really present to another.

Young children know how to be fully present. It is a natural gift of childhood. They hang around. They know what is going on even when we think they are not listening. They may respond to our mood before we recognize it ourselves. Someplace, along the growing-up way, we were taught to ignore our ability to be present. As adults we need to recapture that potent position of being present.

Empathizing

When **attending** indicates that support is appropriate, it needs to be offered in an empathic way. No tough-it-out message such as, *This is not important,* but instead, *I'm hearing you and I care.* Sometimes it includes an offer to help, but often it is just paying attention.

Yolanda tells her dad that her best friend's family is moving. Dad looks concerned, asks where and when, then talks about feelings. "You and Sophia have been good friends. How are you feeling about this?" Or Dad may put his arm around Yolanda or just listen attentively.

Terri is weeping because this is the day her baby has started school. Maggie gives full attention and a hug. "Want to tell me about this morning?"

Ben heard that Nick's wife is ill. "Nick, I hear that Beth is not well. I'm sorry."

Empathy can strengthen even tenuous connections. Sometimes a deeply felt, *I've been there* or, *It was hard for me* is helpful. Usually, *I know how you feel* is not comforting because it is about us, not about the other person. We never know exactly how another person feels.

One of the disturbing findings from the Search Institute's research *The Troubled Journey: A Portrait of 6th–12th Grade Youth* is that although many boys in America have developed appropriate empathy by sixth grade, they lose it by twelfth grade.[3] To ensure that each child values empathy and knows how to respond empathically, parents and teachers need to model empathic behaviors, talk about their importance, and expect them in children of all ages.

Looking after

Besides noticing, being present, and expressing empathy, the question is this: Is there some action I should take, something I should look after?

Gavin is acting more withdrawn than usual. His sister reports that he is being bullied on the school bus. His parents believe that bullying is hard on the victim and is the first step toward violence for both the perpetrator and the victim. They also believe that it is the job of adults to stop the bullying, that asking the victim to handle it very seldom stops the bullying. They decide how they will get the school's attention to stop the bullying.

Parents who ignore bullying risk breaking the parent-child connection if the child feels abandoned by the parents.

When Justin noticed that his wife was consistently fatigued, he asked her about it. She brushed it off. Justin insisted that she get a physical evaluation.

Marshall noticed that one of his employees was often late for work. Marshall warned the employee about the possibility of losing her job. He also asked her what she needed in order to get to work on time.

Discounting—The Opposite of Attending

It is impossible to attend to everything! The world is filled with sights and sounds and colors and people who want us to do things and advertising that urges us to spend our money. We have to learn to screen out lots of information. But we can apply our minds to the things we need to attend to. For parents that means we *can be present with our children, we can look after ourselves,* and we *can be aware of the situations* that affect our children and us. Little things and big things. For friends, relatives, and co-workers, we can do the same.

Discounting is the opposite of attending. It is what we do when we miss or ignore things that we should not have missed.

Discounts can occur at four levels when we act as if there is	To avoid discounting we can ask
1. no problem	Level 1. Is this something that needs to be addressed?
2. the problem is not serious	Level 2. How important or serious is the need?
3. no solution	Level 3. How could this be resolved?
4. nothing I can do	Level 4. Shall I do something to help?

If we discount on any one of these four levels, the issue is not addressed; the problem is not solved. We are not attending, not connecting.

> *Discounting is the opposite of attending, of taking into account, of being aware, and of acting on the awareness.*

The following examples of discounting remind us that we all discount sometimes. Our task, when we realize we have discounted, is to move into awareness and take action.

First level (no problem): Parent discounts a child's school needs

Lauren M. spread out her school project on the table after the family finished eating. Her brother was watching TV and wouldn't turn the set off. Lauren complained about the noise, but neither her brother nor her mother responded. Lauren's mom was surprised when Laura's project was late and she got a poor grade.

Mrs. M. was not **attending**, not noticing that Laura needed support to get her homework done. Mrs. M. discounted on the first level—there is no problem. Mrs. M. could have asked herself, *Is there something that needs to be addressed?* If she had been aware of the problem, she could have turned off the TV, moved the TV, or set up a card table in another room for Lauren to work on. One way of being connected is to notice and respond to what is happening.

First level (no problem): Sometimes a teacher discounts what is happening at home

Andy's teacher didn't notice that his clothes were not clean, that he had circles under his eyes, that he fidgeted a lot and jumped whenever she talked to him. She scolded him daily because the quality of his work had fallen off. The teacher did not apply her mind to wonder what was going on with Andy.

She discounted on the first level by ignoring the problem when she should have asked herself, *Is there something that needs to be attended to?* Andy had lost connection with his dad and because his teacher didn't notice and find out, he was now losing connection with his teacher.

Second level (not serious): A discount at work can spill over at home

A salesman for a cabinet shop, Mr. P. had promised to deliver a cabinet on the way home. The woodworking shop was often late finishing work, and this was one of those days so he wasn't able to make the delivery. Mr. P. shouldn't have made the promise without checking with the shop, so he had to call and listen to a disappointed and angry customer. Mr. P. tightened his lips and vowed not to let it bother him, but instead of relaxing as he drove home he got more and more upset. When he finally swung into his driveway, he flattened a paint set, bumped a little red wagon, and poured his anger on his children.

Mr. P. had discounted twice on the second level, first by not taking seriously the frequency with which work was late and second by not paying attention to the seriousness of his distress. Because he didn't **attend** and make a constructive decision about what to do about his unwise promise at work and about his own distress, he pushed his children from him instead of connecting with them.

Third level (no solution): Discounting a long-term problem doesn't make it go away

A reduction in the retirement benefits plan at Mr. Q.'s company had him worried. His other savings couldn't possibly make up the difference. Everyone in his office was upset, but no one knew what to do about it. Ms. R. suggested the employees join together and hire a lawyer to see whether they had any legal recourse. Mr. Q. thought lawyers made everything worse, so he vetoed that plan. Stopping at a bar after work made him feel better while he was there but not after he finally got home. When his children approached him, he brushed them away and withdrew into silence.

What's the matter with Daddy? Mr. Q. discounted on the third level. He assumed there was no solution to his problem, but he continued to worry about it. He became more and more distant from his family because of his lack of **attention** to his own needs.

Fourth level (nothing I can do): Health problems, when discounted, usually don't go away

The teacher noticed Carolyn's red fingertip. It looked like an infected hangnail, but the teacher assumed Carolyn's folks would care for it. The infection spread under the nail, and Carolyn missed school for two days. The teacher was noticing, but she didn't look after Carolyn by sending her to the school nurse.

The teacher discounted on the fourth level: *I don't need to do anything.* Next time she should **attend** and ask herself, *What can I do to help?*

Fourth level (nothing I can do): Discounting our ability to tackle a social problem allows it to continue

Mrs. K. listened to her children's stories of bullying in the bathrooms, intimidation in the locker rooms, knives in the parking lot, and teachers who looked the other way. Mrs. K. sympathized, worried, wrung her hands, and did nothing.

She discounted on the fourth level and responded as if there was nothing she could do to help. Every day she sent her children to an unsafe school. She could have **attended** by applying her mind to figuring out how to demand that her tax dollars provide a safe place for her children to learn. Mrs. K. might have persuaded her friends to help her support the teachers so they could stop looking the other way and effectively attend to the children's safety. Children need parents whose connection with the school helps keep the learning environment safe.

If You Have Been Discounting

Attending to a problem that has been hanging around awhile can often be expedited by asking

- What am I discounting? My needs, someone else's needs, the situation?
- How am I discounting? Am I ignoring that something needs to be addressed? Am I taking into account how serious the problem really is? Have I looked for solutions? Am I willing to do what I need to do?

The answers to these questions help us focus on what needs to be done. To stop discounting means to start **attending.** We attend when we notice that our children are discounting and insist that they attend to what is really going on. (You can read more about discounting, how to stop it in yourself, and when to confront it in others by reading chapters 20–23 in *Growing Up Again: Parenting Ourselves, Parenting Our Children*.[4])

What Are Some of the Ways We Attend?

There are many ways to **attend:** We nurture. We notice and then make it known that we have noticed. We express thanks for help, gifts, and recognition that others give us. We show respect. We acknowledge that the other person's feeling or response or interpretations are valid for him at the time, even if, with more information, he might respond differently. We notice achievements. Sometimes we acknowledge achievements with special events or rituals. We celebrate others by showing our delight at their existence, by birthday recognitions, and by marking developmental achievements, from a picture of the first steps and the first day of school, to a gift or ritual at the onset of puberty. We offer unconditional love. We provide for the individual needs of children at each developmental stage. We recognize the child's particular learning styles, talents, and interests, and provide activities to support them.[5]

Sometimes you attend by stopping what you are doing, intentionally "parking" your thoughts temporarily, and looking directly at the other person. Other times you attend while you are bending over your mending or driving the car or collecting the trash or cleaning up the tool bench. No matter how you do it, just do it.

What to Attend To

What are the most important things to attend to? That will depend on where you live, your talents, your values, your personality, and the ages of your children. If you let the idea of attending roll around in your mind for a few days, you may be surprised at how easy it is to start noticing what you need to attend to.

Here are some examples.

Obvious needs

Safety is an obvious need, from protecting the toddler by placing a gate at the top of the stairs to helping the school-age child and teenager learn whom to trust, whom it is safe to connect with. This is not as simple as telling children, *Never talk to strangers*. That cuts them off from the world. It limits their curiosity, their experiences, and their chances to practice connecting. Parents who fear kidnapping need to teach a child to stay within their view, remembering that most children who are kidnapped are snatched by someone whom they already know. (Carol Watson's book *Run, Yell & Tell! A Safety Book for Children* is a wonderful help in childproofing a kid against kidnapping.[6])

Health needs are obvious when there are fevers, rashes, or headaches. The symptoms of other health issues such as drug abuse may be less easy to identify. (There is a helpful section on drug abuse symptoms, that does not take a pharmacologist to understand, in *Help! For Kids and Parents About Drugs*.[7])

Misbehavior and defiant, destructive, or violent actions call for immediate attention. Parents need to remember that when they do not give their child the amount and kind of positive attention that that particular child needs, the child arranges to get negative attention. For the child, negative attention—being scolded or yelled at—is better than none. Far, far better. Every human being hungers for recognition, and children will figure out what behaviors their family responds to.

Aggressive behavior in inappropriate places is easy to notice. Boys who use their fists instead of their brains to solve problems need options. In *Reaching Up for Manhood* Geoffrey Canada discusses what it means to be male and explains how to teach boys to be aggressive in sports and gentlemen when they come off the court.[8]

Less obvious needs

Behaviors that are not as noticeable may need as much attention as the ones that are in our faces. Girls are less likely than boys to be physically aggressive. When girls are aggressive, they are likely to tease, shun, and use relationships to control or hurt. These behaviors are not as noticeable as physical acts, but they can be just as damaging as overt aggression, so they need to be addressed. Other behaviors such as withdrawal or isolation or the need to be "supergood" or do everything perfectly may be less noticeable, but they do need attention.

Some health issues may not be obvious. Lack of exercise, poor nutrition, or not enough sleep can sap a person's vitality and need attention.

Grieving can also affect health and vitality. A child can be grieving a loss the parent doesn't even know about. Grieving is a skill that must be taught and supported. (See chapter 20, "I'll Buy You a New Puppy: Helping Children Grieve.")

Noticing, being present, empathizing, looking after—all of these ways of attending strengthen connections.

Mismatches

When parents and children have different personality styles, interests, and talents, parents need to differentiate what appears to be the child's lack of interest or misbehavior from the child's attempt to meet his needs in a way that fits his personality style. Maybe this child's inborn personality traits are such that she does not respond well to the way the demands and expectations of the family are presented, and her parents need to learn a more effective way to approach this particular child. For example, extraverted parents who think as they talk have to learn to wait for their introverted child to respond to a question and not to interpret his need to pause and think as defiance.[9]

Or maybe the child doesn't share the same enthusiasm for and interest in something the parent values.

Dad, an avid sailor, wanted to do something great for his teenage son, Brad. Something that would help them be more connected. Dad rented a sailboat and helped his son collect a crew so he could race two days a week all summer. Brad had trouble getting out of bed on race days and even more trouble explaining why his boat usually came in last. Competitive in other sports, Brad thought sailing should be about long lazy days on the lake enjoying the wind and the clouds. When Brad figured that out, he stood tall and said, "Dad, I know you love to sail and to race. Being captain during a race is not my thing. This racing is not for me; it's for you. I would like to be with you, so if you'll captain, I'll be glad to crew for you." Dad got the message and suggested that Brad drop the races and find times when they could sail together.

Distance and closeness

Connection requires some proximity and when the prevailing culture denies that need, parents may not notice what is happening. The conventional wisdom in America is that children, particularly boys, need to separate, to become independent, to be free of their mothers at a young age. In their wonderful book *The Courage to Raise Good Men* Olga Silverstein and Beth Rashbaum blend personal experience with psychological understanding to point out how following the cultural dictates for distance has resulted in the abandonment of boys.[10] They offer compelling arguments for helping boys stay connected with both mother and father, and poignant examples of what happens to boys and men who don't stay connected.

The assumption that boys can become men only when they deny their affection for and connection with their mothers is a most unfortunate piece of cultural misinformation that has often been accepted not only by parents, but by the boys themselves. Marty's family didn't buy it.

During his teenage years, Marty did his share of testing family values and tolerance. But he remained friends with both parents. He matched wits and humor with his mother, sought her advice about school, and taught her how to surf the Net. Marty was twenty when his father died. Although he was busy at school, Marty made sure to go home at least one day every other week to be with his mom and to help her. His male friends alternately ridiculed, chided, and envied him: "Why are you always running home to Mama?" "Don't let her get dependent on you—that could be a real drag." "I haven't gotten along with my mom since I was about twelve. You act as if you really like your mom. I wish I had a mom like yours."

Besides the great cultural push for distance, seemingly harmless family practices that began for good reasons may eventually create distance.

Mr. B., an avid photographer, started taking pictures of his children to build family history albums that could later be used to recall family stories. He enjoyed taking the children on memory trips through the albums until he started to be aware that he could recall the place and the event, but that he hadn't been part of what the family had been doing. His focus had been on the focus, the lenses, the film, the distance, the light, the framing, and twenty other things that occupy the photographer. He decided what he really wanted was to be with his family, so he stopped taking wonderful pictures and instead took two or three quick shots to capture the place and the action, and then put the camera away.[11]

You guessed it. These very candid, unself-conscious pictures turned out to be wonderful pictures after all because they were often hilarious memory joggers that brought back far more than the place and the event.

Long-term outcomes

Although we often need to pay sharp **attention** to the moment, if we don't also pay attention to long-term outcomes, we may have won the battle but lost the war.

The waitress served drinks, beer and colas, to the adults at the table. Luke, age two, pounded on the table and called loudly, "Op, op." He raised the decibel level until his mother, anxious to let the adults converse, gave him her cola. He quieted and drank. It seemed like a workable short-term solu-

tion. But that evening bedtime was difficult and Luke slept fitfully, waking his parents at least four times.

Mom had forgotten that caffeine hits small bodies hard, that one glass of caffeinated cola has the same effect on a small body that four cups of coffee has on an adult, and that caffeine can be addicting.

Angie seemed to her parents to be a particularly rebellious teenager, so they tried hard to find areas in which they could negotiate for peaceful solutions. Angie refused to stop smoking, so her parents settled for an agreement of not smoking in the house. The agreement reduced the conflict about smoking; it did not take care of Angie's lungs.

Attending means being aware. Sometimes we settle for a short-term solution while we work on the long-term effect. We may be thinking of ways to prevent a problem from recurring and be watching for a window of opportunity, a time or situation where the child will be responsive to us and we can strengthen a connection and then move to the next level. The next time Angie has a cold and cough might be just such an opportunity. Visiting a friend who has lung cancer could be another.

Teaching Children to Attend

When children are not attending to the effects of their behavior on themselves, others, objects, or the environment, we take action or ask questions to help them develop awareness, or we insist they make amends. Many of the examples in the Ask, Act, and Amend chapters nudge, invite, or drag children into awareness of the impact of their behaviors.

Remember the importance of time-in. Practice the art of attending. Attend to others, to the situation, and to yourself. Let the information gleaned from attending help you decide whether you also need to use the Ask or the Act or the Amend puzzle piece.

Being aware and teaching our children to be aware is one of the most significant gifts we can give them.

Chapter 3

Ask

*To speak of "mere words" is much like
speaking of "mere dynamite."*

— C. J. DUCASSE, IN THE *KEY REPORTER*

The time-in puzzle piece **ask** builds connection when we ask a sincere and appropriate question, listen to the response with genuine interest, and use the information to benefit the other person and perhaps ourselves.

Asking builds connection in a number of ways. Asking expresses interest, *Did you enjoy the book?* Asking also honors perceptions, *Is that how you saw what happened?* and honors feelings, *That would have scared me. How did you feel at the time?* We can ask to get information, *Did you clear the driveway?* or to offer support, *Do you need help packing your bag for camp?* We can encourage a child to think for herself by offering choices, *Which day before Sunday can you help me clean the garage?* or by challenging his decisions, *Did you use the clear thinking part of you when you decided to do that?* You may know of many more ways that asking strengthens connection.

Interrogating, grilling, questioning in a critical way, trying to catch or trick or subdue, or not listening to the answer is not what we are talking about in time-in. Interrogating can weaken connection. Asking the time-in way means posing a respectful question and listening (attending) to the response in a respectful manner.

Learn to Listen

There are numerous techniques to improve one's listening skills. All of them remind us to listen to the other person, not to our own internal comments or rebuttals. We can't really hear what others are saying if we are busy writing our next speech. Or if we are hearing with our ears, but not listening with our hearts. We can physically show children that we are listening in a number of ways, depending on each child's preference. When we spend time-in asking questions of children, we notice the way each child likes to be listened to. Some children like the open-body, direct-eye-contact, lean-forward listener. Others prefer to sit side by side and both look out of the window while we talk. Others like us to have our hands busy while we listen. One of my children liked to have us both lie on the floor. (If you do that, be sure not to fall asleep.) Some children like you to repeat what you heard. They say, *Yah, you got it!* Other children feel patronized by reflective listening. They say, *That's what I just told you! Why are you repeating what I just said?*

There are cultural differences about how to respond when listening. Some groups expect children to look them in the eye when asked a question. Other groups teach children to look down as a mark of respect. Do what works for your child, in your culture, but feel free to experiment. And always remember that when one person in a dialogue forces a decision, the dialogue stops. Acceptance or dissension can occur, but the dialogue stops.

The family is discussing what movie to attend. Suddenly Dad says, "Well, I'm not going downtown to a Disney movie. We'll go to the war movie at the local theater."

Only force a decision when you don't want the mutual exchange to continue.

What If I Ask, but They Don't Respond?

If asking is your favorite puzzle piece, you are probably very good at it. However, asking doesn't work equally well with all children. We have to learn the art of questioning, and each child may like a different approach.

Learn to ask questions in ways that work

The Ask puzzle piece is welcomed by children who are highly extraverted and think best when they are talking. When the extraverted child comes in the door, ask him about his day and he may tell you more than you ever wanted to know. *Think before you speak* is definitely not the motto of extraverts, and they sometimes seem to answer a question by starting far from the subject and gradually circling in on it, perhaps with the help of more well-placed questions.

Children who are highly introverted often need to recharge their batteries by being alone, playing music or a computer game, or watching TV. If you must ask them a question when they first come in, try to keep it short. *Hungry?* is fine. These children like to think before they speak. They need time before they answer and then the answer is often short and incomplete. It is important to realize that slow-to-answer people are thinking; they are not trying to irritate, so it is important not to get upset with them. Sometimes it is hard for parents to tell whether a child is thinking or daydreaming.

It was Richard's first day at community college without a car. Dad asked, "How will you get home?" Richard was silent for several minutes. Dad asked, "Richard, are you thinking about how you will get home?" Richard looked out the window as he said, "I don't know." Dad tried again, "What are three ways you could get home?" The answer was immediate, "Hitch-hike, bus to the shopping center and walk from there, or catch a ride with Mike." Dad had asked the right question the second time. Dad didn't ask which option because Richard is old enough to decide that.

Help your child find ways to answer that work for the child

Questions usually get the attention of children who learn well by listening (the ones who are called high auditory learners). Children whose learning preferences are more action oriented (kinesthetic) or visual may take a little more prodding.

Andrew prefers acting to listening. Martha decorated a baseball cap for Andrew. She drew a question mark and a lightbulb. She called it Andrew's fast-action cap. When seven-year-old Andrew wasn't responding to her questions, she touched him on the arm and said, "Run and put on your fast-action cap. I have a question for that fast-action brain of yours." Getting Andrew to move helped him focus on the questions.

Iko was aware that Fubito was quick to notice things (high visual), but often didn't seem to hear her questions. She could get his attention by waving her hand in front of his face, but that irritated him. He was, however, amused when she made colorful flash cards and offered him options. "Fubito, do you want to go to the mall with me this afternoon? Pick a card." She held out a green YES card and a yellow NO card. "Fubito, when do you have time to talk with me? Pick a card: Now, in ten minutes, in half an hour." Since Fubito will need to respond to auditory questions at school, at work, and socially, Iko treated the cards humorously and reminded Fubito that he needed to listen with his ears as well as his eyes.[1]

Ask to get straight answers

Sometimes a child's response to a question doesn't provide the information we're looking for. We can avoid getting sidetracked by sticking with our question. Listen to Scott's dad stick with it until he gets the answer:

"Scott, did you put your baseball glove away?"
   "I used it this afternoon at the game," Scott replied.
   "Good. Did you put it away?" his dad continued.
   "We won, Dad, we won!"
   "Yup. I heard that earlier. So where is your glove?"
   "It's okay," said Scott.
   "I hope it is. So, did you put it away?"
   "I think so," Scott answered.
   "Bottom line, Scott, do you know where your glove is?"
   "Kinda," he replied.
   "I guess you didn't put it away. Where do you think it is?"
   "Someplace in the yard."
   "So what do you do now?" Dad asked.
   "Go and find it?"
   "Yes. And?"
   "Put it away," Scott said, smiling.

If, during a scenario like this, a parent becomes critical, it does not build connection. If the parent remains firm but pleasant, it builds connection. As children grow and get too big to sit on their parents' laps, they still need to stay connected. Some children do this by hassling—by stringing out a communication. Often it helps if the parent throws in a bit of humor. Dad might laugh and say, *"Scott, you are really good at leading me off the track. You almost got me that time. But, not quite, so where is the glove?"*

This sidetracking that children learn to do so skillfully when they want to lead us away from a question is called *redefinition.* By not letting children redefine our questions, we not only stay focused but also teach our children to point it out when we redefine their questions. We can take that in good humor because it holds us accountable, improves communication, and builds connection. (You can read more about redefinition and how to stop it in the book *Self-Esteem: A Family Affair.*[2])

How Asking Builds Connection

When we need someone to do something, it is often more effective to ask than to command. Answering a question requires that the person become engaged in the situation while still keeping his dignity.

To the little one: *Hey, Timothy, did you see that the toys are all over the floor? We are going to pick them up to marching music. Which one will you pick up first?*

To the teenager: *Are you wanting the car any time this weekend? We have a lot going on. Will you help to coordinate our driving schedule?*

To the grandparent: W*e are working on helping the kids be aware of other people's feelings. Are you willing to help with that?*

Questions can build a child's confidence, competence, and thinking skills

Depending on the question we ask, a child will answer from a feeling place, *What do you want?* or from a thinking place, *How can we make that happen?* Both are important. Asking a young child to indicate a desire or preference is asking a question a child can answer from the feeling place. Her answer is correct because it comes from how she feels, and it builds confidence that her feelings will be honored and she can know how she feels. She can answer the question *Do you want some ice cream?* simply by grabbing a feeling. (Except for the two-year-old who is practicing saying no and responds with a no first and then yes.)

But asking only grab-a-feeling questions can build a confidence that is self-centered, so these questions need to be balanced with competence-building, form-a-thought questions. *How can we get some ice cream?* The answer may be correct or incorrect, as the child learns to identify and evaluate options. Asking encourages thinking. The child does not get to practice thinking and problem solving when we tell her how to solve a problem. We have done the thinking and the child does not own the solution.

Saul has a quick mind, a world of experience, and a solution to every problem. He thinks it is his duty, and certainly his privilege, to tell his children how to solve not only the problems they have, but any that they might encounter in the future. "Have I told you how to resolve that problem? Well, first you . . . then you . . . then you . . . "

Walt also has a quick mind, a world of experience, and a solution to every problem. He believes that helping his children develop problem-solving skills is usually more important than finding the perfect solution. He uses questions to challenge his children to find their own solutions to problems that are within their scope of understanding. "How do you want this to turn out? What are some things you can do that would help that happen?"

Saul's children often resent his heavy-handed advice. Walt's children often resent his refusal to give them easy answers. The issue is not about making kids comfortable; it is about helping them become confident and competent. Guess whose children will continue to talk over problems with their dad when they became adults.

If you want a boost in how to ask questions or if your young child has experiences with someone who bullies, read Phyllis Reynolds Naylor's *King of the Playground*.[3] Children need lots of questions that encourage them to identify their feelings and lots of questions that encourage them to think and to problem solve.

Questions can remind children that they are loved

Ramone had started saying, "I know, I know" when his mom said, "I love you." So she changed to a question and asked, "Do you know that I love you?"

"Yes," replied Ramone.

"How do you know?"

"You told me," he said.

Other times he said, "You do stuff for me" or, "You're my mom." One day he answered, "No."

"Well, I do. Very much. How come you don't know?"

"You were so mad at me on the weekend, I guess I wondered," he said.

"I was mad. I didn't like what you did," explained his mom. "And I do love you. Put that in hard-core memory, Ramone."

Questions can remind children they are
a contributing part of the family

When the family plans the weekend activities, Dad often asks, "What shall we do for the good of the family?" At first the kids were perplexed or ridiculed him. "You're the dad; you are supposed to take care of us!"

"I am, and I do. Now what is something we can do that will make the whole family safer or happier? How can we add beauty to our lives?"

Fifteen-year-old Roger suggested cleaning out the car. Eleven-year-old Clara wanted to decorate the house for Halloween. Seven-year-old Marty wanted to go for a family bike ride. Dad agreed that all of these suggestions would be for the good of the family and asked the children to pick which one to do first.

Some questions help children claim, name,
and be responsible for feelings

Telling children how they feel or don't feel is risky. First risk—we may be wrong. Telling a child, *You are really angry* when he is scared and confused doesn't help him understand his own feelings. Second—it may signal to him which feelings you like and don't like, so he may learn to hide a true feeling and express another feeling instead. Telling a child he is not afraid because there is nothing to be afraid of, tells him to distrust his own perceptions.

Questions can help a child claim feelings: *I would have been scared in that situation. Were you scared?* Name feelings: *Were you just a little scared, medium scared, or really scared like terrified?* And be responsible for feelings: *You know that when you are scared, you are to find safety or at least information about the scary event. What did you do? So you hid and that worked. Good thinking. Is there anything else you could have done?*

Questions can encourage thinking and responsible behavior
if the questions are not criticisms or traps

Time-in questions build children's self-esteem and also build their confidence in you and strengthen your connection if the questions are straight.

Don't ask what happened if you know what happened. That is a trap. Ask, *How did that happen?* or *What happened right before . . . ?* or, *How can I help?* If there is criticism in your voice or your body, the message is critical even if the words are not. That breaks, not makes, connection.

Don't ask, *Who started it?* unless there is some unusual reason why you really need to know or unless you want to play courtroom instead of solving the problem. Instead ask, *What do you need to solve this problem?*

Why did you break the vase? is a question begging for an evasive answer. *What made you do that?* is a question that encourages magical thinking: *The devil made me do it.* Instead, after the broken vase is safely picked up, ask, *What happened here?* or, *What do we or you need to do so this won't happen again?*

Sometimes we ask children about rules. *What is the rule about running in the house?* or, *Do we need to put this room off limits for play?*

Warning children about a questionable choice of friends can be done with questions: *I know that you enjoy being with Ted, but he does things that seem risky to me. I wonder, if he keeps on doing the kinds of things he is doing now, what will he be doing five years from now? What do you think? And how will his life be ten years from now? Twenty?* (There are more suggestions about how to ask without criticizing in Chick Moorman's book *Parent Talk: Words That Empower, Words That Wound.*[4])

Play the "what might happen if" game

What might happen if . . . questions encourage children to think more broadly and can be a good family game.

Ask what might happen if

- everyone ran in the house?
- nobody washed clothes?
- we gave all the family money to one family member to spend on himself or herself?
- we were given fourteen million dollars?
- there were no police officers?
- only one person in the family was kind to the others?
- we had to go a whole day without laughing?
- all our toys disappeared?
- there were no television?
- we all hit each other every time we were irritated or angry?
- we moved to another state?
- someone gave us four new cars?

- we had no car?
- we each told every other family member something we appreciated about them every day for a week?
- a family of clowns moved in next door?
- a family who couldn't speak our language moved in next door?
- someone sent you the gifts in the "Twelve Days of Christmas" song? Where would we keep the seven swans a swimming and the eight ladies dancing?

Ask to help a child differentiate a need from a want

People *need* food, shelter, clothing, stimulation, recognition, to be loved, and to be competent. They also need certainty, structure, challenges, and relationship or connection. They *want* toys, brand-name clothes, new cars, faster computers, fame, fortune, freedom, or license.

Teenagers have many wants. Amy wants brand-name jeans. Gerry wants to be captain of the football team. Andy wants big bucks and a sports car right now. Suzy wants a knight in shining armor.

The confusing thing for children and for many adults is that if the basic *needs* are met, then the *wants* can begin to feel like needs. The body doesn't have two sets of desire feelings, one for wants and one for needs, especially when those wants are defined as needs by the media and the peer group. Therefore, it is a challenge for parents to build connection while teaching our children that we will help them get what they need and that they can have only part of what they want. If children got everything they wanted, they would be overindulged. They would be deprived of the need to strive and they would have to invent challenges, some of which we might not like at all.

Tad had been given everything he wanted. When he got his driver's license, he was given a new car and a credit card for gas and maintenance. Tad, with a teenager's belief in his own invincibility, found his challenge in fast driving, knowing that if he totaled his car, he would be given another one.

Telling children, *You can't have it so let's not hear any more about it* may quiet the child, but it does not guide his problem solving. Amy wants brand-name jeans.

"Mom, I want my clothing allowance now so I can get some brand-name jeans. All the girls have them, and I feel out of it."

"Hmm. I know you do, but you also need a jacket for the cold weather. What do you suggest?" Mom asks.

"I wish we had more money," sighs Amy.

"Sometimes I wish that too, but here we are so what can we do about jeans and a jacket?"

"Let me get the jeans and worry about the jacket when winter comes," suggests Amy.

"Nice try, but the jacket comes first. Now how shall we start?"

"Oh, all right. Let's hit a couple of next-to-new shops and see if we can find a jacket I like for a low price. Then maybe I can get my jeans."

"Good suggestion, honey," says Mom.

Gerry *wants* to be captain of the football team, but he is small and poorly coordinated. He *needs* to develop skills. What could he wish for that he could probably achieve?

"Gerry, I know you want to be captain of the football team. What do you think are the chances of that?" asks Dad.

"Possible. The coach likes me," he replies.

"Do you think 'liking' is the top of his list when he chooses the captain?"

"Yah," says Gerry.

"What would be next on the list?" Dad probes.

"That the other players like him. The guys like me," says Gerry.

"Okay. What's next?" asks Dad.

"That he's a good player?"

"I think so. Are you one of the top players?"

"Dad, don't!"

"Gerry, I want you to have the success you want. If your captain is chosen on a basis of popularity, go for it. But I also want you to become proficient in a lifelong sport. Guys like to do sports together at all ages, and it's more fun if you're good at it. Whatever sport you choose, I hope you are willing to practice and become as good at it as you want to be."

Andy *wants* big bucks and a sports car right now. He *needs* transportation to school and enough money for food, clothing, and school supplies. What does he need to learn about earning and handling money?

"Andy, I know you want a car. Want to go car looking with me?" asks Dad. "We can do some price comparisons and then check out insurance costs. Want to look at what the family car cost us last year?"

After some good connecting time exploring the cost of sports cars, and after Dad firmly rejected all requests to pay for the car, Andy reluctantly took the bus, with a promise from his dad that they would continue to look at cars.

Suzy *wants* a knight in shining armor. She *needs* to learn relationship skills to help her connect with both boys and girls.

"Suzy, I used to dream of a knight in shining armor. It's fun. But did you know that sometimes the dragon squashed the knight? Anyway, a white horse would look silly in a parking lot."

"Oh, Mom!"

"We need to talk about the difference between being loved and cherished and being rescued," her mom explains. "Have you thought about what you really want?"

Ask in a way that lets the child have power

It is important for children to learn to be in charge of themselves. They learn that by practicing, making mistakes, practicing some more, and succeeding. Start with small things. When a child has to do something, let the child have some power in deciding when or how. When adults make all of the decisions, children don't have to think.

It was late, but the family was not ready to leave Grandpa's house just yet. Dad saw five-year-old Zach's behavior becoming more and more rambunctious. Dad said, "Zach, you are bumping and pushing. You usually do that when you are tired. You can go lie on the floor or you can sit here by me and rest. How long a rest do you think you will need?"

"I'm not tired!" Zach insisted.

"Well, the bumping and pushing has to stop so try sitting by me. Will you let me know when you are ready to move around quietly?" asked Dad.

Mom knew Rhonda had a busy Saturday. Friday morning Mom said, "Rhonda, I can arrange to do family laundry either Saturday morning or afternoon. I don't know your schedule, so will you tell me when you want to do your part of the wash?"

Ask to help the child gain power: fight, flee, freeze, fix, or flow

Children need to learn to use their power to solve problems. One problem that children and many adults need help with is what to do when the fight/flee/freeze reaction hits. Freeze may not be as widely recognized as fight or flee, but it is also an involuntary reaction.[5] Animals have been observed freezing when they are neither big enough to fight the adversary nor fast enough to escape. The freezing of very young animals, such as the spotted fawn, is well known. Humans sometimes freeze when they see something horrifying. That freeze time is often reported as being short. *I was momentarily immobilized,* or, *I froze in my tracks,* or, *My legs would not move.* Or freezing can last for longer periods of time if a person is depressed. These very deep, very old life-saving impulses are automatic and are helpful to us in many situations. If the place is on fire, get out! If someone is threatening you and you are strong enough to win, sometimes it is appropriate to fight physically or with wit. If the safest way to avoid getting hurt is not to draw attention to yourself by moving, freeze.

But, in many other situations in modern life, fleeing, fighting, or freezing adds to the problem. There are two other F's: fix and flow. They are not automatically triggered in the brain, so they need to be taught and practiced. Fixing is doing something to alter the situation or solve the problem. Flowing is sliding around a problem in a way that avoids it or solves it or at least keeps people safe. (You will find more on fight, flee, fix, and flow in the book *Time-In: When Time-Out Doesn't Work.*[6])

You can use the *how would you* and *what might happen* questions after an incident to look for alternatives or before a problem to build strength and resiliency. These questions can also help kids learn how to opt for fix/flow rather than potentially dangerous fighting, fleeing, or freezing.

Use the five F's before something happens

Dad is using the five F's to teach young Isaac about the danger of fire. "Isaac, we don't play with matches and we have smoke detectors, so I don't worry about a fire here, but let's talk about what we are supposed to do if we were someplace where there was a fire. Let's go through the five F's, fight, flee, freeze, fix, and flow. If you were someplace where there was a fire, would you fight it?"

"Yes, I would be brave!" answered Isaac.

"No, you are a little boy. Firefighters are big people with special clothes and masks and fire trucks. Since you are not to fight the fire, could you flee? Could you get out of there fast?"

"Yes."

"Where would you go?" asked Dad.

"Far."

"Yes, and a safe place, out of the way of trucks and cars. You know what freeze is. It's when you stay perfectly still and don't move. What would happen if we did that by a fire?"

"We might get burned," said Isaac.

"Right. Freeze wouldn't work," said Dad. "What about fix? Is there some way you could fix a fire?"

"If I had a fire extinguisher, I could put it out."

"You are pretty young to do that. But there is something you could do. Who could fix the fire?"

"The firefighters! I could run next door and shout, 'Fire! Call the fire trucks,'" Isaac said.

"Excellent," replied Dad. "Now what about flow. That is when you sort of change the subject or pretend you don't notice."

"That wouldn't work with a fire. Right?"

"Right. You did very well. Flee and get firefighters to fix the fire. I think this weekend our family will have a fire drill so we can all practice flee and fix."

Apply the five F's after a problem

On another day, Isaac's fifth-grade sister, Marie, has told her mom about an incident at school. Mom asks the "what else could you have done" questions to help Marie be more prepared for future problems.

"The girl who has the locker next to you teased you about your hair? I'm sorry. What did you do?" asked Mom.

"I tried to ignore it, but it really hurt," said Marie.

"Let's go through the five F's: fight, flee, freeze, fix, and flow, and figure out what else you could have done. If she does that again, how could you fight?"

"Pull her hair?" suggested Marie.

"Then what might happen?"

"She could pull mine back and we'd both get hurt. We could both get in trouble."

"How could you freeze?" asked Mom.

"I could stand very still and not say anything. I guess that's what I sorta did and it didn't work."

"How could you flee?"

"I could say that I have to go to the bathroom, and go," replied Marie.

"How could you flow?

"I could smile and say, 'Yah, I'm competing in a bad hair day contest today. I think I'll win.' Or I could say, 'I'm starting a new trend. Glad you noticed.' Or I could change the subject and ask, 'What did you think of the math test? I thought it was horrible!'"

"How could you fix?" Mom asked.

"I suppose I could go to the office and ask to have my locker changed," said Marie.

"Fight, flee, freeze, fix, or flow, which one is more likely to work?"

"I think I'll try flow."

Think about the five F's during a problem

The teenager's school friends are having a party this weekend and have excluded him. He thinks through the five F's:

- *Fight—I could crash the party and start a fight. Wouldn't work.*
- *Flee—I could stay away from them forever. Not possible.*
- *Freeze—I could stay home in bed . . . and feel lonely . . . and probably cry. Wouldn't help.*
- *Flow—I could hang around them and act like I don't care and see if they invite me. Might work.*
- *Fix—I could ask one of them what gives? Have I done something awful or have they heard some rumor about me? Might work.*

He decides to go to school and try flow and if that doesn't work, to try fix. That may not work either, but he will have tried something.

In *Poverty: A Framework for Understanding and Working with Students and Adults from Poverty,* Ruby Payne points out that not learning how to flow is one thing that keeps youth trapped in generational poverty.[7] In the social setting where families have been in poverty for several generations, fight or flight may be accepted responses to problems. This puts the child at a disadvantage in school, social life, and work life.

Remember the importance of time-in. Practice the art of **asking**. When you want to give a command, try asking a question instead. Respectful asking is important because it teaches children how to ask and that asking is okay. There may be times in their lives when they are discouraged from asking, and knowing how to ask respectfully will help them get what they need. Practice asking others what they want from you and what they appreciate about you.

Every sincere question followed by respectfully listening to the response, strengthens the feathery, elastic threads of connection.

Take time to ask.

Chapter 4

Act

*Do not overlook tiny good actions, thinking they are of no benefit;
even tiny drops of water in the end will fill a huge vessel.*

—BUDDHA

Actions build connection when they come from a sincere heart and when we are respectful of the response to our actions. Inviting children to participate with us in activities that we and they enjoy builds connection. We also strengthen connections when we involve children in projects that teach them skills or show concern and empathy for others. Safety, care, concern, respect, joy—all of these can be part of the connections supported by using the **act** time-in puzzle piece. When we act in haste and criticize, name-call, or punish, we weaken connection. Fortunately, children survive an occasional slip if they have a backlog of connecting actions, if we make amends, and if most of our actions show that we love them.

The Many Ways We Act

It is easy to offer a plentiful buffet of connecting actions because life is full of activity. Think of all the ways you move in to teach, to comfort, to show love, to support, to redirect. Here are examples of ways to connect through actions.

Touch is action. We strengthen connection every time we hold an infant, pat a shoulder, hold a hand, give a wanted hug.

Talking to children is action. It's important to talk to children of all ages, especially infants. We now know that children learn language by hearing it long before they can talk, and not having been exposed to a rich bath of language puts them at a disadvantage in both language and math skills later on.[1] Parents who worry about children's not talking early can rest assured that a child's understanding what you are saying is a better gauge of language development than when he starts talking. My oldest son didn't talk until he was three, and by the time he graduated from high school he was working as a foreign language interpreter. So relax and talk. What an easy way to connect with your infant. Tell her what you are doing and feeling and what she is doing.

Reading to children seems to be the single most effective way of encouraging children to read. Letting them hear adults read to each other also helps. What an easy way to also build connection!

We also connect with a thousand *acts of service*. Aaron's mom showed support: *"You asked me to mend your uniform. I know you have a game tonight so I got it done."*

Brook's dad did some *teaching*. To twenty-month-old Brook, *"The kitty runs away because you squeeze her. Help me look for her and I will show you how to pet her gently."* To five-year-old Isaac, *"If you don't tie your shoes, today may be the day you learn what happens if you step on your shoe laces."* To his older child, Charlie, *"I hear there is some bullying on the playground. It's time for us to talk about the five F's—fight, flee, freeze, fix, or flow."*[2]

Max's uncle connects by *playing*. *"What will it be, big boy?"* he asked of the six-year-old. *"Do you want to wrestle or shall we play ball?"* Theo and Vanessa's big brother calls, *"Hey, we have to do our chores soon. Let's go out and roll down the hill first."*

Laughing is a wonderful way to connect, as long as it is laughing with someone and not at them. *Grandma laughs when six-year-old Quinn tells jokes even if she has heard them before. Grandpa laughs when Savannah gives him the funny birthday card she made for him. Dad catches the kids being funny and lets them know he likes laughing with them.*

Tatiana's mom connected by inviting: *"Tatiana, I'm going to the mall at 3:00. If you want to go with me, have your room cleaned and you may ask a friend if you wish."* Or, *"I'm planning how to surprise Aunt Lilly when she comes. Please help me think of something we can do that she will like."*

Adults can connect with each other and with kids by *joining*. Tyler's big brother watches a TV program with Tyler and initiates a discussion of it after it is over.

Much of the activity that cares for children takes the form of *prepa-ration*. Think of all the ways we set up connection with children by making preparations, from keeping the mother and fetus healthy during pregnancy[3] to selecting the clothes for the infant's layette to birthday parties to saving for emergencies or the future. Preparation does not always involve getting something new. Often rearranging does the trick.

Mother noticed that the children were throwing all the toys out of the toy box and then saying, "There's nothing to do." The next morning the children found the dolls and bears sitting around the little table with a tea set. The children played tea party, rearranged the toys, and eventually turned the tea table into an operating arena. The next week they found all the toy animals hiding in a cave (blanket over two chairs). No new toys, just rearrangement.[4]

Adults often act by *redirecting* children. Although kids may object at the moment, they have the solid knowing that adults are providing for their safety and welfare: *"Your ball could hit the window. Either take your ball game to the Birchwood Playground or find another game to play."*

Sometimes adults act by *interrupting* children's activities in order to have the children be supportive family members: *"You can finish your game later. Right now I need three people to help me make cookies (or collect the laundry, wrap presents, pack a picnic lunch, clean the tool bench, and so on)."* Children connect with the family by contributing to it and by knowing that their contributions are appreciated—an easy way to raise self-esteem. Other times parents interrupt to get children's attention: *"I'm interrupting this play right now to remind you that people who expect a ride to the mall this afternoon must have their rooms cleaned by noon."*

Often parents *intervene* to prevent future problems: *"I heard you making plans for the weekend. We have to go see Grandpa on Saturday or Sunday. Before you commit to plans, call Grandpa and find out when he wants us. I can go either day."* Parents also intervene when children's behavior gets off track. If a child is abusing or addicted to drugs, asking often gets evasive answers so parents act by insisting on an evaluation or on treatment.

One of the most caring things adults can do for children is to *limit* them until they are able to limit themselves. Learning to put balance in life is a challenge for many of us, and children learn to limit themselves in small increments. *Dad picks up the infant and carries him to a* quiet spot: *"Time to settle down, little fellow. You've had enough stimulation for a while."* Mother turns off the TV and tells the nine-year-old twins, *"Time to go out and play or do some exercises or help me clean the bathroom. You choose."* We all need to be able to set limits on ourselves.

It is as important to know when to quit as when to continue.

Doing chores with children allows adults to teach skills and connect at the same time, especially if there is some humor involved and some joy of accomplishment. If chores are a "have to" for you, make some of them a "get to" and let it rub off on the kids. Avoid using chores as punishment, as that teaches children to avoid them or resent doing them.

Saturday morning Mom said, "I'm going to go play in the garden. You can come out and get dirty with me, or you can start the vacuuming. Whichever your body would rather do this morning."

Celebrations are actions that build connection.

When David, eleven, brought home a report card with an improved math grade, his big sister baked a cake and put little flags with numbers all over the top.

In each of these caring actions the adult moved into the child's awareness with body or voice or both. But sometimes the most powerful action adults can take is to *restrain themselves* from interfering and **attend** before they decide to **act**. Watch and see if the children can work it out themselves this time; wait and see if Johnny *can* get the battery in the action toy; watch the development of the play scenario even though you might *like* to redirect it. Loving looks build connection. Lovers know how deeply meaningful the loving glance can be. Look at the baby and the toddler with loving eyes. Then use touch and words to guide the little ones toward what you want them to do, but keep the loving look.[5]

Since life is filled with action, we may as well be intentional about using our actions to build connection rather than distance.

How Do Children Respond?

How do children respond when we act? Depends. Learning preferences influence how children respond. Some learning preferences show up very early, others later.

Auditory, visual, or kinesthetic?

Children who like to learn by doing, whose preferred learning style is *kinesthetic*, like action. Posted directions, a diagram, or a recipe book help *visual* children get into the action. Children whose learning preference is *auditory* often need words as well as actions.

I grabbed my auditory child and did a simple dance step with her. She followed my lead and we laughed together. When I asked her to do it alone, she said, "I can't. You didn't tell me what we were doing."

When you want to teach a child something, remember to ask yourself, *Does this child learn better if I tell her first, if I show her how first, or if I do it with her first?*

Introverted children often watch before they join in. Extraverted children may jump in before they hear all of the directions. *Bryan paused to watch what his dad was doing before he accepted the offer to join in. His sister Brittany pushed in with a "Let me try it" as soon as she noticed her dad doing something.*

Allow children to enter activities in their own way.

Inductive or deductive?

Children who need the big picture, who prefer to learn *inductively*, may hesitate to join an activity until they understand what it is for or where it is leading. Or the extraverted child, who also needs the big picture, will push in to ask questions rather than to join the activity: *What are you doing? Why are you doing it that way? What is it for? What will you do next?* The *deductive* learners, the ones who like to learn parts and then piece them together, are willing to jump in just for the experience: *Let me help! I can do that!*

Random or sequential?

Children who think *sequentially* need to know how what they are doing builds in an orderly way to fit into the scheme of things. Children
who prefer to learn in a *random* way feel stifled if they have to listen
to a long outline before they can start an activity. Parents with more
than one child and teachers of many children learn to describe a project quickly so the sequential children can comfortably start and to
offer activity soon enough so they don't lose the random organizers.
Ryan and Russell's dad has learned how to do that.

*Dad says, "I'll check what you have packed for camp Sunday evening. Re-
member you will sleep, swim, canoe, ride horseback, and probably be rained
on and bitten by mosquitoes." Sequential Ryan makes a list of items he
needs and then collects and packs them. His brother, random Russell, collects things as he thinks of them, spreads them all over his room (or the living room), and then packs.*

Sylvia Fair has written a delightful children's book, *The Bedspread*,
about two old sisters, Maud and Amelia, who clung tenaciously to
their sequential or random preferences and created a bedspread that
gave equal expression to their preferences.[6]
    Most children learn in a combination of these styles with a prefer-
ence for one. It is up to us adults to figure out how our children learn
best and support them instead of pushing them to learn our way. If
your child isn't responding well to you, try experimenting with one
learning style at a time. Ask yourself

- Does this child learn more easily by seeing, hearing, or doing?
- Is this child more extraverted or introverted?
- Does this child like to know the big picture first or is she willing
  to start with small parts?
- Does this child approach things in an orderly, sequential way or
  does she make sense of things by jumping from one idea to
  another?

Soon you will notice how these styles fit together. You may find that
the child whose styles match yours seems easy to connect with.

> All ways of learning are okay. In fact, they are right for the child who has them. As children grow older, we nudge them toward other ways of learning so they won't limit themselves.

Some Actions Are Continuous

Act to offer structure

Structure, instruction in how to do things and an explanation of the limits, lets children feel secure. Adults too. Everyone feels more sure of what to so (and not to do) when they know where other people stand. Rules are part of structure (more about rules in chapter 9).

Children who lack structure react in various ways. Some become clingy and overly dependent. Children who are more assertive in nature think, *If no one else is in charge here, I'll take charge,* and become bossy. Parents need to be clear about what is and what is not okay. If adults do not intervene on misbehavior, children assume it is all right to continue or they resent not being cared for. If you aren't sure what a child the age of yours needs to be learning, get an age-specific parenting book such as one of the ones listed in the notes[7] or use the age charts from the book *Growing Up Again: Parenting Ourselves, Parenting Our Children.*[8]

Act to teach empathy

Children learn both how to express empathy and that the family values empathic responses by observation and by action. They observe Mom's concern about her brother. They experience Dad's empathy when they skinned a knee, broke a toy, lost a game. Children learn how to express empathy when they join the family in acts of goodwill.

Lorenzo gave each of his three school-age children ten dollars and asked them to make a list of the four foods for the foodshelf that they would most want if there were no food in the house. Lorenzo made a list also. They combined the lists and spent an hour at the grocery store figuring out how many items on their list they could buy with forty dollars. On the way to the foodshelf, they discussed reasons people might need to use a foodshelf. On the way home, the children said, "The children who came to get food looked just like us."

Act to avoid overindulgence

We live in a society that encourages overindulgence. Parents can provide abundance in several ways without being overindulgent.

- Spend more time with your kids and less money on them.
- Help children separate wants from needs. Help them get what they need all of the time and what they want some of the time.
- Sometimes have children give more than they get.
- Insist that children do chores that are appropriate for their age, even if you can afford to hire out the work. Not doing chores deprives children of two great needs—learning self-care and household skills, and having the satisfaction of knowing they are contributing family members.
- Be willing to hear that your family is weird. Remember, all families are weird sometimes. If you want to have a family activity that is fun, ask everyone to define weird. Draw it, act it out, and learn more about each other.
- Don't expect children to thank you until they are at least thirty-one, but probably forty. You may never hear the thanks directly, but you may overhear them tell others how they appreciate what they learned from you.

You can read more about research on how adults who were overindulged as children now feel crippled by it in *Growing Up Again: Parenting Ourselves, Parenting Our Children*.[9]

Monitor

Monitoring means knowing where your kids are, whom they are with, and what they are doing. This may be easy to do when children are young, but there comes an age, about ten or twelve, when children begin to tell parents to "go away." So go. But, not very far. Be less intrusive in the way you ask, but be clear that *everyone* in the family needs to tell another person or leave a note explaining where they are going and approximately when they will be home, because people in this family care about each other. When kids are doing an activity, they can easily report it: *We were skateboarding.* Or, *We were studying for the algebra test.* When they were building relationships with no particular activity, they will report *doing nothing* or *hanging-out.* Then Dad asks, *"So where are you kids hanging out now? Was Tad with you? If you are going to hang out and you don't know where, write that on the chalkboard and write where you might go with a question mark."*

Dr. Stephen Small and his research team at the University of Wisconsin studied more than 100,000 teenagers and found the following:

> Teens who report being closely monitored by their parents, compared to teens who are not closely monitored, are eight times less likely to have used marijuana at least monthly, four times less likely to have been drunk in the last month, eight times less likely to have been sexually active in the last month, and twice as likely to have a grade point average of B or higher.[10]

We invite teens to monitor us when we accept their feedback.

Craig monitored what his mom was doing when he pointed out that she was driving above the speed limit. Mom said, "Thanks," and slowed down.

Ann's dad, an avid golfer, was a regular part of two foursomes. When Ann pointed out that his saying, "I'm going golfing" didn't reveal who he would be with or where, Dad apologized and thanked Ann for reminding him.

Jim, a noncustodial parent, was accused by his sons of being secretive about his travel plans. Since they often had trouble connecting by phone, Jim worked out an agreement with the boys that they would know they could call him at his usual phone if they didn't get an e-mail saying where he could be reached out of town.

When parents expect and accept reciprocal monitoring by their children, keeping track of each other becomes a loving way to care for and about each other, not a prying intrusion.

When Jim's older son, Dana, moved away to go to college, Jim assumed he would no longer want to know Jim's traveling schedule. Wrong. Dana announced that he would fine his dad twenty dollars any time he learned his dad had left town without sending an e-mail message. When Dana made good on his threat, Jim complained, "Dana, I only went to Milwaukee, not Tokyo!" Dana held firm; Jim paid and didn't forget again.

The need to be connected doesn't stop when children leave home.

Act to teach morals

Teaching moral behaviors involves continuous action, whether it is done formally within a religious community or informally within the family, whenever a moral issue arises.

Anna's family attends their house of worship regularly and Anna takes religious instruction once a week. George's family members discuss the importance of moral behaviors in politics, in business and social life, and in their own lives. They challenge each other to resolve moral dilemmas.

Bringing Up a Moral Child by Michael Schulman and Eva Mekler offers an in-depth look at ways families teach moral values.[11]

Celebrate Family Rituals

Family rituals sustain connection, ground children in the family, and add stability to family life. They may be simple or elaborate, repetitive or one-time events. If they are created with joy and the good of the family in mind, they can be deeply satisfying.

Create simple rituals

Here are three examples of simple rituals.

A simple ritual the Becker children enjoy is *listening to Grandpa tell stories* about when he was a boy in the old country. He has always encouraged them to ask questions. Now he is starting to ask them to tell their own stories.

"Grandpa, we don't have any stories. Nothing exciting happens to us. What could we tell?" asked the children.

"Tell what I don't know about," explained Grandpa.

"You know about everything, Grandpa," the children insisted.

"No, I don't. I walked to school. I never rode in a school bus. What is that like? What happens on a school bus? Do the big kids get to drive?"

"Grandpa! You're fooling us."
"No, I'm not. Now tell," Grandpa said.

Telling our stories is one of the most potent ways of building connections. It helps children know about their families, and that helps them know who they are.

One of the simplest family rituals is *eating a meal together.* It is so simple that a busy family may drift away from the habit of doing it, but let's rethink that. Research done at De Paul University in Chicago studied 527 adolescents ages twelve to eighteen. Youth who ate five meals a week with one parent, both parents, or grandparents at home or in a restaurant showed lower substance use or abuse, less depression, higher academic motivation, and better peer relationships than youths who ate with adults three times a week.[12]

Wow! *Why?* you may ask. The researchers do not know why. They only know it works. What an easy way to build well-adjusted children. So, what action can we take? If dinner is not possible, try breakfast, lunch, or a sit-down snack break. If someone has to eat someplace else, let him find a time to sit with the family while the rest eat. Five times a week. Out of twenty-one meals a week we surely can arrange that.

Check out holiday rituals

If the family has been doing some holiday ritual the same way every year and the children seem to be avoiding it more and enjoying it less, check it out.

Mother approached each family member with a stack of recipe cards. "I'm doing a survey about Thanksgiving. Will you write each thing you like about Thanksgiving on a yellow card, and anything you don't like on a blue card, and what you might like different on a pink card? After Mom surveyed each family member, she collected the family for a card sort. Vincent sorted the blue cards and found that nobody liked having dinner at three o'clock and one person didn't like having guests. Mary sorted the yellow cards and found that everyone liked turkey, but only one person liked pecan pie. Two people liked watching football and two liked going for a walk. Mother reported that one person thought it would improve the day to have gifts. Mom said, "Let's agree on one thing to change and one thing to keep and see if that makes Thanksgiving better for the whole family."

For more ideas about how to create all kinds of family rituals, read *The Intentional Family* by William Doherty.[13]

To act or not to act is not the question. We all must act, so let our actions support our family.

Think about which of these ways of acting would help build connections in your family and what you want to teach as well as your family values and your cultural values. In *Parents and the Dynamics of Child Rearing,* George Holden observes that Western parents assume that children are born dependent and need to be taught to become independent while Asian parents assume that children are born independent and need to learn how to become dependent.[14] Perhaps all of us need to learn to become interdependent, to honor each other's souls and encourage each other's goodness. Begin by choosing the actions you think will help your family. If you aren't sure, do the great experiment—try them and find what works for you and your family.

Chapter 5

Amend

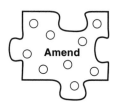

*A bridge broken must be repaired
before the parade can go on.*

—AUTHOR UNKNOWN

Bridges do get broken. They get broken by accident, by carelessness, by intention, or by acts or omissions that we had no idea would break a bridge. But, however the bridge was broken, it must be repaired or the parade will go somewhere else. Even worse, it could disperse in a heap of hard feelings or recriminations.

So how do we rebuild the broken bridge and reconnect with the person who is distanced from us? We learn the art of making **amends.** Making amends does not undo a wrong, but it helps to right it and it helps the amender become a better person. Discipline teaches, but it does not necessarily right a wrong. Punishment hurts, but it does not correct a wrong.

Making amends is an art that, skillfully practiced, sometimes makes a currently frayed connection even stronger than before.

Amends can be made for damaged property, broken promises, physical hurt, hurt feelings, or a damaged reputation.

The **amend** puzzle piece is a special and powerful form of reconnecting. It is the act that says, *I misused or I misjudged you; I am sorry and I want to make it up to you. I also misused myself when I misused you.*

Making amends is about repairing a bridge that you want or need to keep. Sometimes we break bridges because that particular parade should not go on; when this happens, we do not make amends.

Janice broke her engagement to Simon because she realized they were not a good combination. Both of them felt hurt, but Janice believed that connection needed to be broken, so making amends to restore the engagement would not be wise.

Randy broke off his relationship with a business partner when he discovered his partner had been embezzling from the business. There is no need for Randy to make amends. The partner chose not to, so that bridge was permanently severed.

Georgia discovered that a friend at work had been bad-mouthing her behind her back. Georgia broke off the friendship but continued to work with her colleague in a professional way. The colleague did not make amends so the friendship was not reestablished.

What Making Amends Means

So what does making **amends** mean? It means claiming what we have done wrong, deliberately or inadvertently, and doing whatever we can to make it right. Making it right is different from buying people off. Setting something right is different from getting a way out. It is admitting and moving through the negative event to create something better. It is a real healing of the rupture. It means that the person who offended makes compensation or restitution to atone for the wrong and the offended person accepts the offering. It takes time, energy, and perseverance.

Sandy rearranged her early November schedule to be at the airport for the three-hour layover of an old friend. The friend didn't show up or call or leave a message. Sandy was confused, hurt, and angry. Her friend called the next day and said, "I'm sorry. We missed our time together. May I come to your house and cook Thanksgiving dinner? I have no family to join now, and I want to make up for missing you yesterday." Later Sandy said, "It was the greatest Thanksgiving ever! I'm so glad I have him for a friend." In this case, the act of restitution succeeded because the offender offered a specific way to right the wrong and the offended person accepted.

Amends can also be made when the offended person confronts the offender and asks for something, some compensation or some remedy.

Rose was just beginning to establish a reputation for her new catering service. Nell, who was visiting Rose, took a call from a potential customer and neglected to tell Rose. Rose not only lost the sale but also learned that the disgruntled customer had told others that Rose was unreliable. Rose told Nell of her loss and asked Nell to do something to make it right. Nell called the customer and took full responsibility for the mishap. She also set about finding three new customers for Rose. Rose was satisfied and the friendship was restored.

It does not always turn out so well. If Rose had chosen not to feel satisfied with the repayment, or had decided to mistrust Nell, the bridge would not have been fully repaired. Or, Nell could have discounted the situation and refused to make amends.[1] She might not have been able or willing to do what Rose wanted. Or she may have made excuses: *You don't understand how busy I was that day. I just didn't remember it. People do forget things you know.* Making amends successfully is a two-way effort that doesn't always work. The offender may not be forgiven or the offended may not get satisfaction. If you have done all you can to make or to request amends but the other person will not do his part, the bridge remains broken and the reconnection will not be as strong as it could be.

Sometimes it takes great efforts before people reconnect. An adult child of an alcoholic or of incest who expresses her pain about the losses in her childhood may be met with outright denial or hostility. In that case, a reconciliation may never occur and she will have to gather up her life and build strong bridges with people who are willing to connect with her. Or it may take a long time to work through the hurts and reach forgiveness. Being willing to accept responsibility and stick with it until amends are accepted can reach the very core of who an offending person is, and it may ask the offended person to face who the offenders really are as opposed to who she thinks they are. Making amends calls for an honest perception of self. It demands that the offender move beyond shame. Shame, that strong feeling that one wants to hide oneself or else to blame the other, can make it very hard to make amends. Healthy guilt, that knowledge that one has erred and needs to take action to fix the situation, can spur the bridge reconstruction.

Making Amends to Children

When we make amends to children, we attempt to mend, to heal a strained or broken connection. Sometimes it is a little thing such as noticing that we have neglected to introduce the child to an adult we were talking with. We apologize; we say, *I'm sorry! I didn't mean to ignore you. I'll introduce you next time.* And next time we better well remember to make the introduction or we strain the connection even more.

If we err so grievously that we can't fix the error, it is doubly important to make the best amends we can, to compensate in some way.

A fleet of trucks

One Christmas, when a local store was selling a sturdy yellow dump truck at a reduced price, four-year-old Ian received seven. He did not seem disappointed that all his new toys were yellow dump trucks. His mother, however, decided it was not appropriate. Without asking him, she gave six trucks away. Ian searched and searched and cried and cried. Mother told him to be a big boy and dry his tears. She did not hear him sob, "But I'm a garage man and that was my fleet of trucks." The connection was strained. Ian returned to sucking his thumb and two months later didn't know what he wanted for his birthday.

What could his mother have done to mend the rift, to make the best amends? If she had apologized sincerely, if she had made the effort to respect his grief, if she had asked him if he wanted some other trucks, it might have helped. This mother needed to **attend** as well as amend.

Gifts from abroad

Sometimes amends can be made not by doing what the child wants, but by putting a new structure or a new frame of rules around the situation.

"Elena, I have something for you!" Elena's Aunt Fern traveled widely in her job and she usually picked up a small gift for her niece, something connected to the area from which it came. Elena's mom told Fern that sometimes Elena felt hurt because the gift didn't fit or she didn't care for it, so Aunt Fern had

a chat with her niece: "Elena, let me explain something about my gifts. I love you and I always hope the gifts will fit or will please you, but I don't expect that they always will. However, I'm not going to stop bringing them. It gives me pleasure, when I'm traveling, to think about you and to look for things for you. That part is my job as your aunt. In this case, I am the giver. Your job is different. Your job is to be the receiver. That means you take the gift and say thank you for thinking of me. After that you don't have to like the gift; you don't have to use it; you don't even have to keep it. You can pass it on that day. If I bring a gift that is expensive or has historical meaning, I will negotiate with you if you want it or if I should keep it." Elena was surprised, but she was connected with her aunt in a new way and she learned about giving without strings and receiving without reservation.

Helping Children Make Amends

It is important to help children make amends starting at an early age. It helps them feel the power of being able to set things right. It teaches them how to rebuild connections. It builds their self-esteem.

Diane Chelsom Gossen's book *Restitution: Restructuring School Discipline* is written for use in schools, but it offers many ways to help children make amends that parents can use at home.[2] She explains that there are several elements in successful amend making. They do not have to be addressed in a specific order, nor will every point apply in a given situation. The acts of restitution must be made by the offender and not forced by an adult from the outside.

Guidelines for making amends

Diane Chelsom Gossen offers these guidelines for making amends:

- The person making the amends must put forth effort.
- The amends made should support the amender's values or the family or school values if the amender is young.
- The amends made must be related to the problem.
- The amends should help the amender become a better person.
- The amends must be satisfactory to the victim.

You may ask an offending child to think of three things she could do to make amends for a hurtful action. Read the following scenario and then check the five guidelines in making amends to see how many were reported in Caitlin's story.

Caitlin wore Morgan's blouse without asking. Morgan was furious. She had ironed the blouse carefully and planned to wear it at her sixth-grade concert. Morgan asked Mother to help get Caitlin's "borrowing" stopped.

"Caitlin, you have been using Morgan's things without asking, and you know we don't think that's fair," Mother said. "Today you really upset Morgan's plans. You need to make amends to her for wearing her blouse, and you need to think how to remember that you don't borrow without permission. What could you do to make amends?"

"I could tell her I'm sorry," said Caitlin, sheepishly.

"That's not enough, Caitlin."

"I could let her wear my blouses," suggested Caitlin.

"You know your blouses are a size too small for her," replied Mother.

"I could buy her a book. She loves books."

"No, this is about a blouse, not a book," explained Mother.

Caitlin thought for a moment and then offered, "I could offer to iron her blouses for the next three weeks."

"Do you know how to iron well enough to please her?"

"I could learn," she insisted.

"Okay, that's one option. Let's have two more."

"I could buy her a padlock so she could lock her closet."

Mother laughed. "That sounds pretty silly to me, but it is about not wearing her clothes. You could offer that. Now, one more."

"I could promise not to wear her stuff without asking and if I ever do, I have to do her chores for a whole week."

"Okay, ask Morgan if she will accept any of those amends."

Morgan said she kind of liked the idea of the lock on her closet door, but she chose the last option because if she got the lock, she would be doing the work and if Caitlin stopped taking things without asking that would be even better.

For a young child, you might offer two or three ways to make amends for the child to choose from. To three-year-old Libby: "Libby, when you kicked my leg you hurt me. Now you must do something to make it better. You can get me an ice pack from the freezer or a Band-Aid from the bathroom." To five-year-old Janet: "Janet, you cut Annie's doll's hair and Annie doesn't like that. You are not to damage each other's toys. Now you have to do something to make it up to Annie. You can offer Annie one of your toys, or you can offer to straighten up her doll house for her, or you can ask her what she wants you to do. You must find something Annie says is okay and I say is okay."

Asking a child to say he is sorry for causing hurt or pain is usually not a good idea because that is our thinking, not his. If the wrongdoer is uncomfortable about what he did, that is hopeful. If he is genuinely sorry for what he did, so much the better. If he is angry and upset and blaming the other child, this is probably not the time to teach him how to make amends and it may be better for you to choose some consequence for his actions.

Here is a story in which a young teen made amends successfully.

Jason and his friends were spray painting graffiti on the back of a neighbor's garage. The neighbor came home, recognized Jason, and called his mom. When Jason got home, Mom said, "I know that you spray painted the Carlsons' garage. I'm really sorry you did that. How can I help you with this?"

"I didn't do it," said Jason.

"I asked, 'How can I help you?'" Mom repeated.

"There were other kids there. I wasn't alone," Jason explained.

"I asked how I could help you. You will have to think of a way to make it up to the Carlsons. Well, think about it. Your dad will be home soon. Will you tell him what you did or shall I tell him?" asked Mom.

"I'll do it," sighed Jason.

When Jason told his dad, his dad was quiet for what seemed to Jason a very long time. Then his dad said, "Right now I am not proud of you. How can I help you?"

Mom and Dad sat with Jason while he thought of options. He could pay to have it repainted, but he didn't have any money. He could apologize and offer to mow the Carlsons' lawn. He could buy paint remover and try to remove the paint. Dad suggested that Jason ask the Carlsons what they would accept. Jason was afraid to do that, but Mom and Dad insisted that he talk with the Carlsons and offered to go with him.

At the Carlsons, Jason's parents sat silently and let Jason negotiate. Luckily for Jason, Mr. Carlson said he had been planning to repaint the garage so Jason could be at his house at 8:00 A.M. on Saturday in old clothes and with a paint brush and they would paint the whole garage. Jason accepted and Jason's parents approved. They decided to say nothing about the "friends" who had run off and who did not appear to help with the painting, but to let Jason figure out that lesson for himself. Jason returned from the day of painting exhausted, but satisfied that he had made things right with his neighbor.

Review the list of elements on page 55 in making successful amends and notice how each of them is reflected in Jason's experience.

Chapter 7, page 72, contains further examples of making amends. Four-year-old Laney tore Hunter's book. Teenage Noah left the family car's gas tank empty. And in chapter 6, pages 62–63, five-year-old Jamal hurt Carlos's feelings. *Time-In: When Time-Out Doesn't Work* offers several more examples of amends making.[3]

Time and effort

Since helping children make amends takes both time and effort, choose the times when you will teach it with care. If young children are to make amends, it should be done immediately or very soon after the offending incident to be sure they know why they are doing it. You might give yourself and an older child time to think by saying, "By tomorrow I expect you to have several suggestions of things you might do to make it up to Charlie" or, "We will talk about amends tomorrow so I have time to think what I'll be willing to accept as your amends." It often benefits older children to have to sit on their discomfort for a day or two. Adults need to make amends as soon as they recognize they have offended.

Helping children make amends from an early age is important because it teaches them not only how to rebuild connections, but also how to restore themselves to wholeness. It also teaches them how to be accountable to other people.

Teenage Lorenzo has a quick temper and a vicious vocabulary. When he calms down, he can't understand why the person he has ravaged acts withdrawn from him. He is "over it." He is smiling and pleasant so he thinks the other person should forget it, let it go. Lorenzo doesn't realize that when you savage others, they move away from you even if you later say you didn't mean it. And if they have to be near you, if they are in your family, your school class, or your workplace, their faces may look the same, but they have moved their hearts back to a more protected place. And they will not offer you things that you will never know you missed. If Lorenzo's parents had insisted that he make amends for his attacks when they first started, this lad might not hold the misconception that others should ignore his bad behavior. Learning to make amends now could help him see himself and others in a new way. This means truly making amends, not buying people off by being pleasant.

Amend

If a child is denying the need to make restitution, look for ways to counter by reviewing "Discounting—The Opposite of Attending," chapter 2, pages 14–18.

> *Time spent helping children learn when and how to make amends is a priceless gift.*

Making real amends changes behavior. Making amends rebuilds connections when it offers a chance to start again, correct a mistake, compensate for an injury or loss, and make a change for the better.

Chapter 6

Putting the Four A's Together

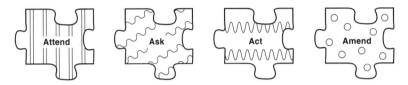

When what you are doing doesn't work, try something else.

—HARRY ILLSLEY (MY FATHER)

How shall I put the four puzzle pieces—Ask, Act, Attend, and Amend—together you ask? Any way that works. Any combination. In any order.

To establish a new connection, try Attend, Ask, Act, Amend in that order or any other order!

To strengthen a connection, start with the one that person likes.

With children, use all four at some time. Be especially sure to model making amends when you have been at fault.

For discipline, use as few puzzle pieces in any order as are needed to teach the lesson the child needs to learn. That leaves more time for fun and work with the child.

Sometimes, to make discipline effective, more than one puzzle piece is needed.

Using All Four Pieces—Laughing at Hurts

Here are examples of different ways the four A's could be used to deal with a child who laughs at another's pain. Please notice that each of these examples could have come from Rae's home or from the preschool at which she teaches.

*Rae's pattern of using time-in when a young child has hurt another child is to start with **attend**. She has the child who inflicted the hurt stand or sit beside her while she applies first aid if needed. She avoids giving lots of attention to* *the perpetrator because she doesn't want to reinforce the idea that hurting someone else is a way to be the center of attention. She is compassionate, but also avoids oversympathizing with the victim. She doesn't want to reinforce the idea that being victimized is a way to get good strokes, or positive recognition. Instead, she empowers the victim by helping her stand up for herself. In the following example Rae uses all four puzzle pieces.*

Example: Natasha fell and hurt herself but not seriously. No big deal. However, Natasha was upset because Rachael laughed at her.

Attends: Rae stands or sits beside Natasha.

Acts: Rae says to Rachael, "Rachael, Natasha has been hurt. You get the first aid box and then stay beside us while I help Natasha."

Asks: Rae says to Natasha, "Natasha, do you remember what we say about laughing at hurts?" Natasha nods yes.

Asks: Rae says to Natasha, "Natasha, can you tell Rachael that rule by yourself or shall I stay right beside you while I tell her?" Natasha says, "We don't laugh at people who are hurt. We help them."

Asks: Rae applies the Band-Aid and asks, "Natasha, do you want to tell Rachael how you feel?" Natasha says, "I'm mad at you and I don't want to play with you." Rachael says, "I don't care."

Amends: Rae tells Rachael, "Rachael, Natasha just reminded you of our rules about using put-ups instead of put-downs, and laughing at people who are hurt is a put-down. Whether you care or not, I expect you to make some amends to Natasha. That's how we do it here." Rachael says, "I forgot that dumb old rule." She thinks awhile and then makes an offer. "Here, you can play with my doll, Natasha." Natasha takes the doll and says, "Okay, you can play house with me." Rae says to Rachael, "That was a nice offer, Rachael. Good thinking."

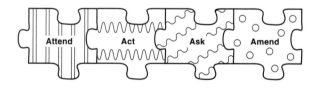

Rae believes that amends made by young children require an action. Occasionally a child will show some empathy and spontaneously say, *I'm sorry,* but Rae does not push for that or expect it. She believes that having children *act* their amends teaches a better lesson than urging them to *say* they are sorry when they may not be.

When a child hurts someone, helping that child make amends encourages thinking, promotes problem-solving skills, and teaches empathy. But the amends process often takes time because the perpetrator must find an amending offer that the victim is willing to accept. When a child is making amends to another child, the supervising adult must also agree, because adults are in charge of determining safety and appropriate behavior.

On another day Rae doesn't have time to work through to amends. Upon hearing one child laugh when another child's Lego project got broken, she might use **ask** with the one who laughed: "Jamal, do you remember the rule about laughing at hurts?" Or **act** (intervene), "Jamal, remember what we say about not laughing when someone's building gets ruined!"

Sometimes a child knows a rule but does not follow it because he does not believe it is important or because he does not know what to do instead. In this case, **act** to help the child think about the rule. Help him make sense of it for himself, and give him options about what to do instead. Explain the rule briefly to a young child; discuss it with an older child.

Listen to Rae talk with a five-year-old child. Rae **acts**: *"Jamal, when we laugh at someone's loss, we can hurt their feelings. Then they have two hurts. Instead, ask if you can help them."* Then **asks**, *"Can you think of a way you could have helped Carlos?"*

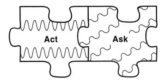

Or if Jamal is older, Rae asks, *"Jamal, why do you suppose we have a rule about not laughing when something gets ruined? Tell me three things you could do that would help Carlos."*

Putting the Four A's Together

If she had time, Rae might have used **amend** first. *"Jamal, you laughed at Carlos's ruined tower. That was a put-down. Now I expect you to make amends. Do you want me to help you think of ways to make it right? Your amends will have to be okayed by Carlos and by me."* Jamal says that he could say he is sorry, or he could help Carlos rebuild the tower, or he could let Carlos play with the pumper truck he had been playing with. Carlos chooses to play with the truck.

When the child has made amends, the adult encourages him to see himself as stronger and as a better person: *"Jamal, I'm delighted that you thought of three things you might do. Are you proud of the way you asked Carlos to choose? You did that well."* Rae avoids saying, You are a good boy. That doesn't tell Jamal what he did well or what to do next time.

These examples apply to young and school-age children. If you review the Jason spray painting story, chapter 5, page 57, you will notice that although the parents had determined that Jason would have to make amends, they also used **asking**, **acting**, and **attending** to accomplish their goal.

Use your experience, your thinking, and your intuition to help you decide how to combine the four A's.

Time-in occurs whenever you are attending, asking, acting, or amending in respectful ways, and that's what builds connection.

SECTION II

Discipline That Builds Connection

Chapter 7

Time-In for Discipline

> *The single most important factor in successful discipline*
> *is the bond, the relationship, the connectedness*
> *between parent and child.*
>
> —MADELYN SWIFT, *DISCIPLINE FOR LIFE*

When a child misbehaves discipline is called for. This is true when a child is just having a grumpy day or when parents are working on relieving an underlying contributor to unacceptable acts. The goal of discipline is to teach the needed lesson, to help the child become more responsible, and to strengthen rather than rupture connection.

It is not our job as parents to raise good children. It is our job, instead, to help children stay in touch with and develop the goodness within themselves and to act upon that. As we look for ways to help children find their own goodness, let's not forget that the connection we have with children is the most important part of discipline. In fact, the degree to which babies under a year old obey their mother's verbal commands has been shown to be strongly related to the mother's responsiveness to the child and practically unrelated to the use of rewards and punishments used as discipline measures.[1] Think about the lessons from the Holocaust. The long-lasting effects of disciplinary methods are reflected in Samuel and Pearl Oliner's *The Altruistic Personality: Rescuers of Jews in Nazi Europe*.[2] Almost all of the more than four hundred rescuers interviewed for this book reported that their parents had disciplined them by explanation and argument rather than punishment. Eight percent said this about their rescue efforts: "I had to do it. I could never have stood idle and watched injustice being done." Hitler, on the other hand, was beaten mercilessly and daily as a child, according to his half-sister.[3] So let us use the disciplinary methods that produce empathy and moral behavior. Let us think about ways to use time-in to strengthen our relationship with the child as we teach. Let us never try to break a child's spirit. Rather than breaking it, protect it. His spirit is a gift.

To Discipline Is to Teach

The ancient meaning of *discipline* is "to teach," not just to respond to misbehavior. Teaching is one way we connect with children. Teaching includes everything from helping a child learn to dress himself, to managing his wardrobe, to caring for an automobile, to getting along with others and learning when and how to connect with others. Today, the word *discipline* is often used to describe how one intervenes to teach a child about inappropriate or unsafe behavior.

While thinking about what intervention to use, a parent might ask

- Is my child learning that rules are made to keep her safe and to help her?
- When my child is doing something I wish she would not do again and there are natural consequences that would not be hurtful, do I let her experience and learn from the consequences?
- Do I let her learn to deal with the results of her own behavior and with her discomfort over other people's responses?
- Or instead do I try to protect her from all discomfort and thus teach her that she need not be responsible for her misbehavior?
- Does my method of discipline help me connect with my child, or does it create distance and separation?
- Does my intervention focus my child's behavior in a way that supports family values?

Harriet Heath, who founded the Parent Center at Bryn Mawr College, has written an easy-to-follow book, *Using Your Values to Raise Your Child to Be an Adult You Admire,* to help identify values and choose ways to parent with values in mind. It also takes developmental stages, the child's temperment, and learning style into account.[4]

All discipline teaches something. Keep asking, Am I teaching my child what I want her to learn?

Advantages of Using Time-In for Discipline

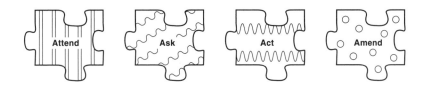

In section 1 we looked at the four puzzle pieces of time-in as they help parents and children connect. These four puzzle pieces, **ask**, **act**, **attend**, and **amend**, can also be used as forms of discipline.

One big advantage of time-in as discipline is that it keeps the child in *loving contact* with the parent. Children do not learn life skills in isolation; they develop them within relationships. Time-in discipline teaches without criticism, shame, or punishment. It strengthens the parent-child bond, builds the child's trust in the parent and in self, and assures the child, *My mom is on my team. My dad is there for me. My grandma cares about me.*

Although time-in can deal with the behavior, it will not remove the cause of the behavior if the cause is external to the child or if the child has some need that is not being met. (For more on why kids misbehave, see chapter 10.) Using time-in may, however, help you discover the root cause of misbehavior.

Using time-in as discipline also teaches the child *how to succeed* and *how to be responsible.* It teaches problem solving and conflict management skills. The goal of discipline is well stated by Madelyn Swift in her book *Discipline for Life: Getting It Right with Children.*[5] She says that every child and every adult needs to understand and believe that "I am responsible for what I choose to do and for what happens to me and others as a result of my decisions and actions."

This means that our job as parents and caregivers, through the years, is to teach children to take charge of their own behavior for themselves.[6] It is not helpful or healthy for children to be placated or to be paid to be good. Even children who initally need external rewards need to learn, over time, that behaving in a way that reflects the values of the family and that upholds their own values is satisfying. Paying kids for being good or doing well promotes a *What's in it for me?* attitude. Children need to learn to behave appropriately because that is their job. It is in their self-interest. And they need to do some chores because they are part of the family.

Another advantage to using time-in, and it is a big one for some of us, is that this approach encourages us adults *to be clear in our own minds* about our rules and to make sure the children understand them. If you waffle on rules or have too many, you may want to devour chapter 9 right now and do some thinking about rules before you start thinking about which of the time-in A's to use when you need to discipline.

Steps for Using Time-In for Discipline

As you use time-in for discipline, keep the following steps in mind.

1. Stop the unwanted behavior as soon as you become aware if it.
2. Ask yourself, *What do the children need to learn about this?* Don't tell them the answer—give them a chance to learn it themselves. Give them tools; give them words; give them something concrete to do.
3. Ask yourself, *Would a natural or a logical consequence help the child learn?* Natural consequences are natural results of a behavior: *You don't eat—you will be hungry.* Logical consequences are used when the natural consequences would be either unsafe for the child or inconvenient for the parent: *You left the gas tank empty—you pay for the next two tank fulls.* Logical consequences are related to the offense. *You left the gas tank empty—you don't get to watch TV* is neither natural nor logical. Natural consequences may follow an **act** intervention: *Your toy is broken so you won't have it to play with anymore.* The **amend** puzzle piece is itself a logical consequence: *You broke her toy and I expect you to make amends.*
4. Keep discipline simple. Use as few puzzle pieces as possible for any one discipline problem. Spend more time on children's successes than on their misbehavior.
5. Use the pieces in any order and any combination.
6. Notice the pieces that this particular child responds to. Use those rather than the ones you would respond to.

Ask, Act, Attend, Amend (In Any Order)

You can copy this reminder card and post it on the bathroom mirror, the kitchen cupboard, the car dashboard, or tuck one in your wallet.

> **Time-In: Discipline**
> 1. **Stop the behavior.**
> 2. **What is the lesson?**
> 3. **Consequences?**
> 4. **Keep it simple.**
> 5. **Ask, Act, Attend, Amend.**
> 6. **Do what works.**

Deliberately examining the four parts of time-in—**attend, ask, act, amend**—may help you think about discipline in a new way. Remember, when you can handle a discipline incident with one puzzle piece, you are keeping your discipline short and effective.

If an object is broken or a person is hurt, start with **attend**. Attend to the object or the person who is hurt. Focus on the results of the behavior to teach about responsibility. Mariella spilled her milk. *"Mariella, you know what we do about spilled milk."*

Or you may start with **ask**: *"Do you remember the rule about . . . ?"* Do this only if you are sure the child knows the rule and is old enough to state it. Do not ask, *"Did you break this plate?"* if you already know who broke the plate. Remember, if we want the truth from children, we must make it safe for them to tell the truth. Ask to get information, not to criticize, ridicule, or vent anger. Ask to encourage the child to think, not to tell him what to think. If the child responds positively, encourage the child and don't use more puzzle pieces.

Or start with **act** to intervene, interrupt, distract, invite, redirect, support, or teach. If the child has broken an important but unstated rule, act to set and teach the rule.

Jimmy is accustomed to asking for treats at Grandpa's house. When he and Dad visit Dad's friend, Jimmy asks for a treat. Dad acts to intervene, "Jimmy, we are having our treats when we get home today." On the way home, Dad acts to explain a new rule: "We can ask for treats at Grandpa's house, but at other people's houses we must wait until they offer."

Parents **attend** by noticing what usually happens before a child mis-behaves and then **acting** to restructure the situation to reduce the stress.

Often Natalie explodes just before the family is ready to go somewhere. Does everyone get into a big hurry? Does Natalie not feel safe where they are going? Has she been out too much? Are there too many transitions in her life right now? Did the parents neglect to give her the information about where she is going and what will happen there?

Amends can be used as part of discipline. If a child knows the rule she violated and recognizes the hurt to someone else's property, feel-ings, reputation, or person, and if she is a kinesthetic child (more comfortable doing than talking), start with amends. *"Laney, you tore Hunter's book. You need to do something to make that up for him."* The amending act must be approved by the adult and the wronged per-son before it is carried out. *Four-year-old Laney may say she is sorry or swap her undamaged book for Hunter's torn book or help the adult tape up the book.* Amends need to be directly connected with the child's mis-behavior. An amend can be an act of service or appreciation or some-thing the offending child makes. Making amends may involve discomfort for the child as she faces up to her behavior, but it does not include "equal suffering." Instead it is some action that will help her feel more competent and will raise her self-esteem.

When children make amends, they are allowed to grow from their mistakes by becoming more responsible rather than being dimin-ished by them. To sixteen-year-old Noah, *"You left the car with an empty gas tank. Mistake—big time! I was late. How are you going to make it up to me?"*

In this situation, the parent has options. She could **act** and enforce a previously known penalty: *"Noah, you left the gas tank empty. You know the penalty—no gas, no driving for ten days."* But often, especially with older children, making amends is more powerful than being pe-nalized. When a parent sets penalties, the parent has already done the thinking. Making amends demands that everyone involved thinks. It may take awhile for Noah to come up with a satisfactory offer, but this teaches thinking and problem-solving skills and Noah may end up raising his own self-esteem and feeling competent in-stead of resenting a penalty or a punishment. Also, at times a conse-quence, such as no driving for ten days, is more of an inconvenience to the parent than it is to the child. What did Noah offer? *"I could wash the car. I could do errands for you Saturday morning. I could take the car in for an oil change if it needs one. I could write a tardy note for you to take to your boss."* Humor helps as long as the parent doesn't let it discount the seriousness of the problem.

Helping a child who has damaged or neglected something to make amends teaches responsibility. Since, in order to learn, the offending child must be part of the decision making about what amends to make, this process often takes time.

Must discipline be immediate? Very young children need discipline while they are still thinking about what happened. With older children it is sometimes better to let everyone cool down for an hour or a day or longer: "I hadn't expected you to do this. I will have to think about what we need to do. You think about it too. We'll talk about it tomorrow."

Ask and Act Puzzle Piece Stories

Getting out of bed: ASK—remind of a rule

It is past three-year-old Rosa's bedtime, but she has climbed out of bed and is at her mother's elbow. Very calmly, Mom says, "Rosa, you have had your bath and a story with a cuddle and a tuck-in. Do you remember what you are to do after that?"

"Get up?" Rosa replies.

"Nice try, honey," says Mom. "What is my little honey to do after her tuck-in?"

"Stay in bed?"

"You remembered! Good thinking. Now, do you go back by yourself or shall I walk with you?"

"You come. 'Nother story?" said Rosa hopefully.

"Nope. Bed. Come on."

Act—If Rosa throws a tantrum, Mom picks her up and puts her in bed. No words.

Whining in the car: ASK—promote cause-and-effect thinking

*Aunt Jane is taking Allison and two of her friends to the park. Allison has been whining instead of using her big-girl voice. Now she is whining about her seat belt, her place in the car, and so on. Very calmly Aunt Jane **asks** Allison, "Do you think girls who whine are apt to get to go to the park the next time they want to go?"*

Aunt Jane does not expect an answer.

The ball in the house: ACT—interrupt

*Mr. Z's grandson Deon hasn't responded well to their talks about where to throw the ball. Deon's eyes glaze over and no behavior change follows. Grandpa decides to use a kinesthetic **act** interrupt with no words at all. Over the familiar sounds of children playing, Grandpa hears the thud of a ball hitting something. He dashes to the scene, grabs the ball, and puts it on the toy shelf. He turns toward the children, looks at them, and waits expectantly. His grandson says to the playmates, "We're not to throw the ball in the house. Come on, let's play with the trucks."*

Mr. Z. got the desired behavior. It doesn't matter whether the child responds grudgingly or willingly. If the child is kinesthetic and responds better to actions than words, give him a high five or thumbs up or just a smile and leave. If it happens again, Mr. Z. will put the ball in the toy jail for three days. The toy jail is where toys wait while children think about the rules of play.

Dress up: ACT—support

The dress-up play changes tone as the children wrangle over who can wear what. Aunt Gina walks in with a twinkle in her eye and an armload of something. "Look! Listen! Come here!" she says, inviting her visual, her auditory, and her kinesthetic dress-up players to attend to her. "I have an old bedspread and a shawl and a scarf to add to the dress-up box."

If the children reach for the new props and resume play, the **act** puzzle piece was enough.

Dress up: ASK—redirect

If instead, Molly whines, *"Jennifer took my shoes and Wade won't let me wear the sword belt,"* Aunt Gina looks at Molly sympathetically and says, *"Oh,"* acknowledging Molly's protest without oversympathizing. Taking Molly's hand, Aunt Gina **asks**, *"Would you like to tie this scarf around your waist like a dancer or wear it over your shoulder like a super hero?"* If the play group seems to need further help, Aunt Gina **asks**, *"I think this tablecloth would make a fine tent, but what else could it be?"*

Bullying: ACT—intervene

Four boys swimming off a dock should mean fun for all four. But it isn't fun when one boy bullies another and the other two boys do not intervene. They are *bystanders*, or people who do not help someone who is being victimized. An adult neighbor walking by, stops and watches the action, then calls out, *"Hey, guys, make it fun for everybody."* The bullying boy shouts, *"It is!"* The man nods toward the victim, *"No it isn't fun for everyone."* The man looks at the bullying one who protests loudly and continues his abusive behavior. The man folds his arms, stands firm, keeps watching, and repeats at intervals, *"Make it fun for everybody."* The other three boys try to act as if the neighbor isn't there. After the fifth *"Make it fun for everybody,"* the bullying one grabs his bike and leaves. The other boys continue to play. Notice that the intervenor does not say, *Stop that,* or *Don't . . . ;* he says what to do, very simply and very assertively, and uses his confident body posture to reinforce his words.

Telling children what to do is far more helpful than telling them what not to do.

For information on using all four time-in puzzle pieces together, see chapter 6.

How to Start Using Time-In for Discipline

Know the puzzle pieces

Study the puzzle pieces **ask, act, attend, amend** and think of times when you have used each one. Make several copies of the puzzle reminder card on page 71 and use them as reminders to use the four A's in any order. Put one in your wallet and post the rest where you can easily refer to them.

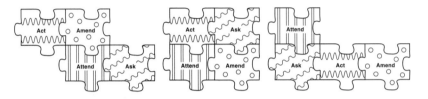

Start using time-in with the puzzle piece that is easiest for you. Experiment with the number of puzzle pieces you need to use at one time. Use the fewest number possible to get the response you want. Think of yourself as a guide or a coach.

Decide when

Use time-in for discipline when you decide it is important to intervene on behavior, when modeling is not enough. Use it when you are willing to let the child experience discomfort over his behavior. Parents who try to be buddies with their children may forget to provide the protection, the structure, and the opportunity that children need to experience the consequences of their behaviors.

> *Children don't need parents who are friends; they need parents who are friendly.*
> —Ada Alden

Use time-in to keep discipline positive and be careful not to slip into punishment or criticism. Recently a parent asked me, "But, with the four As, when do I get to really discipline, to punish?" Since the lessons from punishment are more about violence than about good behavior, we use the four A's to avoid punishment. Keep a calm attitude of, This is not my problem; this is your problem, I am here to help you. Make sure your voice and body language are not judgmental. Use making amends only when you have time and patience. (Diane Chelsom Gossen's book, *Restitution: Restructuring School Discipline,* is written to be used in schools, but the information is straightforward and many of the wonderfully enlightening examples are from the home or could easily happen there.[7])

Have clear rules

If the rules in your household aren't clear, write them out in a short and clear way and post them. (For more on rules see chapter 9.) *Growing Up Again* has helpful information about non-negotiable rules and negotiable rules and when to use each.[8] When you ask your child if she remembers a rule, you need to listen carefully to her response. When you discuss or teach about a rule, be sure to include and listen to the child's feelings: *"I hear that you are angry about that rule sometimes, but we have to keep it because it is about safety. How would you feel if that happened to you?"*

Select your focus

When one child has hurt another, remember that empowering the victim is important for the victim. It also keeps the offending child from getting that wad of attention she may be aiming for. Remember to center yourself and think about your long-term goals in parenting. See this as an investment. You are the teacher, the helper for your child. If the offending child refuses to cooperate, *"Aaron started it,"* insist that the offending child be responsible for his behavior: *"No matter who started it, we don't destroy each other's things."*

Give yourself time to learn

What, you say, *four pieces to time-in?* Too hard? Too long? Not so. You probably use several of the pieces with great skill already. Learning this discipline method won't take as long to learn as how to play softball or bridge or how to use a computer. Some people shorten the learning time by role-playing common problems with another adult who plays the role of the child.

Discipline using the four A's helps build, not break, connection. It teaches without criticism or shaming and can empower the child and raise self-esteem.

> *It is up to parents to build on the child's need for attachment to promote self-control around particular issues and, even more important, a lasting inner commitment to be, or at least to become, a disciplined person.*
> —*Bruno Bettelheim,* A Good Enough Parent

Remember that it takes a long time and many tries for children to learn life's lessons. Get help when you need it. Parenting is too important a job to do without support. Because you are your children's most important teacher, using positive discipline skills is an investment in their futures and yours.

Chapter 8

What about Time-Out?

Call time-out before tempers flare . . . remember that
if kids learn to take a break before they blow up,
there won't be any misbehavior to punish.

—MARY SHEEDY KURCINKA,
RAISING YOUR SPIRITED CHILD

Does time-out help your child feel connected with you or does she feel distanced, abandoned, or rejected? That depends on how you use it and on what she decides about it.

What Is Time-Out?

Time-out is a technique for calming an overexcited child or for interrupting misbehavior with a time to think. For the latter, the misbehaving child is sent to a predetermined time-out space or chair or to his room to be quiet for a period of time, usually not more than one minute for each year of the child's age. The child is to think about how to behave. When the child comes back to the family, he is expected to act appropriately. The goal is to encourage the child to think about how to be responsible for his behavior.

When time-out is used as a calming technique, the child is removed from the stimulating environment to calm himself before he is expected to think about his behavior. He can choose to be alone or to be accompanied by the adult who will soothe and comfort him. This takes as long as it takes—the goal is to help the child recognize when he is getting overstimulated and to remove and calm himself before his behavior gets out of bounds.

Time-Out as Punishment

Time-out is punishment if it is held over the child's head as a threat, a negative consequence for misbehavior. Time-out, when not used as a punishment but as a gift of time and space to help the child, is a positive interruption of behavior or overexcitement, a time to pull back, and a chance to start over. Used that way, time-out can be a prelude to time-in. If time-out is used as a punishment, it is apt to cause the child to disconnect. One of the problems with punishment is that, since it is imposed from the outside, many children use their discomfort to fuel blame and anger at the adult rather than to become self-responsible.

Advantages of Time-Out

Time-out has several advantages. It is an easy, instant way to interrupt misbehavior. If the child has already been taught how to calm himself, he may do that. If the child has a secure parent-child bond, the child may be able to use some calming time to remember a rule or choose more appropriate behavior. The introverted child may welcome some alone time for peace and quiet, time to get her energy restored, and time to think, to do a favorite activity and therefore become more calm. The child whose caring adult stays with him during time-out may find the support comforting. For a visual child, the chance to stare out the window or look at the rules poster may promote thinking. For the auditory child, calming music and the directive, *"Think about how to tell me what you can do differently next time,"* may be helpful. The kinesthetic child may be calmed by time alone to jump up and down or push things around. Using his moving body often helps him unfold the thinking process. Parents can also take time-outs: *"Leave me alone for five minutes. I need time to think about what to do about this."* This break benefits both the parent and the child who misbehaved. In his excellent book, *T. I. P. S.: Time-In Parenting Strategies*, Otto Weininger describes all time-out as destructive for the child. Any calming he classifies as time-in.[1]

When There Are Problems with Time-Out

Time-out doesn't help if the child doesn't understand what behavior led to the time-out or what new behavior is expected. Children may regard time-out as punishment to be resisted or resented rather than time to become calm and think. Children may interpret time-out as abandonment or as rejection of their noise, crying, or raging. Making noise is natural for children. *I'm not yelling; I'm playing,* they insist, and crying and raging are ways that children release tension and let us know that they are sad or frustrated. Otto Weininger says,

> Forced to attempt to deal with such strong feelings alone and away from adult support, a child may become physically ill, or unusually withdrawn—with either response being potentially damaging to emotional development.[2]

A child who is extremely distractible may stare at the crack in the wall instead of thinking about her behavior. Children whose personality style is to process experiences with feelings first and thinking later may shut down feelings and therefore shut off thinking during a time-out.[3] The auditory child may need to be talked to and listened to before quiet time is productive for him. If she needs to move in order to think, the kinesthetic child may have such difficulty keeping her body on the chair that she gets more agitated rather than calmer. While physical touching and holding will reassure one child, another child will be overstimulated by it and need some time alone to calm herself. Parents can watch for clues from each child to figure out what works with that particular child.

Children who are naturally extraverted may need to talk in order to think, so being alone in time-out can shut down their thinking. If the child lacks information about the problem or its solution, time-out to think does not provide it. For some children who are upset, time-out by themselves may seem to be a withdrawal of love—a very frightening thing for a child.

Time-out doesn't work if the parent is angry. The child needs to be guided, not forced. If time-out has been followed by a penalty or violence, the child will probably focus on dreading the penalty rather than on improving his behavior. If the parent is using time-out as part of a power struggle to prove *I can make you sit in time-out,* the child will think about ways to win the struggle. If the parent gives in and doesn't insist on the desired behavior, the child may experience a subtle form of abandonment. Time-out imposed by the parent is often not effective after a child reaches eight or nine years of age. Hopefully, by that age, the child will be taking his own time-out to calm himself and think.

Dr. Peter Ernest Haiman, child-rearing consultant and former tenured chairman and professor of the Department of Child Development and Early Childhood Education at the University of South Carolina, takes a dim view of time-out in his article "'Time Out' to Correct Misbehavior May Aggravate It Instead." He asserts:

> Cries and misbehavior from children and adolescents are, in a way, very much like a sore throat, stuffed-up nose, aching muscles or a fever. All are symptoms. All have causes. When parents correctly diagnose and provide remedies that address the needs of children and adolescents, the symptoms of crying or misbehavior will also disappear. The purpose of a cry is to obtain the kind and quality of parental love and care that will properly attend to unmet needs and, therefore, establish feelings of security in the child. Older child and adolescent misbehavior serves the same purpose as the baby's cry—it announces that needs are frustrated. . . . For the frustrated and uncomfortable child, time-out offers enforced silence and the feeling of being rejected by one's parents. . . . A frustrated child who must sit quietly and alone in time-out frequently becomes angry. Although they dare not express this anger when in time-out, children often express it by becoming angry and defiant sometime after being released from time-out. Time-out sends the message that one should bottle up uncomfortable emotions. . . . Children desperately need to stop the painful feelings going on inside them when they are upset in time-out and unable to express these feelings. . . . To cope, they learn to ignore and/or distract themselves from the energy of their hurt and angry feelings, and thus, they learn to repress them. In the process, nervous habits emerge, such as thumb sucking, fingernail biting, hair pulling, skin scratching, tugging at clothes, self-pinching and many other similar behaviors. These behaviors serve to ward off uncomfortable feelings. . . . As a result, being unaware of true feelings often can become a characteristic feature of a person's life.[4]

Time-Out as Connection

Mary Sheedy Kurcinka, in her book *Raising Your Spirited Child,* explains how to use time-out for calming and not as a punishment:

> If we have taught them that Time-Out is an opportunity to pull out of the action to rest and relax rather than a punishment to endure, they can feel comfortable taking a break. . . . They need to understand that a Time-Out is not over until that sense of peacefulness fills their bodies. That's why you can't just send young children to their room

alone. You have to go with them, talk softly, rub their back if they like it, and stay with them until that rosy, good feeling is inside of their bodies. . . . call the Time-Out before tempers flare. . . . remember that if kids learn to take a break before they blow up, there won't be any misbehavior to punish. . . . This is preventive discipline.[5]

Madelyn Swift in *Discipline for Life!* describes time-out as *"a gift of time and space given to upset children. . . . Misbehaving children do not go to Time-Out: upset children do."*[6] The gift of time and space for the upset child may be a quiet time sitting in a chair, but a high energy, intense child stays upset longer if asked to sit still. This child needs to rock in a chair, jump, run, climb, or swing. The misbehaving child needs the intervention, the teaching/discipline, one or more of the four A's that will help him learn what he needs to learn.

If a child is upset and has misbehaved, a time to calm down can be followed by an A and can promote connection. **Ask:** *What did you decide to do?* or, *Do you need some help?* or, *Ready to tell me how you are going to do better next time?* **Act:** *Show me how you can do that differently.* **Attend:** *Now come with me and we'll look at what you broke and decide what to do about that.* **Amend:** *Now that we have both calmed down, tell me what you can do to make things right with your brother.*

Of course, if calming time were used before misbehavior occurred, no intervention would be needed.

You can notice how your child responds and decide if and when a calming time-out is an effective way to help you connect with your child.

Chapter 9

The Role of Rules

*Children need rules because they do not have the long eye
for the future that is part of mature thinking.*
—ANONYMOUS

Rules are tools, tools the family uses to build structures that create a safe, productive, and convenient place in which people can live, love, grow, and connect. In order for time-in to be used to connect with children and teach them to internalize and follow the rules, an understanding and appreciation of rules is helpful. If you are comfortable with setting and enforcing rules, and if your child seems to understand the family's rules and usually responds well when you remind him of a rule, skip this chapter. If not, use the following ideas to help you think about your family's relationship to rules.

Mom is on the phone. Elliott, four, tugs on Mom's sleeve. He is carrying a small bag of toys and crackers. Elliott tugs again and whines, "I'm running away." Mom says, "You can go as far as the door and that's as far as you can go; that's the rule." She continues her conversation. Elliott calls twice more; Mom repeats the rule in a clear, noncritical voice and continues her phone conversation. Elliott sits down by the door and eats his crackers.

Lucky Elliott. Elliott lives in a family that has rules that protect him and that he knows will be enforced. Children like rules. Rules help them feel safe and secure. Rules help children feel connected to their families.

Alexa, four, sat on a stool at the kitchen counter, swinging her legs and eating her snack. Her friend, Sophie, was telling her about sneaking next door to throw mud and rocks in the neighbor's fish pond. Alexa looked at her friend with scornful eyes and muttered, "Your mom lets you do that?" a question that clearly implied that Sophie's family was not taking good care of her.

Older children also need the support of clear rules. *Felipe, fifteen, was urged by his friends to get drunk. Saying that he didn't want to didn't deter his friends, so Felipe called up the power of the family rules: "My folks would kill me."* Family opposition to teen drinking is a more powerful deterrent to drug abuse than peer influence, according to research done by Peter Benson of the Search Institute who surveyed more than 46,799 youngsters for the report titled *The Troubled Journey: A Portrait of 6th–12th Grade Youth.*[1]

Why Are Rules Important?

Some people, some personality types, like straightforward rules and like to know exactly what they are and what they mean. They regard rules as friends that help them know how to succeed. Other personality types prefer to go about learning rules, or being reminded of them, somewhat indirectly. Either way, children do not like the chaos that comes from the lack of rules or from rules that are inconsistently enforced. Children need to have a safe space in which to be individuals and to be creative, and they need to be challenged to think. To do that they need clear, consistent structure, and that includes protective rules.

The five cousins attended an elementary school where breakfast was served. Every morning they quarreled as they left the house to catch the school bus. Admonitions to stop quarreling or to get along had made no difference. One morning Robyn decided to try giving the children a specific directive at which they could all succeed. She stopped them as they went out the door and said, "Remember to eat a big breakfast." They trooped off without a squabble so Robyn repeated the directive every morning.

After about three weeks, when Robyn said, "Good-bye, I love you, and eat a big breakfast," the seven-year-old asked, "What else should we do?" Robyn was startled, but she recovered quickly, smiled, and said, "Obey your teacher." A couple of weeks later the eight-year-old said, "We are ready for our next rule." As the months progressed, the children asked for more rules:

- *Eat a big breakfast.*
- *Obey your teacher.*
- *Learn something new.*
- *Make good friends.*
- *Make good choices.*
- *Smile a lot.*

The children chanted the litany as they left each morning. "Smile a lot" was added by the five-year-old.

I have not heard how long the list was by the end of the school year, but I have thought much about these fortunate children. They left home each morning with rules (their word), telling them how to be successful. They acquired their rules at their own pace; they reinforced each other; they were connected to each other and to family values. It certainly beats quarreling on the way to the bus. Lucky kids. Wise mom. Easy discipline.

What Does Your Family Teach about Rules?

Before you decide to call the limit setting or directing part of your structure *rules,* think about how you feel about rules. Listen to what the adults in your family are teaching about rules. Use the following example sheet to record what your family is teaching.[2]

1. Think about the question and write a word or two that describes how you respond to it or how you feel about it. Your words might be *resentful, annoyed, troubled, angry, fearful, scared, safe, secure, relaxed, glad, I agree,* or *I disagree.*
2. Read the example.
3. In the "our words" space, write in an example from your family if that question hits home.

Do you think or feel

- that rules are a burden?

   Feeling: _____

   Oh, groan, we just got another set of rules and regulations at work. This means more meaningless paperwork.

Our words

_____

• that you should know the rules without asking?

Feeling: _____

I made a mistake at work. It was something we have never done before, but I should have known.

Our words

_____

• that rules are stupid or thoughtless in design?

Feeling: _____

What a stupid rule! I wonder who thinks up these things!

Our words

_____

• that it's okay to break rules as long as you don't get caught?

Feeling: _____

Padding my expense account gets by my new supervisor. She doesn't notice.

Our words

_____

• that rules are to be broken, finessed, or ignored?

Feeling: _____

Well, there is another rule we will have to get around.

Our words

_____

• that rules benefit adults at the expense of children?

Feeling: _____

You know the rule. Children don't ask questions when adults are talking.

Our words

_____

• that rules are made to be helpful?

Feeling: _____

I'm glad there is a rule that we all drive on the same side of the road.

Our words

_____

- that rules should be evaluated?

  Feeling: _____

  That rule no longer seems to fit. Let's think about how to change it to be more helpful.

  Our words

  _____

- that you value your family rules because they protect and respect everyone in the family?

  Feeling: _____

  I'm glad we have a no put-down rule in our family. It helps us think about how to be helpful instead of blaming each other.

  Our words

  _____

You can decide whether you should change some of the messages you are sending. Even if your messages are clear and consistent—that rules are to benefit the family and are to be followed—your child may still be doing more than occasional rule testing. If so, check out the messages from the child's school and peer group. You may need to take a stronger position on family values. You may need to ask your child to find a more supportive peer group. Do what you can to get the school to change. Start by talking to a teacher. It's amazing what one determined, tenacious parent can accomplish in a school. Remember, schools work for us. We pay for them. They exist to teach our children academic and social skills in a safe setting.

Reminding about Rules

Notice how your children respond to the way you remind them about rules. Some children like a direct reminder: *Hey, go brush your teeth.* Some like humor: *I heard about this guy that didn't like to brush his teeth, and after a while he didn't have to.*

How do you feel about rules? If you do not view rules as your friends, maybe you need some friendlier rules.

If you feel apologetic about enforcing rules, or if you are not able to be matter-of-fact in enforcing them, you can use indirect ways to offer structure. You can say, *This is not the way our family does this* or, *We expect our children to leave their toys in the garage, not on the driveway,* or, *It helps all of us when everyone carries dishes to the sink, so bring yours now.*

If your family or child believes that rules are a burden or are to be avoided or manipulated, or if you or your child bristles at the mention of the word *rules,* avoid the word and ask the *Do you remember . . .* or *Can you think why . . .* questions.

- Do you remember when we talked about put-downs?
- Do you remember when we practiced petting the puppy gently?
- Do you remember where to put toys when you are through playing?
- Can you think why I need to know one day ahead when you plan to take cookies to school?
- Can you tell me why everyone writes on the chalkboard where they are going and when they'll be back?
- Will you tell me three reasons it is important for you to refill the gas tank when you have used the car?[3]

Rules Themselves Are Teaching Tools

Family rules, by whatever name you call them, need to provide physical and emotional protection for all members of the family, and children need to understand that the rules are devised to help all family members. Before you set rules, ask yourself and others in the family, *What do you need; what do I need; what does the situation call for?*

In making rules for young children, consider these guidelines.

- Have as few rules as possible. Try five or fewer for children who are five or younger.
- State each rule clearly: *Hang jackets on the pegs.*
- Create rules that tell what to do, not just what not to do: *Use put-ups instead of put-downs.*
- Post the rules. Long before children can read, you can emphasize a rule by taking the child to the rules poster and pointing to and talking about a rule. Pictures help children identify each rule. Having posted rules also reminds parents to be consistent.
- Apply rules to everyone. If Dad leaves his bowling ball in the entryway instead of the closet and Mom leaves her craft supplies in the eating area, expect difficulty in enforcing a "Put toys on

shelves" rule. A no-hitting rule has to mean no hitting for every-one. If children are not supposed to hit, but adults do, the children learn that they can hit when they get big.

Here are some examples of family rules for preschoolers, school-age children, and adolescents.

> **Our Rules[4]**
>
> 1. Touch people gently—hitting hurts.
> 2. Put markers and crayons away so Baby won't get them.
> 3. Wash face and brush teeth before bed.
> 4. Say please and thank you often.
> 5. Eat at the table with TV off.

As children reach school age, housekeeping rules are often presented in a concrete but whimsical way.

House Rules

- If you take it out, put it back.
- If it is hungry, feed it.
- If you sleep in it, make it.
- If you open it, close it.
- It it's dirty, clean it.

Interpersonal rules deal with more abstract concepts and are impor-tant for older children, adolescents, and adults.

People Rules

- Speak for yourself, not others.
- Listen to others; expect them to listen to you.
- Ask directly for what you need.
- Be responsible for yourself and toward others.
- Respect yourself and others.

Rules Can Be Enforced Many Ways

Remember, once a rule is made—*by* parents when the children are young and *with* children as they grow older—enforce the rule if the rule is enforceable. Sometimes a situation necessitates **action** in the form of a direct command, or reprimand, or consequence, or one of the other A's. (See chapter 7.) Sometimes it is desirable to help the child internalize rules by modeling and patient expecting. If the family has a rule about taking off shoes when entering the house, parents can take theirs off and then wait by the child while he takes his off. Often no words need be spoken.

Some Rules Cannot Be Enforced

Rules about safety should be clear, even if they can't always be enforced.

Maria gets home from work two hours after school lets out. She has a rule that no neighbor children are allowed in the house unless a parent is at home. Maria can't enforce the rule because she isn't there, but she believes it is important. She could set up a video monitor, find an adult to monitor the children, or find an afterschool program for the children to attend. Since none of those options are feasible, she tells the children that she wishes they would not invite other children into the house, but since she can't enforce it, she will have to trust them. Then she makes sure they understand why others should not be allowed in and discusses how important trust is. She calls the children on the phone periodically to ask how they are doing.

Keeping Rules Up-to-Date

It is important to review family rules periodically. Use this list to check yourself regularly or hold a special rules-update family meeting and listen to the children's answers to the questions.

- Does everyone understand the rules?
- Are any of our rules outdated?
- Do any of our rules need adjustment?
- Do we need any new rules?
- Are we negotiating more and more of our rules as the children grow old enough to understand the importance of the rules?

- Are we consistent in our enforcement?
- Are we affirming good behavior?

Helping Children Internalize Rules

A mom who thought she had made it clear through the years that the rules were for the children's welfare decided to test it out when her children became teenagers. "I know that you know the rules now, but being that I'm a mom and I still think I should remind you about them, would it be okay if we numbered them so as you leave the house I can just say, I love you and remember 8, 17, and 31?" The teenagers thought that was silly but they agreed. They never did assign a specific number to a rule, but if Mom didn't remember to call out some numbers as they left, they challenged, "Mom, aren't you forgetting something?" Mom hoped that the random numbers would remind the kids of the rules they needed for that day. The kids playfully ridiculed the practice but secretly enjoyed the trust their mother placed in them. They amused themselves by bringing disbelieving friends home to witness what they described as their mom's ridiculous way of saying good-bye.

Clear, appropriate rules help children feel safe and be successful and stay connected with the family. The need for certainty that clear structure brings is present all of our lives. You can learn more about making and using rules as tools for structure and about negotiable and non-negotiable rules by reading Clarke and Dawson's book *Growing Up Again: Parenting Ourselves, Parenting Our Children.*[5]

Structure is not a sometime thing.

Chapter 10

Now What? Why Kids Misbehave

Cries and misbehavior from children and adolescents are,
in a way, very much like a sore throat, stuffed-up nose,
aching muscles or a fever. All are symptoms.

—DR. PETER ERNEST HAIMAN,
"'TIME OUT' TO CORRECT MISBEHAVIOR
MAY AGGRAVATE IT INSTEAD"

Sometimes children misbehave. Even if we feel deeply connected with them. Even if we love them dearly and they know it. Even if we have lots of time-in.

Mostly, Grace is cooperative and agreeable. I love it when she says, "I'll help. What do you want me to do?" She can be empathic and thoughtful when she wants to. But, other times, when I ask her to do something, she ignores me or scowls and whines, "I don't want to!" or, "Later!" She even breaks rules and denies that she knew the rule. I feel helpless when she hisses, "I won't and you can't make me!" I think, "Now what?"

Why do children misbehave? Since children are complex beings with changing needs, and since children live in family systems that are also complex with changing needs, it is futile for us to look for a single reason. Seductive, but futile. If there were one simple reason why children misbehave and if we could find a single effective response or child management tool, the task of raising children would be magnificently easier. But this is not to be. Instead, we must become detectives and do the work of figuring out why this misbehavior at this time. Only then will we find the solutions that have long-term positive effects.

Reasons for Misbehavior

Here are some of the reasons for misbehavior that parents have discovered. You can probably add to this list. When your child misbehaves, especially if you can't see a reason why, try using this checklist. You could ask a caring friend or relative who has observed your child to fill it out also. Of course, trust your own judgment and make your own decisions, but it frequently helps to get input from other people who may see things we don't notice.

Could this be the reason for this particular misbehavior?

Yes Maybe No

___ ___ ___ 1. Does this child have a health problem? Does she not feel well, not hear well, not see well?

___ ___ ___ 2. Is this child not getting enough sleep?
Fatigue can cause a child to have a behavioral meltdown.

___ ___ ___ 3. Does he eat the foods his body needs?
When toddlers and young children misbehave, look first at their diet. If they are hyped up, look for caffeine. When they are grumpy, see if they are hungry.

___ ___ ___ 4. Is this child overscheduled or does she not have the time or the skills required to manage the many transitions in her day?
Young children who were happy at home and are put in day care before they are mature enough to handle the many transitions that involves often respond with fussiness, sleep disruption, or loss of appetite. Too little sleep, drop in grade level, and surliness toward family members may be symptoms of overscheduling of older children.

___ ___ ___ 5. Is this child sad, angry, embarrassed, frustrated, or confused about something?

___ ___ ___ 6. Is my expectation too advanced for the child's age or developmental level?

___ ___ ___ 7. Has my structure been so lax or inconsistent the child doesn't believe or realize that the rules need to be followed?

___ ___ ___ 8. Has my structure been so tight, my rules so rigid, that my child is rebelling against unnecessary restrictions?

Yes Maybe No

__ __ __ 9. Does this child not understand the rule; does he not believe it is a rule because others don't follow it; or does he not see any sense in the rule? (See chapter 9.)

__ __ __ 10. Have I unwittingly or deliberately set up competition for love and attention within the family?

__ __ __ 11. Do conflicts between family members escalate because I need better conflict-resolution skills?[1]

__ __ __ 12. Is there stress in the family system due to the arrival of a new child, illness, job loss, addiction, dissension, divorce, or for other reasons?

Children know when something stressful is going on, even if the adults don't talk about it or insist that it is not a big deal. Children often express that stress for the family by doing things that are hurtful or disruptive or look dumb.

__ __ __ 13. Does this child have an extraverted nature and need more interaction with other people?

__ __ __ 14. Or is he introverted and reacting against being overstimulated?

__ __ __ 15. Are this child's inborn personality traits or learning styles such that she does not respond well to the way the demands and expectations of the family are presented?[2] (See chapter 7.)

__ __ __ 16. Does he lack the kind of positive attention and contact that this particular child needs, so he arranges to get negative attention instead?

Remember, negative attention is better than none. Far, far better. Every human being has a strong, basic hunger for recognition, and a child will do what his family responds to, even if it is hurtful to him.

__ __ __ 17. Is the family so busy that this child feels disconnected from other family members and is looking for ways to get attention?

__ __ __ 18. Has this child been watching too much TV with the barrage of messages to solve problems quickly with violence or easily with a drug, or playing computer games that simulate destroying people?[3]

Yes Maybe No

___ ___ ___ 19. Has this child been given a label, such as clumsy, slow, or dyslexic, that she uses as an excuse for misbehavior?

___ ___ ___ 20. Is something hurtful or stressful happening to this child, such as being bullied at school?

___ ___ ___ 21. Does the child just feel contrary on this particular day?

> Adults have days when they "get up on the wrong side of the bed."

Dr. William Doherty observes that many families are overscheduled outside of the family and underscheduled within the family. He recommends that families schedule time to eat together, talk together, play together, hang out together. His helpful book, *The Intentional Family,* suggests many ways to do that.[4]

Could This Be Normal Behavior?

One of the reasons children misbehave is that they are doing what comes naturally and haven't yet learned that their adults find that particular behavior unacceptable. Some of the normal behaviors become misbehaviors only if the child does them too long. Let's take lying as an example.

The dictionary says a *lie* is a false statement deliberately presented as being true. But small children do not read the dictionary, so often their lies are not deliberate attempts to deceive. Many children, especially three-, four-, and five-year-olds, tell tall tales. This is a very important way they develop imagination and creativity and sometimes deal with their own fears and frustrations. You can encourage tall tales and enjoy the fancifulness of the stories. When four-year-old Danny tells how he used his toy fire engine to put out a real fire, his family encourages him to give details and then says, *"Thank you for that good story. Maybe you will be a firefighter when you grow up."*

Sometimes what sounds like a lie to us is not a false statement, but the result of the child not understanding what we mean. *Put your toy away,* means *put it on the shelf* to us, but it could mean *take it out of the middle of the floor* to the child, so she puts it under the sofa. In that case, we do not tell the child she is lying when she tells us she put it away. We teach her *where to put the toy away.*

Tattling may seem like lying because it often leaves out part of the truth. Kathryn M. Hammerseng's little book *Telling Isn't Tattling* is helpful in teaching children when to tell and when to take **action**.[5]

Children will sometimes lie to get a rise out of an adult. In this case, give the child more attention at other times. All children need to be noticed.

Often children lie to protect themselves or to please others. The child thinks, *If I say I didn't break the glass, she won't be angry.* We can take **action:** *"Broken glass is dangerous. You stay on the chair while I clean it up. Next time you see broken glass come and get me right away."* Later, glass-carrying practice or placing-the-glass-safely-on-the-table practice can be an enjoyable activity: *"Big kids know how to carry glasses. Try it again with this plastic glass and then we will practice with a glass glass."*

We need to make sure the child understands whether the discipline/teaching is for the lie or for the misbehavior that was lied about, and sometimes that requires two separate discipline/teachings. The example above is about the misbehavior. Mom offers discipline about the lying when she asks, *"Do you know what happens when children don't tell the truth?"* She then negotiates about what **amends** the child will have to make to restore her trust.

As we help children learn when and where and how much of the truth to tell, we need to remember that the development of a conscience as an inside behavior guide takes many years.[6] We also need to remember that children learn from watching us. When we say, *"It is important to be kind to others,"* and then we ridicule our child, is what we said a lie? If we already know a child did something, and we ask if he did it, is that a lie?

We can talk about the importance of morals and of truth telling and how a person who is lied to no longer trusts. This trust must be rebuilt, earned over time. If the school-age child has not separated fantasy from reality, or deliberately tells lies, it is time for adults to use the four A's to convince the child it is safe to tell the truth and to make lying uncomfortable. If the child over age six frequently tells obvious lies or consistently lies to be in control and using the four A's doesn't help, get professional help.

It's important to remember that calling a child of any age a liar encourages him to feel bad about himself and may even program him to lie. Teaching him how to tell the truth and to be successful encourages him to be responsible. Love and structure help the child develop a conscience.

*Dis*behavior Messages from School and Peers

Remember that your children may be spending part of their day in settings where misbehavior is not only accepted but applauded. When the *Minneapolis Star Tribune* invited schoolchildren to write about *dis*behavior for a feature called *Mindworks*, more than five thousand students responded.[7]

The students agreed that disrespect for peers is a universal problem. One fourth-grade student said, "I think the teacher should put a brick wall around each of our desks." Their list of causes of *dis*behavior included getting into trouble for a thrill, competing for the most demerits, feeling good when peers laugh at their misconduct, believing that *dis*behavior is cool and enhances their reputation, and believing that they will look stupid if they don't behave badly. They reported having *dis*behavior excused by teachers because they have attention deficit disorder or because they are angry. The most frequently listed cause of *dis*behavior was because students don't get consequences for it.

Add to the school and peer influences the constant media messages that children's impudence is amusing and expected, that violence is an acceptable way to solve problems, that delayed gratification is unnecessary, and that a short attention span is not a disability but is definitely cool.

We parents who are attempting to raise responsible, respectful, responsive children do not have the cultural support we need. In our current situation, good parenting is often a countercultural activity.

Counterculture, going against the dominant cultural values, is difficult. We all need to find some group of families, however small, that share our values and are determined to help our children withstand the cultural pressures to misbehave. We may have to organize to put pressure on the school, or we may need to move our child to a different school that doesn't tolerate misbehavior.

Making Changes

If the detective work you did by examining the list of reasons for misbehavior, or by **attending** to what is going on for your child at home and away from home, points to anything other than a contrary day, think about the underlying problem. Many of these problems can be resolved by getting information and then practicing new parenting behaviors. Of course, if the child's underlying health problem is severe—for example, if a child has been diagnosed with brain damage or fetal alcohol syndrome—parents will need and deserve professional help. In fact, parents should get professional help for any problem that feels too big to handle on their own. Part of the job of parenting is knowing when to ask for help. (For more on how to ask for help, see *Growing Up Again: Parenting Ourselves, Parenting Our Children.*[8])

If there are several problems, remember that working on one at a time is usually easier on the family system than trying to attack several at once. Ask your caring relatives and friends to support you with this specific effort. Stick with it, give it some time-in. And what happens? Sometimes the child's behavior gets worse at first. Many children respond to any change, negative or positive, with disruptive behavior. It seems to be human nature to try to hang on to a familiar system, even if it isn't working. Then, after some time, depending on the consistency of the grown-ups and the personality traits of the child, the child's behavior will improve. No matter what the reason for a child's misbehavior, parents can try using time-in for discipline. (See chapter 7.) The book, *Time-in: When Time-Out Doesn't Work,* has additional information on misbehavior.[9]

Take the time to connect with a child so that the child feels listened to and held accountable in a loving way. When the parent-child connection is strong, children want to behave in an acceptable way.

This time is an investment in your child's self-esteem and future success. It is also an investment in your future. What a child learns today can be built upon in the future, making the parenting job easier. Relationships banked today can be drawn upon or built upon in the future.

—Madelyn Swift[10]

Chapter 11

Why Do Children Respond Differently?

If there were only one good way to raise children, we would all be using that way, and all the children would be wonderful

—ANONYMOUS

Children Are Unique

Discipline methods that help you connect with one child may seem to cause distance with another. Why do children respond differently? Children respond differently because children are different! That sounds so simple, but sometimes that fact is difficult to remember and frustrating to deal with.

First, children's experiences are different. Even if they are living in the same family with the same parents, each child's experiences are specific to that child. Birth order alone is a powerful shaper of a child's environment. Other factors such as early trauma, health problems, death in the family, divorce, adoption, and foster care all create special sets of circumstances that require unique responses.

Second, and perhaps most significant, is the indisputable fact that children are born with differing personality traits. *Understanding Temperament* by Lyndall Shick offers suggestions for responding to and managing your particular child's combination of traits.[1] Children who are extremely active and do life on fast forward, who respond lightning fast to whatever isn't working for them, can be especially taxing. Linda Budd, in her book *Living with the Active Alert Child,* calls these children active alerts; Mary Sheedy Kurcinka, in her book *Raising Your Spirited Child,* refers to them as spirited.[2] If you live with such a child, you deserve the support and suggestions of such books. If you try the suggestions in these books—look at the child's personality traits, diet, exercise, and response to stress—and the child's behavior does not improve, by all means have your child evaluated for a possible biochemical imbalance. Some parents report that when a chemical imbalance is effectively treated, the child's behavior changes within twenty-four hours.[3] No matter what the diagnosis, it is important to teach children the steps in problem solving and to refrain from using the label as an excuse for inappropriate behaviors.

In this chapter we will futher explore the learning differences described in chapter 4 by focusing on two sets of differences and by thinking about matches and mismatches between parents' and children's preferences. Many children show auditory, visual, or kinesthetic learning preferences at young ages, and all children demonstrate personality traits that can be placed on an extravert/introvert continuum. These differences help explain why children respond differently to the four A's: **attend, ask, act**, and **amend.**

Extraverts and Introverts

We'll begin by looking at how these extraverted and introverted children differ.

Mother Atwood's story: "Our first child, Kristen, was a very easy child. She responded well to time-out. I didn't have to use it very often but, when I did, I liked the quiet times and she always seemed calmer, more thoughtful, and more responsive after she had a short sit in her yellow thinking-time chair. I thought I had discipline all wrapped up. Then came Kyle. He wiggles and squirms, whines, and slides off the chair so much that a five-minute time-out becomes half an hour. Afterward, when I ask him what is going on, he is more belligerent than before. He doesn't respond well to me.

"His Aunt Betty has better luck with him than I do. When he is rough with her, she gets excited and says, 'I want to talk with you, but let's do some jumping jacks first.' He loves to count and he loves to jump so that seems to work. When Kyle won't do what his grandfather asks, Grandpa, generally a quiet man, watches his grandson a bit and then grabs him and tickles him lovingly. Kyle laughs and then Grandpa says, 'Okay, Kyle, I know you don't want to do this right now, but come along. You and I have to be helpers, not blockers.' Kyle says, 'Okay.'"

Kristen responded well to quiet time. An introverted child tends to be inside herself and needs to be by herself some of the time. Such a child re-energizes herself by being alone, by listening to music, by zoning out in front of TV, by playing Nintendo. She can be seen as an *easy child* to an introverted parent. Perhaps Mother Atwood and daughter Kristen are both introverts.

Kyle needs interaction. Kyle may be the kind of extraverted child who needs to talk while he thinks and needs lots of interaction with others. Both his aunt and his grandpa engage directly with him, so he finds it easier to connect with them and what they want of him than with his mother and her request that he withdraw and be quiet.

To a parent who is highly extraverted, an introverted child may seem unresponsive.

Extraverted Dad wants to talk about everything they saw at the circus, and introverted Mario wants to get home and play it out with his toys or draw it or listen to music or just look out the window. After the demands of a day at the circus, Dad needs interaction to recharge his batteries, and Mario needs time alone.

We can build connection with our children by noticing these qualities in them and letting them do their recharging and learning their way even if it is different from our way.

> *A mismatch of personality styles, unless the adults become aware of and honor the child's natural way, can lead a child to feel strange, different, dumb, unimportant, or disconnected. And the adults can feel ineffective.*

Nathan, a small introvert in a family of giant extraverts, believed that he was slow, tongue tied, and stupid. Nathan didn't feel connected with his family. As an adult, Nathan had friends and co-workers who pointed out that his slower thinking went deeper than theirs and was greatly valued, but Nathan still felt stupid. Early decisions about oneself can be hard to shake, and Nathan will need to find ways to accept himself as he is.

Little assertive, extraverted Elizabeth pushed her way through childhood in a family of introverts. Her personality was attributed to her red hair and assumed to be something she would need to get over. Elizabeth felt like an outsider. When they were adults, Elizabeth's musician brother observed that it must have been hard for her growing up in a family of Brahms when she was a John Philip Sousa.

Parents can notice how a child prefers to re-energize and ensure that the family patterns allow for both time for interaction and time for quiet. For more information on extraverts and introverts, see Mary Sheedy Kurcinka's book, *Raising Your Spirited Child.*[4] Elizabeth Murphy's book *The Developing Child, Using Jungian Type to Understand Children* expands on the topic and explores ways to develop positive relationships with children of varying personality types.[5]

To Hear, to See, or to Do—That Is the Auditory, Visual, or Kinesthetic Question

Children and adults also differ in the ways they like to approach learning and problem solving. While some children seem comfortable with all three approaches—auditory (listening and talking), visual (seeing and drawing), and kinesthetic (moving and doing), most children, even during the early months of life, begin to show a preference.

Megan, at four months, was not only more responsive when she could see who was talking to her but was also uncomfortable when she could not see where the noise of family activity was coming from. When she was brought into a new room, she needed time to stare all around the room before she was ready to be responsive to the people. She will probably have a strong visual learning preference.

Remember Mother Atwood's story? Mother Atwood and daughter Kristen may both be auditory. Talking and listening are easy ways for them to communicate, so, because of their similarity, Kristen is described as an *easy child*. Kyle, however, may be very kinesthetic. A quiet time-out doesn't work for him. He has to *do* something with his body first. Kyle's aunt may be kinesthetic herself, so jumping jacks feel natural to her or she may prefer to talk and listen (auditory) but has learned that Kyle can listen better after he has moved. Grandpa asked Kyle to *do* something—be a helper—and Kyle responded positively.

Perhaps some highly visual children respond well to time-out because it allows them to *look at* what is going on before they have to talk, listen, or do something about it.

Notice what works

By trying all three learning methods—auditory, visual, kinesthetic—adults can discover how to get information from children in the way the children can best give it. One child will prefer to talk and listen (auditory). Another will respond to a request to draw or write about the situation (visual). A third child will act out a situation (kinesthetic), probably with words, but also with body movements that tell you more about the situation and his feelings than the words do. Parents can notice whether children respond better to asking or to acting.

Some parents learn to read kinesthetic children by the sounds their movements make. Joey's mom reported, *"I can tell what kind of day Joey had by the way he comes in the door and walks down the hall. If it sounds good, I call out, 'What's up?' If it has been a particularly hard day, since he is an introvert, I just say hi and I don't ask him to talk about his day until after dinner."*

Notice what doesn't work

When Roberto isn't hearing, his auditory dad's impulse is to sit him down and talk some more, to say it again, to explain it better. Meanwhile, kinesthetic Roberto, his eyes glazed over, really isn't listening. He has zoned out. He needs to move. Roberto can think better if he and Dad move while they talk: *"Roberto, I want you to do something different. Let's go for a bike ride while we talk about it, and then we'll practice doing it the new way together."*

The visual parent, when daughter Gabriella isn't responding, tends to point the way again, to show her the mistake again, to write the recipe, to draw the map on the chalkboard, to make Gabriella watch one more demonstration. Auditory Gabriella, who has been avoiding eye contact for a while, has gone elsewhere in her mind or inside to her clutched feelings of never doing it right. When Gabriella asked for pizza, Gabriella's busy visual mom turned to her and, pointing to the kitchen, said, *"Gabriella, you are old enough to make pizza. You have sat at the counter and watched me do it dozens of times. You know how to do it."* To Mom's surprise, auditory Gabriella's response was, *"But mom, you never told me what you were doing!"*

The kinesthetic adult may insist that the child come for a walk while they talk. Walking could turn the auditory or visual child's awareness away from the problem at hand.

Kinesthetic Dad expects Jared to help him figure out how to hook up the new VCR, without looking at the directions. Visual Jared needs to look at the diagram. When Jared doesn't respond, Dad patiently or angrily tells Jared to try it another way. Jared, feeling inadequate, tries to think about something else or slips away physically until his dad finishes the job. Jared needs to get a visual picture or pattern before he can act. Dad could say, "Jared, take a look at those instructions and see what we do next."

When kids or adults zone out, don't do more of what you are already doing. Do something else.

Auditory, Visual, Kinesthetic, Extravert, and Introvert Chart

On the following chart, place your name in the box or boxes that indicate your usual preferences. Then place the names of other family members where you think their preferences are.

The Atwood Chart

	Auditory	**Visual**	**Kinesthetic**
Extravert	Aunt Betty		Kyle
Introvert	Mother Kristin	Grandpa	

Your Chart

	Auditory	**Visual**	**Kinesthetic**
Extravert			
Introvert			

- Ask other family members where they think they are.
- Ask them where they think you are.

- Notice how each person responds to you when you tell, when you show, and when you act.
- Notice whether your family provides enough alone time and space for introverts to regenerate themselves.
- Notice whether your family provides enough stimulation and listening time for extraverts to regenerate themselves.

Although children need to be able to learn through the different methods in many situations, they learn better if they have been affirmed and respected for their learning preference instead of having been labeled slow, stupid, clumsy, shy, unwilling, or rebellious.

Attending to children's introverted or extraverted auditory, visual, or kinesthetic preferences respectfully honors the child and builds connection.

Chapter 12

Looking at Discipline in a New Way

Honor thy father and thy mother.
—THE TEN COMMANDMENTS

What if we look at honoring thy father and thy mother in a new way? What if it does not mean that children shall pay homage to, bow before, praise, and respect their parents no matter what those parents do? What if it really means honor the gifts given by the parents? The gifts of life, of body, of mind? What if it means pay attention to the strengths and the talents that are the genetic and the environmental gifts of your parents? What if it means honor your parents by developing those gifts and using them to benefit the family, yourself, the world? Is this what is meant by *from those to whom much is given, much is expected*? Are we not all given much, if we take the trouble to envision the possible impact of our gifts?

If this is the case—if we are to honor and develop the gifts of body, mind, and spirit with which we are born—there are profound implications for parents and parenting. Instead of viewing our children as either dependent, burdensome beings whom we must make independent or as independent, selfish beings whom we must make cooperative or dependent, we can view them as gifted beings whose gifts we must help them discover. Instead of trying to *make* our children be good, we can *help* them find and grow the goodness within themselves.

It is a gift in this world to have a parent who always has your best interests at heart.

This means that we **attend** in ways that help us learn who this child really is. And, when we do this kind of attending and as we guide the child into the ways of the culture, we find that he honors us with a natural willingness to cooperate, and eventually with heartfelt appreciation of our gifts and efforts.

But, you ask, *Does this mean that we let him do whatever he wants? Isn't that license?* No, indeed. If *whatever* he wants is hurtful to himself or others, we stop him. No, this is not license. Giving a child license is a form of child neglect. The lessons of discipline are an important part of helping the child uncover and develop his gifts.

So, you ask, *How do we do that? What does work with children?* The discipline that works with any particular child is what works with that particular child. But the starting point always involves paying attention to the uniqueness, the feelings, and the experiences of that child. We can explore this kind of **attending** in three ways: *being present, showing interest,* and *honoring feelings.*[1] All three build the trust that helps the child feel connected and helps him want and expect to cooperate.

Laying the Groundwork

Think about how we lay the groundwork for later discipline with babies. When they cry we go to them immediately; we **act**. This does not spoil babies. It tells them we are reliable. We are *present* for their needs. We try helping them in many ways until we meet their particular need and they stop crying. If they don't stop crying, we know that we are unable to meet their need and we just live through it. But we stay *present*, trying to be helpful to them and being careful not to blame them or get impatient. Meanwhile we use our *interest*; we attend. We keep listening and looking and feeling for cues. We *honor their feelings.* Feelings tell children what is going on inside their world, and long before they can talk, children try to tell us what their need is by crying and fussing in differing ways. If we cannot meet a need, it becomes our problem.

What is the problem? Sometimes it is, *I haven't been touched enough* or, *I have been handled too much* or, *Touch doesn't feel good because my skin is sensitive or hurting.* Sometimes the problem is bigger, such as an immature nervous system or an illness or an allergy. Sometimes it is the baby's response to too many changes or to other stresses in the family. Sometimes we never do find out what the problem is. In that case, in time, either the problem gets solved or the child makes an adjustment, and we hope it is a healthy one, not one that is costly to the child like withdrawing or having to be overpleasing. So, even with infants, adults are practicing the three great supports to discipline: *being present, showing interest*, and *honoring feelings*. All three ways of interacting express love.

Older Children

As children grow and become verbal, adults can respond to them more easily. Children who can talk can tell us what is going on. Sometimes. But we still need to be present, to **attend,** and we learn how to be interested without hovering. We continue to honor children's feelings even as we are teaching them how to express their feelings in ways that do not hurt themselves or others.

Sometimes, with teenagers, we feel as if they are babies again. We stay present, but they may not tell us what they need. We offer time-in and they say, *Leave me alone*. We back off and they say, *You never have time for me*. We learn to express interest without prying, but we don't let them push us away. We honor their feelings even when we don't understand them. Teens recycle all their earlier developmental tasks and it is often hard for parents to keep up with their swings.[2] They can be very young one day and amazingly grown-up the next. They also practice *teenage logic: They express a burning desire to be different and don't feel okay unless they are dressing exactly alike*.

Even though we probably did this ourselves, we may have forgotten how right adolescent logic seems to an adolescent. So, as parents, we need to offer the three supports to children of all ages and to all family members. If we didn't know how or were unable to offer these supports to our children at earlier ages, we can start now. Whatever their ages are. Now. Today.

The Three Supports: Being Present, Showing Interest, and Honoring Feelings

The three supports can be used with all four time-in puzzle pieces.

Being present

Being present means being there. The baby cries, the mother, attuned to the call, is on her feet before the other adults hear the cry. She is *present*.

The preschoolers are playing and there is a crash or a change in sound of the tone of the play. The caregiver moves immediately to the scene, is *present*, and then decides which time-in puzzle piece is appropriate.

It is the child's first ball game, recital, or concert. Dad is there. He is *present*. Or if he cannot attend, later that evening or on the weekend he says, *"I wanted to be there for you but I couldn't. Will you help me almost be there by telling (or showing or acting out) what happened?"* He listens, responds, ask questions. He has moved from *being present* to *showing interest*.

Showing interest

Showing interest means connecting with a child by finding out what is going on with the child. Parents ask, listen, read homework, celebrate achievements, visit school, talk about TV and movies, get to know friends. Parents ask if what they did was helpful and, if not, they make it right. These are all part of time-in: **ask, act, attend, amend.**

Elizabeth is to perform in a dance recital. Her stepmom asks, "Do you want me to come?"
    "Oh, yes," replies Elizabeth.
    "Would you like me to bring your cousins, Denny and Rob?"
    "Let me think about that," Elizabeth says, pondering.
    "Okay, but I'll be there," her stepmom reassures her.

Honoring feelings

What does *honoring children's feelings* mean? Does it mean that when children are scared we should get even more scared or when children are angry we should get mad at them? No. It means that we respond in a way that honors their specific feelings, that we accept that they have that feeling. If Elizabeth had responded, *"No, please no! Don't ask Denny and Rob. I'd be too embarrassed,"* her stepmom would have assured Elizabeth that she would not ask the boys.

Sometimes we talk about feelings. We say, *You seem really angry. What happened?* Not, *You have nothing to be mad about.* Honoring feelings also means that we respond to the level at which those feelings are expressed and we mirror the intensity of those feelings. This kind of honoring is sometimes called *reciprocal affect*. If a child is very up-set, it does not mean the parent gets equally upset, but rather that the parent brings a physical intensity and level of concern that matches the level of the child's concern. If the child is hysterical, the energy with which the adult listens to and attempts to calm the child lets the child know the adult is aware of the child's level of anxiety.

Some adults assume that they should not mirror a child's level of feeling for fear the child's feeling will escalate. But a child who is very excited or upset can feel disconnected from an adult who is deadpan calm and seems not to notice the intensity of the child's concern or pleasure. She may escalate even more to try to get the adult to re-spond. When the adult wishes a child would calm down, the adult can match the child's intensity and then start to breathe more slowly, speak more softly, and the child will usually calm down as the parent relaxes.

On the other hand, the child who casually remarks that no one at school likes him may be reassured by an equally casual, *Good thing I like you,* but could be put off by the adult who immediately responds by excitedly heaping love, acceptance, and praise all over him.

At times *reciprocal affect* means matching the degree of the child's feeling with the same degree of another feeling. When the child is very upset, for example, the parent is equally protective or respon-sive. Other times it means matching not only the intensity, but also the child's exact feeling as in being joyful when the child is joyful.

Honoring feelings also means accepting and encouraging the full range of feelings in both girls and boys. William Pollack in *Real Boys* reminds us that parents often, without being aware that they are do-ing so, handle boy's and girl's feelings differently from infancy, thus providing what he calls *gender straitjackets*.[3]

Why is honoring feelings so important? Children learn about their inside world and how to shape their responses to the outside world from their feelings. So when we honor children's feelings, we honor their knowing. We also encourage their intellectual growth, accord-ing to Stanley I. Greenspan. In his book *The Growth of the Mind: And the Endangered Origins of Intelligence* he proposes the following: "In-telligence gets its boost more from emotional experience than from cognitive stimulation."[4]

Do you find that your children learn faster if their feelings are at-tended to before you offer a lesson?

Combining All Three—The Baby Bailey Story

Let us look at how the Baileys combined *being present, showing interest,* and *honoring feelings* in response to their infant.

Baby Bailey had a very busy and stress-filled week. Day care, the sniffles, and trips to the doctor on Wednesday and Saturday. On Sunday he was included in the noisy group that watched the football game. So far, so good, still smiling. Then off Baby goes for his weekly visit with his grandparents when Mom and Dad Bailey have some time to themselves. Grandma is delighted and Baby is smiling, but as soon as he realizes Mom and Dad are gone, Baby wails. Nothing will console him. Grandpa tries to help, but Baby wails even louder. Baby Bailey had one more outing than he could handle. Thank goodness for the telephone. "Mom and Dad, I think Baby wants you and needs to go home." Grandparents showed presence and interest and honored Baby's feelings.

Mom and Dad arrive quickly (presence) and ask for a full description of Baby's behavior (interest). Dad picks Baby up with concern and energy, his voice and facial expression matching the intensity of Baby's feelings (honoring feelings). Dad tries to jolly Baby in the way Baby usually loves. Baby wails. Dad offers a rattle. Baby wails. Dad offers a bottle. Baby wails. Dad says, "Mom, you try. What I'm doing isn't working" (presence and interest). Mom takes Baby with willingness and energy (honoring feelings) and holds Baby in her lap in the sitting-up-with-his-head-near-her-heart favorite position. She gently rocks back and forth, protective arms tight around Baby, repeatedly kisses him gently on the head, lightly rests her chin on his head, all the time crooning over and over with heartfelt sympathy, "Baby, I'm so sorry. We didn't understand. We are here for you. We will take you home. It's all right. Thank you for telling us it wasn't working for you. I'm so sorry. It's okay. We just didn't understand. We are here now." Baby looks stoically and seriously straight ahead for the first minutes of this comforting and then relaxes into Mom's arms. Ten minutes later he is willing to take his bottle from Dad.

Mom Bailey successfully honored Baby's feelings. Her level of concern and sympathy matched the level of Baby's distress *and* her responses matched Baby's type of concern. Baby needed to reconnect through care and comforting. Dad's jollying and offering a rattle didn't work because Baby likes being entertained only when everything else is okay. Baby's need was for the familiarity and rhythm of his own household and for his parents to understand and accept that. For help on understanding what infants and children through age three need at each age, read Berry T. Brazelton's *Touchpoints: Your Child's Emotional and Behavioral Development.*[5]

Continue through the Years to Offer the Three Supports

Children need *presence.* They need someone who cares and is there. Baby Bailey needed the people he has bonded with. The older children get, the more they can accept *presence* from people beyond the immediate family or whoever is providing the primary care.

> *Children need presence more than they need presents.*
> — *Sue Murray, co-author of* Mom to Mom, Heart to Heart

Children need interest. They need the present person to be willing to learn what is important to each child. Showing interest is what adults do when they are learning to recognize the child's introverted or extraverted tendencies and when they honor the child's preference for auditory, visual, or kinesthetic expressions.

Adults need these supports too. We show presence and interest for other adults every time we use the **attend** puzzle piece with them:

- You are late. What happened today?
- You look tired. What can I do for you?
- You are grinning. What's up?

Children need to have the feelings they are expressing *validated* by adult responses that accept the *content* of what they are feeling and match the *degree* with which children are expressing the feeling. Rather than telling a child how to feel—*That should make you happy* or, *I know this will make you mad* or, *You are not scared of that* or, *Don't be mad at me*—notice or **ask** how the child does feel, and then **act** or **attend** directly in response to that feeling.

If the child feels sad, offer comfort or compassion. Add comforting touch if the child wants it.

If the child is frightened, provide safety or information to help the child make herself feel safe or, depending on the event, offer information about why that situation is not hazardous. Hold the child's hand, hug, touch him on the shoulder. Hug or massage a baby or wrap her more firmly and securely in her blanket.

If the child is angry, take the anger seriously and treat it as a signal that the child needs or wants something. If it is a need, help the child get the need met. If it is a want, help the child get the want if it is appropriate, or help the child accept anger as an understandable response if he will not get what he wants. If he holds the anger for more than a few minutes, try to find out if there is an underlying need or want that is bubbling up from underneath.

If the child is confused, offer information or help her get information for herself. Validating a child's feeling shows respect for the child's struggle.

If the child is feeling satisfied or confident, notice, nod, smile. Maybe give him a pat on the shoulder or a hug.

If the child is joyful, respond joyfully and celebrate with her, if she wants you to, or let her know that you expect her to celebrate within herself. Some children do that by walking and humming a happy tune, some by dancing, some by making or buying a small object or a book to remember the occasion by, some by daydreaming, some by talking.

If the child is loving, receive the love willingly, honor it, and offer love, appreciation, and delight in return if you can. If you can't love a child, the essence of a child, the potential of a child, sincerely try to find out what is stopping you. Whatever a child's behavior, there is a lovable person hiding in there somewhere. Sometimes you just have to take this on faith when children are acting horribly.

If you know a child who is not getting the love he needs, offer it if you can. Research on resilient children, youngsters who are disadvantaged by poverty, violence, or neglect, shows that one of the constants in these children's lives is someone, a relative, a neighbor, a teacher, who loves them and believes in them.[6]

We build connection when we find out what children need and feel and want, and then respond to children on their terms, not on just what we want. Being present, showing interest, and honoring feelings are ways of putting love into action and building a firm foundation on which to provide effective, positive discipline. If this requires us to look at discipline in new ways, let us have the courage to do that.

> And do not be conformed to this world, but be transformed by the renewing of your mind.
> —*Romans 12:2a*

Actually, what works with children also works with adults. Reread the "Continue through the Years . . ." section in this chapter and substitute for the word *child* the word *friend, sister, brother, grandparent,* or the name of a spouse or partner or your name and see how closely it fits and which parts help you feel connected.

SECTION III

Obstacles to Connection

Chapter 13

When There Are Problems Using Time-In to Discipline

She was not really bad at heart, but only rather rude and wild.
She was an aggravating child.

—HILAIRE BELLOC, "REBECCA"

One of Those Days

There are days when nothing seems to go right, when you wish you could stop the day and start over or, better yet, skip the rest of this day and start fresh tomorrow. On *one of those days*, we all need help.

Young Children's Days

If the children are having one of those days, when they march right through the middle of your patience and you snap at them, *Stop!* What to do? Tell them you are sorry. Give them a hug if they want one. Let them hug you if they want to. Remember that your most important job is to take better care of yourself so *their day* doesn't get to you—so you can shake your head and laugh about what landed on your plate today instead of letting the plate crush you.

Evaluate their patterns. How often are they having one of those days? What triggers them? What change of schedule or extra support do they need right now? Do they need more sleep? Or better eating habits? Caffeine, any caffeine from a soda, chocolate, medication, or junk food, can make young children restless.[1]

If children aren't responding positively to time-in, there could be several reasons. Go back to chapter 10 and look for clues to problems underlying misbehavior.

Children Learn by Playing—Play Is Their Work

If this is one of those days when children's play turns to tears or fighting or whining, perhaps you can help. Sometimes young children misbehave because they aren't getting what they need from their play. If parents are overzealous about connecting with young children during their play, children don't have time to work out their own play scenarios. On the other hand, if parents do no more than provide toys, children may be overwhelmed by the jumble in the toy box. In their book, *The Play's the Thing,* Elizabeth Jones and Gretchen Reynolds describe how to stimulate creative play by arranging toys in new ways.[2] They also describe the ways teachers participate in play. It is interesting to think about parents in these same ways: parent as stage manager, mediator, player, interrupter, scribe, assessor, communicator, or planner. All of these roles involve the **act** puzzle piece. If we use one of these, say the interrupter, to the exclusion of the others, that might be why time-in isn't working. If we interrupt to teach safety rules, we enhance the play. When we interrupt for our own pleasure, we often stop the play. Children learn valuable organizational, leadership, and problem-solving skills by being allowed to play in their own creative ways without adult interference—as long as the play is safe.

Arnie's children, ages three and five, had been bugging him to arbitrate their quarrels, which usually ended up in "you started it" arguments. Arnie decided to see if rearranging toys, acting as stage manager, would reduce his role as mediator. Here are some things he did after the children had gone to bed. He started with arrangements like a masking tape road with cross streets on the floor with cars and trucks placed on it. A couple of nights later he arranged a band of stuffed animals and dolls with drums, rattles, any musical instruments or noisemaking toys. Another time he cut a door and a window in a packing case and set magic markers beside it. Later he propped the biggest teddy bear up with a book and set the other toys in a circle around the storybook reader.

Another time he placed the toys in ways that didn't clearly signal what the play scenario might be. One night he lined up the stuffed animals along a wall, all facing the wall. Another night he put four plastic horses under a table.

Soon the children became focused on creating play activities and spent less time quarreling and blaming. Arnie played with them sometimes if they invited him, but at the end of playtime he always asked them what they had been playing. He listened for evidence that they were doing children's work: using their imaginations to create play activities that required them to learn how to organize, to lead and to follow, and to solve problems. If they were finished with that activity, he helped them put the toys back on the shelves. If not, they negotiated about leaving the play scene in place until the next day.

Older Children's Days

Older children may have one of those days because of pressures from outside of the family. Then we **attend** and **ask** to find out whether we can help. We match the child's concern and we are careful to help the child to cope, not to take her discomfort on ourselves. If adolescents are having many of *those days*, we think about hormones, love, achievements and disappointments, peer pressure, safety, depression, and drugs. And we get help whenever we need it. From our friends, from the school, from social services, from a clergyperson, from a therapist.

The Parents' Day

Sometimes children have one of those days because their parents are having one of those days. Time-in will probably not work if you are having one of those days when you are too busy and pay attention to your child only when a rule is broken. On these days, she is probably not going to give up misbehaving unless you give her more time and attention when she is cooperating.

On a day when you are feeling rigid about rules and forget to take the child's perspective into account, the lesson that your child learns is that you are unreasonable, and he may become resistant or resentfully compliant.

If you forget that calling a child names labels him as the problem, don't be surprised if he acts out what you called him—bad boy, destroyer, troublemaker, turkey, scatter brain, or Mr. Clumsy. Children tend to do what we call them.

If you laugh at your child's misbehavior, you give a most powerful permission for misbehavior. Enjoying a child's misbehavior reinforces it. If you act as though the behavior is cute, if you laugh, smile, wink, or tell stories about it with glee in the child's presence, the child will remember that you like it and will repeat it. Children will do almost anything to please their parents, even behavior that is self-destructive.

These ineffective parenting behaviors are more powerful than time-in or time-out or almost any other disciplinary method. If you have done some of those things sometimes, but have decided to be more positive in your parenting, practicing time-in can be helpful. Try it a bit at a time and forgive yourself if you don't do it smoothly at first.

Time-In Doesn't Work If . . .

Think about how you are offering the four A's. Using time-in for discipline doesn't teach responsibility or create connection if it is used carelessly or is turned into a punishment. Here are several ways that could happen.

- If the adult ignores the child's feelings, the child may experience time-in as manipulative and cold instead of supportive and helpful.
- If a parent pushes for quick responses, the child may learn how to please the parent, not how to be responsible.
- If the adult is critical and is using time-in as a punishment instead of a teaching tool, the child will resent it.
- If making amends or restitutions that take a lot of time and energy are used too often, they can become a burden to both the adult and the child.
- If parents let children who are good at verbal manipulation or conning circumvent the rules, the lesson of the discipline is lost.
- If children who are shy or naturally introverted need alone time to think or to recharge their batteries, they may resist **ask**, **act**, or **amend**.
- If children are not getting enough attention at other times or enough positive response to their appropriate behavior, they may find misbehaving to be the only way to get an adult's time and attention.

- If children are upset about something else in their lives, they need to have those feelings heard and attended to before they can respond to time-in as discipline.

If you wish you had fewer of *those days* or think time-in should be working perfectly, stop. Think. Nothing works all of the time. And children don't need perfect parents. They need parents who love them and do the best they can—parents who care about the safety of their bodies and the growth of their minds and souls. They need parents who make mistakes, admit them, and correct them. Remember, parenting is not only the most important task we do, it is probably also the most difficult. During *those days* practice using the Instant Calming Sequence Steps referred to in chapter 14, page 128.

If you are short on love, pick up the book *101 Fun Hugs* by Ed Fischer and think of all the safe people you could ask for one of those hugs.[3] Or read *25 Things You Can Do to Feel Better Right Now* by Bill Chandler.[4]

Children do better when they are with caring adults whose own needs are met.

Chapter 14

What about My Anger?

When your mom is mad at your dad, don't let her brush your hair.
—FROM *TRUTHS LITTLE CHILDREN HAVE LEARNED ABOUT LIFE*

But what about my anger? the parent asked. *I think I understand time-in, but I get so angry when my child pulls the same old tricks! The only way I want to connect is with a swat. I can't keep it positive.* Ah, yes. Who among us has not felt anger, despair, or even rage when we have done the best we could, have other worries, and are probably tired, hungry, and in need of recreation or love ourselves?

Many of us have heard about anger management—take ten deep breaths, beat on a pillow, go for a walk, take a relaxing bath, and so on. But if we are trying to use time-in with a child who has been picking at the edges of our tolerance all day, ten deep breaths *don't make a dent.* If a child has just run away, this is not the time for a long walk. If the youngster just tried to drown the gerbil, a relaxing bath just doesn't fit. If we are dealing with a kid who just smashed a lamp or hit her brother, it is hardly the time to beat on a pillow, which could increase our anger rather than making us less apt to hit a child.

Two common ways parents vent anger are criticizing and spanking. But these methods often produce a different effect than the parent intended. Criticizing is meant to offer structure, but it usually comes off as verbal punishment. Spanking, which is meant as an attention-getting device or a deterrent, is physical punishment.

Criticizing and Shaming

Criticizing may help the parent feel better for the moment because it lets out angry feelings, but it creates distance instead of connections.

Criticizing is discouraging to a child, not empowering. It programs negative behavior. It teaches kids how to fail. Calling a child clumsy or selfish tells him how to behave—to be clumsy or selfish. Criticizing can also attribute negative characteristics to the child. For example, telling a child she is stupid lets her know you think she can't learn. It doesn't teach her *how to succeed.* Criticizing creates shame. Shame is disconnecting. It breaks the trust bridge between parent and child. It invites children to give up parts of themselves and to view themselves as defective and lacking the ability to succeed. In addition, shame can be an aggravating problem in relationships throughout life. (See chapter 15 for more about shame.)

Spanking

Spanking also breaks connection. Although it may help the parent feel better by letting angry energy out through the arm, and the child may respond quickly, sometimes the spanker finds it hard to stop. Furthermore, spanking doesn't teach the child new skills about what to do instead of the misbehavior. Hurting the skin and flesh on the buttocks does not necessarily send the correct message to the brain. Spanking does teach the child that people who love you hit you. This can cause major problems in adult relationships. Spanking when you are angry usually teaches the child more about your anger than about his behavior. Spanking, even though we do not intend it to, teaches that violence is okay.

If you are worried about sparing the rod and spoiling the child, read *Spare the Child: The Religious Roots of Punishment and the Psychological Impact of Physical Abuse* by Philip J. Greven.[1] Remember that the good shepherd used his rod or his staff to nudge, direct, or lead his sheep, but never to hurt them.

Spanking breaks connection, even if the adult tries to reconnect with the child afterward.

Aida remembers that when she was little, her mother would take off her shoe and hit Aida on her bottom until it was red. Then the mother, perhaps out of guilt or maybe out of wanting to reconnect the bond with the little girl, would scoop Aida up and rock her and sing to her for what seemed like a very long time. Aida was as angry about the rocking as she was about the hitting. She has no memory of what she was being punished for, only of total confusion.

A sincere apology is the only thing that rectifies spanking or slapping, and it will not always be sufficient. *I'm sorry I hit you. I shouldn't have. People should not hit each other. I will find better ways to teach you how to act.* Sometimes the child will accept the apology as a way of making **amends**, but probably only once. In the long run, spanking breaks connection and produces overcompliance, rebellion, or violence rather than internalized self-control.[2] Use time-in instead as a way of both connecting with your child and teaching better ways of behaving. Parents who have been hitting and decide not to must substitute loving ways to discipline. Substituting spanking with the withdrawal of love or making love conditional on good behavior is an insidious type of rejection and disconnection, and it is shaming to the child.

Anger as a Sign

Anger is always a sign there is something that we want to keep or to change.[3] Either the thing we want to keep is threatened, or we feel ineffective or powerless to change the thing we want to change. When I want to change my noisy, conflict-filled house to one of peace and quiet and I can't seem to do so, it is normal, natural, and appropriate for me to feel angry. This is self-affirming anger.[4] It tells me that I need to pay attention to my needs, especially when my anger is triggered by some little thing—the straw that breaks the camel's back—and my anger is out of proportion to the offense. Maybe I have to get an hour of peace and quiet somewhere else. Maybe I need to look at my rules about peace and quiet. Do I really need quiet or do I think others think a quiet child is the sign of a successful parent? Maybe I need to learn some new parenting skills about conflict management. Learning takes time, and I will need to give up the wish that a new skill will give me instant gratification. Or I may need to accept that one of my children is wired on fast forward and learn how to deal with that and take care of myself at the same time. Read Linda S. Budd's book *Living with the Active Alert Child* and Mary Sheedy Kurcinka's book *Raising Your Spirited Child* for specific help on this subject.[5]

When I am angry at my child, when I want to change my child, I can remember to view my child's misbehavior as her experience and not perceive it as an extension of myself. Then I am free to help the child change herself, to face what she has done, understand the implications, make amends, and figure out what she needs. I can be helper and guide rather than angry adversary.

What about My Anger?

This does not imply that my child never knows my anger. Anger is an honest feeling and our children have the right to know all of our honest feelings.

*When two-year-old Jeremy bit his uncle Bob, Bob yelped, pushed Jeremy away, and flashed him an angry look. Bob rubbed his tooth-marked hand and calmed himself. Switching to a strong, structuring position (**acting**), he showed Jeremy the teeth marks and said very firmly and sternly, "No biting. Biting hurts people. No biting!"*

*When eleven-year-old Martha wore her mom's favorite sweatshirt without asking, Mom let her anger show. Then, instead of giving a directive as Bob did to a very young child whose reasoning skills were not yet developed, Mom put the responsibility on Martha to think by **asking**, "What do you need to do so you can remember to respect other people's property?" Since Martha is old enough to remember about asking, Mother asks Martha to identify a penalty she will impose on herself if she chooses to take her mom's things without asking. If Martha continues to "borrow" without asking and pleads that she "forgot," Mom will recognize that as passive aggressive behavior—behavior often designed to "get back at" other people. Mom **attends** and attempts to discover why Martha is so out of tune with the family or with her own competence, her own goodness.*

If we are angry again and again at the same misbehavior, we need to seriously look at what is going on. When we discover that a teenager is using drugs, we make our anger clear, not with name-calling but as an expression of our own deep angst.

How could you do this? Drugs are no way to solve problems! How can you think that momentary pleasure is worth the great losses that drugs bring with them? Your behavior causes me deep pain! You are too smart to do this to yourself! I did not believe this of you! Do you realize what you have done to my trust in you? Either you stop immediately or off we go for counseling right now! What will it be?

Without name-calling, this parent gives an **action** wake-up call that this is a problem the parent demands and expects the teenager to resolve. Get the substance abuse stopped first; then help the child find what is missing in his life. Help him reconnect with his own inner self-respect, his inner goodness.

Put Anger to Work for You

Remember, your anger is a reminder to do something about what you want to keep or change. Here are seven things you can do to help you put your anger to work for you.[6]

1. Use it as a clue that there is something you want to change or keep.
2. Look at the list of reasons why kids may be misbehaving (chapter 10, pages 94–96). If you discover that your anger has an underlying cause, go to work on that even if it means changing yourself. It is worth doing for your child and for your peace of mind.
3. Find some sympathetic, non-blaming support. Turn off self-criticism and shame and go about solving the problem.
4. Remember that what works with your child may not be what your father or your sister or your neighbor thinks you should do.
5. Take your own personality style into consideration before you start to solve the problem. Introverts may need some time alone. Extraverts may need to find a safe place to do a Tarzan yell.
6. Find a good counselor if you need one. Going to counseling for anger help is as important as going to the doctor for a broken bone. You may have an old anger you are not even aware of that is spilling out on your child.
7. Meanwhile, before you rain on your child, try Robert K. Cooper's Instant Calming Sequence Steps from his book *Health & Fitness Excellence: The Scientific Action Plan*[7]:
   Step 1. Uninterrupted breathing—long, deep breaths
   Step 2. Positive face—smile
   Step 3. Balanced posture—stand tall
   Step 4. Wave of relaxation—loosen whole body
   Step 5. Mental control—focus on a solution

Breathe! Deliberately. Relax your face or make it positive—smile if you can. It will change your emotions. Pull your head high and relax your shoulders toward your back. Flash a wave of relaxation from the top of your head to your toes, or from your feet up to your head, whichever feels better to you. Then repeat to yourself, *What is hap-*

pening is real, and I'm determined to find the best possible solution right now. Too fast? Too simple? Try it! Thank goodness there is one thing we can do that is fast and simple. Reading Harriet Lerner's book *Dance of Anger* is a good way to learn more about anger.[8] It is subtitled *A Woman's Guide to Changing the Patterns of Intimate Relationships,* but men can learn a lot from it too.

Your anger is your friend. It signals you that there is something you need to keep or to change in order to be free to connect with your children.

Chapter 15

What about Shame?

Shame on you
the father said.
The little fellow hung his head and went
and hid beneath his bed
and wondered what to do instead.

—ANONYMOUS

Shame! That debilitating feeling that *we* are bad. Not that we have *done* something bad, but that we *are* bad. Or, if *bad* isn't the right word, it may be a combination of *inadequate, incompetent,* and *inappropriate,* not for anything we did but just because we exist. For some of us, it is an all-consuming preverbal feeling that has no name, no words, but we know there is nothing we can do that will be enough to be okay, so we make work an obsession rather than a joy, or we find a way to dull the pain with drinking or clowning or whatever. We can't know our true selves because we are so busy creating a facade that looks okay to others. Shame can be a global, invading, all-pervasive feeling. Shame is different from guilt, the knowledge that we have done something wrong and we need to correct it.

We all know about shame because we all have experienced it, even if we have buried it deep and forgotten it. Some of us have let shame make us depressed or incompetent or obsessed. Some of us have talked about it. Some of us couldn't. Some of us have read about it. Some of us wouldn't. Some of us use it to help us know when we have strayed away from our true selves or have lost touch with our spiritual path.[1] Some of us don't want to think about it. It can smash connections in an almost irreparable way or it can nudge us to respect and rebuild our connections.

Some of us want never to experience shame, but wish fervently that other people would. That tells us why shame is bad and how it can be useful.

Shame That Harms

The many authors who write about shame disagree about its effects. Some say all shame is bad; others think some shame is necessary and therefore good; still others explain that shame is only used to control people and began with disenchantment, the disconnection of people from each other and from nature that began four thousand years ago and culminated in Newtonian science. You can read more about shame and its origins and some of the authors who have discussed those ideas by referring to the notes section.[2]

For the purpose of this book, let us consider how shame is currently used and how it affects us now in our personal lives and in our families. Let us focus on helping children deal with feeling ashamed, with shaming others, and with holding fast to their own goodness and worth.

For example, shame is bad when it is used by someone else to violate us, to humiliate us, to degrade us. Shame is bad when it has put us out of integrity with ourselves, when we have done something we are not proud of and we go beyond the feeling of guilt (which energizes us to make amends), into the depth of incapacitating shame. We want to hide, to run away, to deny, to blame the other, to forget, and we want others to forget.

Shame is harmful when an individual or society uses it to diminish innocent people. For example, the shaming of children born out of wedlock is diabolic. It is also harmful when a group or society shames people for being who they are, as in racism, sexism, and ageism. It is harmful when it is used to keep people within roles that require them to give up parts of themselves, to be less competent, less creative, to stifle their gifts.

Make Shame Help Us

When I listen to people who say they are *recovering from shame, that they hate being shame-based, and that they are never going to feel ashamed again, that they aren't going to "should" on themselves anymore,* I feel confused. Surely it is debilitating to have grown up in a family, a social group, or a religious institution that used any mistake you made to convince you that you are a bad person. We definitely need to recover from that.

But, no *shoulds*? That is scary! I want to be with people who have a strong enough sense of nurture and structure that they believe they *should* behave as good citizens, honest workers, kind friends, and caring parents, even on the days when they don't feel absolutely gleeful about doing so.

Shame is useful when our determination to avoid it bolsters our will to do the right thing for ourselves and for others, helps us strengthen our own healthy boundaries, and motivates us to keep our connections within those boundaries appropriate. It is helpful if we recognize that we have created shameful boundaries that harm other people and then become determined to change those boundaries. When we use the threat of shaming ourselves to help us stay true to our higher selves, we make shame our friend.

Some would argue that we should not need shame as a motivator, that we should be so responsible, so loving that we will always do the right thing. Maybe. But most of us have enough tired, rebellious, or weak days that a little deterrent in the back of the scene helps us stay on track.

Shame as a Wake-Up Call

I listen to arguments about public figures who have done serious boundary breaches that have far-reaching negative effects. Some people say, *Kill him,* others say, *It wasn't illegal, so forget it. Excuse him.* There must be something in between these two extremes. Shame has been used through the ages to prevent behaviors that would threaten the welfare of the group, the tribe, or to send a wake-up call to someone who has done harm, to hold that person accountable.

I asked a British friend, "When you were living in England was there a way society shamed a person whose behavior harmed the group?" "Oh, yes," she said, "they are put in Coventry." She went on to explain:

> "Lady Godiva, who lived in Coventry, was concerned about her husband's harsh treatment of the peasants. When she begged him to treat

them better, Lord Godiva insisted that they were no better than animals so it didn't matter. The lady insisted that they were not only human beings, but good, respectful ones. Lord Godiva challenged her to prove it. She made a proposal: 'If I ride nude through the village and no one looks at me, will you grant that they respect me and will you treat them better?' The lord agreed, knowing that it was impossible because the whole village would leer at her. You know the rest. She sent out the word. They went inside, closed their doors, and latched their shutters. The lady, clad only in her hair, rode through the town. But, alas, one fellow, Tom, took a look, so the lord declared she had lost and he need treat them no better. From then on, the villages treated peeping Tom coldly. They were polite but used no more words than absolutely necessary. No one would work with him, walk with him, sit by him, chat with him. In this way the villagers shamed him for harming the community."

So it became a custom, when someone harmed the group as Tom had, or harmed another person in the group, as a wife beater does, to "put that person in Coventry"—to shun him until he felt remorseful and changed his behavior. No fun for the offender. No fun for anyone really. The offender could dive deep into debilitating shame, or he could choose to hear the wake-up call and feel the remorse. He could behave differently, make amends, and perhaps be reaccepted in the group.[3]

This "putting in Coventry" did not involve physical punishment, incarceration, or ridicule. Do you think this kind of wake-up call is helpful to society? How do groups you belong to hold members accountable if they have harmed the group or a member of it? Do those methods provide a way for the member to make amends and become reestablished in the group? How is it done in your family?

Shame Is a Stopper That Pops Out Later

Because shame is such a stopper, adults can use it to stop unwanted behavior in children. It does that. It stops them cold. Trouble is, it leaves them cold. It does bring them to their knees, but it is very hard for children to get up again. Some never do. They go through life displacing their shame onto other people and persecuting them. For example, in her writing, Alice Miller recounts the ridicule and beatings that Hitler and many of the Holocaust perpetrators experienced in childhood.[4] History shows that physical punishment, psychological punishment, any extensive, repeated punishment is deeply shaming. It teaches the child *he* is bad. The results of such shame can bubble up in later life in ways that shock the rest of us. Shaming by physical punishment doesn't teach people how to live peacefully.

Because shame is a stopper, we can use it to keep ourselves and our families from healing from being hurt or from hurting others. Recognizing a long-standing behavior, such as codependency, is embarrassing at best, especially if we have been using it to the detriment of ourselves and others for years. But, if we go beyond embarrassment to pull up a blanket of shame and pull down the blinds to hide, we can keep ourselves from practicing new, healthy behaviors.

If we are recovering from an addiction—any addiction—and have moved past denial, it can be tempting to hide in shame. Facing shame takes courage, and it is courage that separates those who recover from those who don't. Limit the bouts of feeling ashamed to five minutes, and then spend ten minutes making amends to self or others.

By pledging allegiance to our shame, we keep ourselves locked in dishonesty.
—*Connie Dawson*

Helping Children Deal with Shame

If the child feels ashamed

A parent or caregiver can help a child who feels ashamed of her action(s) by guiding her through the **amend** piece of time-in. If she can move from shame to remorse, she may realize that although she may not completely undo the hurt, she has done the responsible thing by making amends and she will no longer need to hide.

If the child has been shamed

Helping a child who has been shamed by others is trickier. Usually it involves some combination of empathy, affirmation of being, information about the motivation of the shamer, and coping skills. Sometimes adult intervention is necessary to confront the shamer or to stop bullying.

What about Shame?

Verbal shaming

*Teresa came home tearful because the kids at school had ridiculed her for still playing with dolls. Mom did not see this as anything Teresa should feel remorse for, but as humiliation. Mom **asked** and **acted** to help Teresa recover her good sense of self and not hang on to the shame. Mom said, "Oh, I hate it when someone makes fun of me for doing something I want to do. You do like your dolls, don't you?"*

"I guess so." Teresa kept her eyes downcast.

"Maybe for a while we should think of ways you can play with them without the girls knowing," suggested Mom.

"But I want to play dolls with a friend." Eyes still downcast.

"It's been awhile since we've had Polly over for a weekend. You love to play dolls with her. She goes to another school. Shall we call her?"

"Yes, I guess so." Eyes peeked up beneath bangs.

"Teresa, I wonder why those girls made fun of you. Don't they play with dolls?"

"They say they're too big." Eyes downcast again.

"Well, maybe. Or maybe they don't have pretty dolls. Or maybe their moms or big brothers ridiculed them for liking dolls. Or maybe someone broke their dolls. That could have happened and they could be passing that hurt along to you."

"That's awful!" exclaimed Teresa.

"Sure is," agreed Mom. "So let's be sure you don't take their hurt in. You know, some little girls who loved to play with dolls turn it into a prosperous business when they grow up. Remember the lady we talked to in the doll store in Stillwater?"

"Yes."

"Do you think she might have liked playing with dolls when she was a little girl?"

"Maybe. Yes, I guess so," said Teresa.

"I wonder if she ever stopped. I haven't. When I make doll clothes for your dolls, I'm still playing with dolls. Let's go see if any of the doll clothes need mending."

"Okay." And Teresa, head up, runs off to survey the doll clothes.

Notice how Mom **acted** and **asked** to combine empathy, affirmation for being, information about the motivation of the shamer, and coping skills.

Physical shaming

Rob came home from school and hid. When his dad finally found Rob and got him to tell what had happened, he learned that on the way home from school, Rob's playmates had held him down, pulled off his pants, thrown them in a ditch, and then ridiculed him. Rob begged his dad not to do any-thing about it (to hide in shame with him). Dad said, "What they did is def-initely not okay. This is a job for the grown-ups. I will do something, but let me think about it. I'll think of several things I could do and then let you choose. This kind of bullying needs to be stopped by the adults. You should not have to put up with this." Dad's **action**, his firm stance, moved the blame off of the victim and back onto the perpetrators, and the respon-sibility off the victim child onto the adults.

If the child has shamed others

Children who shame other children may do so for a variety of rea-sons. When parents **attend**, they may notice that Adam uses racial or sexual slurs because he has heard the words but does not know what they mean. Dad **acts** and **asks** and may ask for **amends**: "Adam, you need to understand what that word means. It means . . . and that is hurtful. I'm sorry you used it against Victor (the victim). I understand that you didn't know what it meant. Do you think it would be better to apologize to him or just not to use that word again?"

Barbie uses racial or sexual slurs because her crowd is doing it. Mom **acts** and **asks**. "Whoa, Barbie. I just learned that you and your friends have been calling Vicky a . . . That is racist (or sexist or what-ever) and our family doesn't do that. Now, what can you do to make sure that doesn't happen again?" If Barbie is fearful of being the next target of the group's ridicule, Mom will help her explore fight, flight, freeze, fix, or flow. She might flee—leave the group. She might fight— take on the group leaders and try to get them to change. If she froze, she would stay perfectly still and do and say nothing. She might try to fix—get the group interested in activities other than gossip and ha-rassment. She might flow—stay in the group, but try to sidetrack the gossip or quietly withdraw when they harass. (You can read more about fight, flight, freeze, fix, or flow in chapter 3.)

Charlie has been using sexual and racial slurs. He hears them at home. In this case, the whole family will have to face up to their be-havior and change their attitude and way of speaking.

Dena has been using sexual and racial slurs and her parents don't know why. Time to **attend.** Time to figure out what Dena needs so she will feel good enough about herself that she won't need to put others down.

Bullying

A report from Eddy's teacher reveals that he has been bullying other children on the playground. Bullying is hurtful and shaming of the victim. His parents **act** and **attend.** The action is doing whatever it takes without isolating or breaking the connection to get the bullying behavior stopped and then helping the child regain his positive sense of self so he doesn't need or want to hurt others.

If the bullying has become a habit, it may be hard to stop. Or, if the child thinks it is not serious or the parents won't carry through, he may need a wake-up call. What will stop it may vary from child to child. You know your own child. Here is a suggestion from therapist Bernie Saunders who has had success using this method with children who need a serious wake-up call.[5]

STOP!

1. Tell the child the bullying behavior must stop, totally, now.
2. Tell the child that if he does that kind of behavior one more time, he will experience a penalty that will be four times worse than he expected. Don't tell him what it is.
3. If he bullies again, enforce the penalty. Think of one penalty that might fit; then make it four times as big. This is to get the child's attention. Choose penalties that do not break his connection with you or shame him in front of others. Tell him if he does it again, it will be ten times as big.
4. If he bullies again, make the penalty ten times as big. Choose something you can live with. Grounding may penalize the parent more than the child. The idea is not to harm the child but to make the penalty so outrageous that it will get his attention and he will understand that he has to stop bullying.

As part of the above method, one family took the wheels off the bicycle. Another family canceled a much-longed-for trip. One family boxed and moved to a rental storage all video games, CDs, and other cherished toys. Another family removed all furniture and clothing from a child's room except for a mattress, sheets, and a blanket and two changes of clothing until the child asked why, sincerely, and was willing to listen to the need for remorse and the urgency of learning respectful ways to treat people.

At the same time the STOP! action is going on, parents are carefully **attending** to reasons their child may be bullying. Why does he think it is okay to ridicule and beat up others? Why is her self-esteem so low that she treats others disrespectfully? Many children who bully have been bullied by someone else. Is he being bullied at school? On the playground? At home? If so, take whatever adult **action** is needed to get that bullying stopped.

Sometimes the four and ten ways of getting the child's attention is enough, and she finds better ways to get along. He finds new ways to make friends. Sometimes, however, the cause is too deep for parents to search out and they get help from a coach, counselor, or therapist. Parents need to keep searching until they find a way to help children who have been shaming others to get back on track with respectful behaviors toward others and to rediscover the goodness within themselves. Further readings about the origins and effects of bullying behavior are listed in the notes section.[6]

Many grown-ups who have been shamed also need help. Otherwise they may have difficulty keeping connections intact. Sometimes professional help is needed. Other times, we can generate our own creative solutions.

Someone told me that, in the time of apartheid, in certain villages in South Africa, a village member who had been humiliated by a racist incident was helped by the whole village. He was not to hide, but to return to his village and report what had happened so he could be sung to. The village then sang him back to health. They sang constantly until he felt reconnected with his village and himself. People came when they were free and went when they needed to, but they made sure someone was singing until the shamed one was healed.

What a beautiful thought. To be sung back to health. To be sustained through the grieving. No blaming. No excusing. No discounting. Just a continuous bath of music that says, *We see the pain the shamer transferred to you. It is not yours. We will help you remember who you are.* What a supportive way to say you are important to us, you are okay with us, you belong here.

Recovering from shame always involves grieving. After having been shamed, things can never be exactly as they were before, but we can help each other recover from it. Each family could develop its own way of singing a shamed member back to health. It might not be singing, but it could be another ritual, another activity that the shamed person knows will be there so it will not be necessary to hide, only to say, *I need the ritual.* And to be reconnected with the family and with the health of self.

So, there it is. Shame. We want never to experience it, but the awareness of it nudges us all to use our behavior for the good of ourselves and the good of the group, even when we don't feel like it.

Shake yourself out of being shamed into healing and health. Shake yourself like a dog shakes off water. Move out of feeling ashamed into making amends and rebuilding connections.

Chapter 16

What If a Child Doesn't Connect?

And yet they are a close and loving family, as families go.
—OLGA SILVERSTEIN AND BETH RUSHBAUM,
THE COURAGE TO RAISE GOOD MEN

Most children are adequately connected to their families, but if you have a child who doesn't seem to connect or won't respond, keep trying. When the personality traits of the child and parent don't mesh, connecting may not come easily for either of them. Sometimes a trauma that the parents may or may not know about makes a child wary of connection. Some children connect more easily than others. Some children find it difficult to connect because for some reason their early bonding and attachment weren't secure. Some have suffered from brain injury.

Before we talk about early attachment and its effects, think about what you mean by connection. How do you expect your child to show you that she feels firmly connected to you? If you show emotion easily and your child is less demonstrative, that may be a personality trait difference, not a lack of connection. Look instead for willingness to participate in family activities, evidence of loyalty to the family, expressions of empathy, concern, and support for family members.

Is He Connected or Isn't He?

Some children connect without showing the connection in a way that the parents can easily recognize. Sometimes the parent-child connection becomes obvious only when parents see their values reflected in their children's behavior.

Bryan had a difficult birth and almost died. His father moved out when Bryan was a baby, saw him infrequently, and died when Bryan was four. John, Bryan's stepdad who later became his adoptive dad, spent time with Bryan, worried over him, played sports with him, taught him to play the guitar, and helped him get the musical education he so desired. Bryan was physically present but emotionally distant, often unresponsive. As an adult, Bryan moved to another state and did not initiate contact with John. When John called him, Bryan was often cool or resistant. Other times they talked about music for an hour. Imagine John's surprise when he learned how Bryan described his fathers to his peers. "I've had two dads. Earl was my birth dad, but he didn't stick around to be my dad. John is my real dad. He didn't always know how to do the right thing for me, but he was always trying. He was always there. He still is. He is solid and loyal." Bryan is solid and loyal and helpful to his friends, like the dad he connected with.

Some Children Don't Ever Seem to Connect

Sometimes, no matter how hard a family tries, they are unable to forge a strong connection with a child.

Derrick was two when he was adopted into the warm, loving Hurtado family. No one knew much about his prenatal or birth experience or his first two years of life. Mrs. Hurtado was a full-time mom and glad of it because Derrick's needs were enormous. He had muscle coordination difficulties and a learning disability. Despite the Hurtado's consistent efforts to connect with Derrick, care for him, and teach him their values, when Derrick hit adolescence, he took off. He joined a gang, did drugs, and dropped out of school. For six years he occasionally came home to be cared for and to steal from his parents. They finally had to grieve for the life they had expected for this boy, tell him they would always care about him, and bar him from their home until he changed his behavior.

Did the Hurtado's efforts to connect with Derrick have a positive effect? It is impossible to know. So far, Derrick has not maimed or killed another person. We can only guess what would have been Derrick's life path if he had not been cared for by the Hurtados. The Hurtados' second adopted child, Dulcie, made a fine, warm connection. Bryan, Derrick, and Dulcie all had rough and bumpy starts and all three involved adoption. Two children connected and one did not. We still have much to learn about how to help adopted children connect.

There is more information about bonding and adoption in *Growing Up Again* and in *Adopting the Hurt Child: Hope for Families with Special-Needs Kids: A Guide for Parents and Professionals.*[1]

Sometimes a baby born to two loving parents and living in a stable home doesn't seem to want to connect. We can get information or get counseling to find new ways to help that child connect. Some parents need help in learning how to be in charge, to cuddle the baby who pushes away, to hold responsible the older child who seems not to care. Sometimes there has been a traumatic experience with a babysitter or a relative or a neighbor, or at a place of child care, that the parents don't know about. Any number of reasons could convince a child to give up on other people. Our job is to provide the kind of parenting that will invite him to trust us, to want to be *attached* to us.

What Are Bonding and Attachment?

Infant bonding is the name for the close connection that is forged between infant and mother, father, and/or other caretaker before and immediately after birth. Genetic programming, personality predisposition, and the birth experience combined with the prenatal experience affect the assurance with which the infant enters the process of after-birth bonding. In their helpful daily calendar, *Affirmations for Your Healthy Pregnancy,* Cheryl Kilvington and Robert Brunjes not only identify some aspects of fetal growth, but also suggest affirmations of support to enhance the prenatal bonding experience: "Darling baby, you are filled with creative intelligence."[2]

Here are my general affirmations that support the baby in the womb:

- I celebrate that you are alive.
- Your needs and safety are important to me.
- We are connected and you are whole.
- You can make healthy decisions about your experiences.
- You can be born when you are ready.
- Your life is your own.
- I love you just as you are.[3]

These messages set the stage for the initial outside-of-the-womb bonding and later attachment.

Parents who weren't able to send these early messages or who didn't get to hold their baby right after birth can still help him make a firm attachment if they are careful to gaze at him, to touch him, to talk to him, and to be consistent and reliable in response to his needs. Helping children form a firm attachment with parents is an investment in their future. It forms the template for future connections and bonds. Bryan's difficult birth and subsequent abandonment by his father suggests that his template for connections included great wariness. We can guess that Derrick's early months were very difficult, but that Dulcie received warm, loving care. The need for adoption gives any child a rough and bumpy start, but the degree of disturbance can vary greatly. Since all children need loving, supportive homes in which to grow, we need to figure out how to give greater support to both birth and adoptive parents during those crucial early years.

Robert Karen, in his book *Becoming Attached,* traces the history of the research on how children attach and what that implies for their later success.[4] Karen credits John Bowlby for his pioneering research on attachment and loss.[5] The identification by Mary Ainsworth of levels of attachment is especially useful to think about.[6] She noted that children need to use parents as a secure base from which to explore the world. From her studies of the mother-child relationship in the early years of life, Ainsworth offers such descriptors of attachment as avoidant, ambivalent, or secure. It is during the first eighteen months that the child sets a pattern to be used for later relationships. The secure child is sure about her caregivers and learns to trust them. The ambivalent child is not sure that adults will always be dependable and has a shaky trust base. The avoidant child seems to have given up on being cared for. He doesn't reach out for care. He acts too independent too soon.

These behavior styles seem to be directly related to parenting styles, and they seem to influence the development of both intellect and social skills. If you suspect that your child, for whatever reason, hasn't made a secure attachment to you, use time-in, especially **attending**, while you learn more about this subject and get a professional evaluation by someone who specializes in attachment disorders. You can read Dan Hughes's *Facilitating Developmental Attachment: The Road to Emotional Recovery and Behavioral Change in Foster and Adopted Children.*[7] Foster Cline and Jim Fay are specialists in helping with attachment problems. Their books *Parenting with Love and Logic* and *Parenting Teens with Love and Logic* are helpful to any parents wanting to raise responsible children.[8] To the extent that time-in says, *Yes, I am here for you to help you in getting your needs met, and I am reliable,* it can reinforce early positive decisions about trust and counter or call into question early decisions based on faulty bonding and attachment.

Older Children

Sometimes a child with whom we had a good connection seems to pull away. If an older child is resistant, complaining, and manipulative, but sticks around to fight with you, you and he may need help. On the other hand, fighting and arguing means making contact and maybe this child cares about you but is ambivalent about the difference between family values and the values and behaviors of his friends and school peer group. There are not generally accepted and supported norms for social behaviors of children and young people right now. Some settings admire politeness, others applaud rebellion. The media offers violence and instant gratification. It is not surprising if young people today are deeply confused about what to believe and how to behave, and who better to accuse than their parents? We may not be culpable, but we are the safest ones to fault. And as the children push against us in an effort to deal with their confusion, it is especially important for us to **attend**, to be present, and to do our part of the connecting.

As adolescents pull away to establish their independence, let us, as parents, monitor ourselves to be sure that we are not pushing them away. Sometimes fathers, out of deep caring and respect for the incest taboo, pull away from adolescent daughters at the very time the girls need assurance that they are loved and attractive. These dads need to get clear about the difference between sex and nurturing and learn to continue to give nonsexual, nurturing touch to their daughters. One dad discovered that side-by-side hugs were loving and safe. The book *Reviving Ophelia* by Mary Pipher, helps parents look at the way we have shortchanged girls.[9]

Sometimes both moms and dads, but especially moms, pull away from teenage boys in the mistaken belief that distance will help them become strong men. If you think this might be happening in your household, run, don't walk, to get a copy of *The Courage to Raise Good Men* by Olga Silverstein and Beth Rashbaum, or *Reaching Up for Manhood* by Geoffrey Canada, or *Real Boys* by William Pollack.[10]

A father with three daughters read *The Courage to Raise Good Men* and recognized that he had been pushing his oldest daughter away because, after all, she was eighteen and an adult. As he reestablished loving, supportive contact, their relationship improved dramatically. She still pushed, but without the hostile edge that had grated on their relationship.

What Next?

If the structures you are setting and the values you are teaching are different from those on TV or even in your neighborhood, remember that in this time of cultural overindulgence and neglect, good parenting is often a countercultural activity. So get lots of support.

If we have done everything we can and our late-adolescent or adult child will not accept our values and morals and will not connect with us, at some point we parents have to grieve and let him make his own way. That will be painful, but we can always hold that child in love in our hearts. Remember, our job is to offer the best that we can, to learn better and better skills about how to invite connections, and to expect the child to respond. But children decide what to do with what we offer.

> *Parents are responsible for the process; children are responsible for the outcome.*

Do you believe this? I have three children and no matter what I wish for them or try to get them to do, eventually, they decide what they will do with their lives, how they will treat themselves and other people, and in what areas they will direct their life energies. And often they make far better choices for themselves than I would have made for them. They know themselves better than I think I know them.

If it is true—that parents are *responsible* for the process, that is, the setting, the environment, and the adult interactions—then it is the parents' job to offer both love and structure and to be *aware* of that process. Parents must be willing to change or to improve it as the children grow and their needs change. I hope using time-in will help you create the process you want for your family.

Chapter 17

Families Don't Blend:
Sometimes They Bond

And they all lived happily ever after?
—JEAN ILLSLEY CLARKE

The Reality of Stepfamilies

Children need families in which to grow. The families that support that growth come in different forms. Fairy tales remind us that many of these families have been with us for ages. Sleeping Beauty and Tom Thumb lived with two parents. The orphaned heroine of the fairy tale "The Spindle, the Shuttle, and the Needle" lived with her god-mother. Stories of children from single-parent families include those of Pinochio, Jack and the Beanstalk, and Aladdin. Some fairy-tale children were fostered; some, like Mowgli, even by animals. Cinderella and Vasilissa lived in what we now call blended families. But the adjective *blended* does not appear in the old tales, and the stories were more about courage, tenacity, and survival than happy family homogeneity.

Let us think briefly about the type of connections we expect in each of these various families. We expect children living with both parents will bond with both. We expect children in single-parent families to bond with the caretaking parent and we hope with the noncustodial parent. We also hope that children in single-parent families will have consistent, caring contact with other adults of both sexes.[1] We expect children in extended families will have the opportunity to bond with grandparents, aunts, and uncles as well as parents. We hope that adoptees will bond with their adoptive families and manage to hold both birth and adoptive parents in their hearts.[2] We wish that all children in foster care find themselves in families

146

that provide them the nurture and structure they need, and that the children are able to accept it and thrive.

We fervently wish that children who have been abandoned by one or both parents will find a family circle of love. Professionals who work with families recognize that these children who have two families, the adopted and the foster children, have a great deal of grieving that they need help doing before they can bond with new caregivers. There is also recognition of the dilemma these children face: *If I let myself love this second family, will I be disloyal to my birth family?* These are not easy tasks and choices, and we should celebrate every foster or adopted child and family that is successful. This is not to imply that raising children in a birth family is a snap. Raising any child anywhere takes love, willingness, determination, and dedication. But the special needs of foster and adoptive children demand an extra measure of maturity, patience, and perseverance from parents.

In the fairy-tale families, often a man whose wife had died took a new wife whose husband had died and they brought their children together. They were called stepfamilies. In our present time, we have new families with children whose birth parents are alive, perhaps living with another spouse or partner and their children.

Parents in these families have special needs. One of the most helpful sources of information and support for these families comes from the Stepfamily Association of America, founded in 1979 by Emily and John Visher. They have advocated, through their writing and through workshops, for stepfamilies and have trained countless professionals to address the clinical issues in working with stepfamilies. Their books are widely used and appreciated.[3]

The Myth of Blending

Stepfamilies have their own characteristics and special problems. But I believe we have added another one, a highly unrealistic expectation. We have asked these families to blend. Many helpful supports are available to stepfamilies, and many of these families are succeeding in providing loving, carefully and safely structured environments in which children thrive. But asking stepfamilies to blend, without societal agreement on what that means, can place a heavy burden on stepparents and may be an obstacle to the child's process of connecting. So in this chapter, I am not describing the successful stepfamilies; I am only addressing the myth of blending and describing how the attempt to blend could shove aside the need to grieve and could make the process of connecting more difficult for both child and stepparent.

If you have created a new family with children from former families and the new family is bonded, the connections are sound, I offer you deep congratulations; you may skip this section. I wrote it for all the children I know who didn't want a divorce or a stepparent or new siblings and who are doing the best they can, especially in situations where the adults are not helping the children understand and deal with their deep confusion. Many of these children are saddened and even ashamed because they believe they caused the divorce. We all need to remember that children often don't have the capacity to understand their parents' problems and that divorce can seem like a tragic break of the implicit parent-child contract that says your parents chose to have you and they will stay together and raise you.

Of the other families that we hope will bond, the adoptive and the foster families, we do not say that we expect them to "blend." That word has come into use since divorce has become common. The lessons of the old fairy tales don't tell our children how to succeed in families where birth parents live in two different homes. Some children feel that their divorcing and remarrying parents are being very selfish and don't realize how important the child's needs are.

I believe it is impossible for stepfamilies to blend as many people understand that word. We have a blender in our kitchen. I know what happens when you push the blend button—everything ends up looking alike. So when we blend children from two families, do we expect them to look alike and be happy to be together? This is not going to happen in a real family. Think what would happen if we stopped putting the *everybody happy* expectation on stepfamilies and said, *Make the best connections you can. We expect you, the new Mom and Dad, to develop a strong bond. We urge you to maintain the bonds with your own children. If you do bond with a stepchild, hurrah. If you don't, be the friendly stepparent and offer the love and structure of an additional caring adult. But help your children grieve their losses and if they won't let you help, find someone who can help them.* Many children thrive in stepfamilies, but I do not guess that those are the families that ask their children to just put-on-a-happy-face and love your new brother.

Listen to this stepmom who remarried with high hopes and the best of intentions:

Families Don't Blend: Sometimes They Bond

"I love Bill and I care about his kids. While we were dating, my kids and his seemed to get along. They all seemed wonderful at the wedding, although if they weren't I was too excited to notice. Then we moved in together. It's been fight and snipe and compete and complain ever since. Both sets of kids insist the others are getting more than they are: more space, more clothes, more rides, more attention. Except for Emily. She doesn't ask for anything and she stays out of the way. She is a darling. But, I'm upset. I want so much for us to blend. I want them to accept my mother as a grandmother but they ignore her. It's six months since the wedding, and I don't even see signs of a truce. I wish I had a fairy godmother who would wave her wand and make our family blend."

Hear the good intentions of this mother? This is no wicked step-mother. This is a fine, caring, loving person. This is also a person in pain because she can't make her new family match her new vision. She does need a fairy godmother. A friend or counselor, or a wise part of herself who is willing to challenge the fantasy in her vision. One who is able to see things as they are and is courageous enough to send a wake-up call. Listen to her wake-up call:

Come on mother, stepmother, wife, wake up! Think about what you are wishing for. Children are not carrots and green peppers and cucumbers that you put in a blender, whirl on razor-sharp knives, and pour out in one homogeneous blob that can't even stand up for itself.

Your job—mother, stepmother, and wife—is not to help your children blend, but to help each one of them grieve their losses and survive with their individuality intact. Youngsters need to belong, and you are asking them to leave their old place of belonging and "blend" into a new place that they did not choose and about which they may feel grateful or deeply resentful or some of both. You, new wife, you got to choose. You have what you want. You got your Bill. The children didn't get to choose.

It is your job to make this unfamiliar place an accepting, loving, supportive setting where children will want to forge a new connection. If you and your new husband have already "blended," have merged yourselves in each other and given up your individuality, get help. That is codependency and it is not good for children. If, however, you and Bill are forging a healthy, loving bond between yourselves, you are offering a positive model for the children.

But even if both of you adults are totally loving and accepting, a stepchild must still find hostility, even if he has to create it. Remember the dilemma in which your children find themselves. They are always missing something that is important to them. If your new husband is awful to them, that is hard. If he is wonderful to them and they like him better than their birth father, that is hard. If they like him so much they wish he had always been their father, that is hard. Sometimes they will be mad at him for not having been with them all of their lives. Then they feel disloyal to the birth dad and that is hard. It is deep in the nature of every child to be loyal to a birth parent. Even if he was awful. Even if he deserted the family. There is still a part of the child that knows in deepest knowing that there is something to be loyal to. Many people don't figure out what that something is until they are middle-aged adults, but even if children never learn of redeeming traits, they know that their father is in themselves. One-half of their genetic characteristics, their looks, their inherent strengths, and their talents came from that first dad and his ancestors. Of course, if that dad is around and is wonderful to them, that is hard because they will feel disloyal to the stepdad. If the birth dad is acrimonious toward you or the new marriage, that will make it harder for everyone. So forget about blending. The best thing that can happen is that over time (some who study remarriages say five years), the family, or part of it, will merge. The new family members will make connections, not instead of the genetic connections, but in addition to those connections.

So forget about blending. Pretend you are a camp counselor and you want to take the best care you can of each child, and you hope to have some peace in your cabin. Be the caring adult who aids learning. If some of the campers eventually choose to bond with both counselors and with the other campers, that will be wonderful. But don't set your heart on it or you may get in the way of it happening. And tell your mother to wait. Step-grandparents have to be chosen by the stepchild when the child is ready. Sometimes that happens. Sometimes it doesn't.

Now let's look at each of your children. There is Ben, twelve. Your youngest. Even though Emily is quiet and withdrawn, he torments her at times. Why not? She took his youngest spot. Unless you let him remain your youngest, in addition to his other losses, he will have to grieve giving up his birth-order position and accept a new position in the family, a change he did not request. Remember that even in birth families children often resent a new baby. And Emily is no baby, she is ten and stringy haired and awkward for gawd's sake.

Think about Ben and your new husband. I know you want him to be Ben's new father, but Ben has a father, so don't ask him to call this interloper Dad. "Bill" will do just fine. It is not disrespectful unless Ben makes it so. It is disrespectful to ask a twelve-year-old to call a man who is not his dad by that name. If Ben bonds with Bill and chooses to call him Dad or some other affectionate name, that will be genuine. I heard of one little boy who calls his stepfather "Two Dad." When he calls to his stepfather, he chants, "Hey Dad, Two Dad, where dat Two Dad?" Your Ben is older. Let him find his own way to name Bill.

Now think about Shelby and Spencer. Both are sixteen, and they fight like cats and dogs. Well, look at them. Your Shelby is gorgeous, full-breasted, sexy looking with her long shiny hair and her flashing eyes. Bill's Spencer is tall and appealing with his boy-man handsomeness and his broad shoulders. It isn't enough that he has lost his place as oldest, but there is the problem of Shelby. His Adam's apple moves up and down every time Shelby comes into the room. You can imagine what else happens, both physically and in fantasy. Their attraction is not intentional. It is hormonal. They are a matched pair of surging hormones. They don't have the incest taboo that is instilled from birth in birth families. You have them in bedrooms next to each other and they share a bath. What do you want them to do? Fall into each other's arms? Think again. How would you have handled this situation? Recognize that they may be coping remarkably well at keeping themselves apart by fighting. I admire their resourcefulness. And change the bedroom arrangement!

Then there is Peter, your eighteen-year-old. It is his developmental job to be separating at this time, and you want him to blend! You'll be lucky if he merges. He may, of course. But he has his path to find, and this new house, with four younger sibs instead of two, may not fit it. Keep your own connection with him and hope.

Well, that about wraps it up for the kids. Oh, except for Emily. Wonderful, quiet, agreeable Emily, who takes care of herself and stays out of the way. At ten years old. Does this sound like age ten? For a few weeks perhaps, but for half a year? She lost her mother three years ago. What is she losing now? How can you help her connect? Did she lose some special role when you came into the picture? Has she finished grieving for her mom? If she hasn't, it will hamper her connection with you. I am most concerned about Emily. You get some good help for her right away.

You can do this. You and Bill love each other and you are both people of goodwill. You are courageous and determined, so get busy helping each kid grieve the losses, the physical losses and the loss of the dream. Help each become who he or she really is and maybe, just maybe, the children, or some of them, will choose to bond and the merger will happen. If it does, consider it a bonus. But don't let your happiness depend on it.

SECTION IV

Unresolved Grief:
A Barrier to Connection

Chapter 18

Let Grief In

I locked the door and kept grief out,
but grief crept in and shrunk my heart.
—ANONYMOUS

The Power of Grief

Grief unfaced and unresolved can hang over a relationship and fray even the strongest of connections. Or old griefs, unrecognized and dishonored, can hinder the development of new relationships and keep them at superficial levels. Grief accepted, shared, and resolved, on the other hand, sometimes makes the threads of connections stronger, more flexible, more empathic. If grief, then, has such a powerful influence on connections, why are so many of us inept at handling it?

If you are an expert at dismissing the personal and cultural messages to deny grief—you willingly move through your own grief and use it to strengthen connections—and if you have excellent skills at helping others through the many stages of grief, you can skip this section and go directly to section 5. But if you haven't recognized the insidiousness of the "don't grieve" messages, if you are unfamiliar with the stages of grieving or don't know how to help others who have losses, read on.

Grief Is Not the Enemy—Let Grief In

Hear the protest:

Let grief in? Like a guest? No! Grief is not a guest; it is a thief. It should be enough to have already lost something, but just as I say, "I can live without it," grief muscles in, a rough giant that fills the rooms of my house and crowds the rooms of my mind. Or grief is a silent interloper that rolls under sofas and into corners like beads from a broken string. Or, a slippery elf, it crawls into small holes and scratches places I thought were sealed off. Grief is a fountain of tears. Unquenchable. Lock the door; keep grief out. I don't want your words; I don't want your hand; and I did **not** want a new puppy.

Grief, however, does come in, or more correctly, grief is already present. Neither guest nor thief, it is a constant, human part of us that surfaces whenever we lose something. Each time we are disconnected from some person or place or thing or belief or dream, when we lose anything we value, grief is ready. Ready to stop us, ready to say, *Pay attention*, ready to say, *Walk the grief path all the way so you can be healed and stronger and able to make the next connection more fully, more surely, more realistically than you did before. Otherwise the bluebird of happiness will pass you by, and hope will be a flutter instead of a beckoning light.*

Children Grieve

Grief in small or large doses is a regular part of life. Let us think of a child's bonding and attachment and need to grieve in this way:

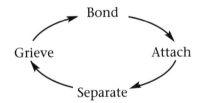

The infant's early bonding is reinforced by attachments and connections over a period of time. As the child grows, the push of physical, mental, and emotional development causes the child to experience a long series of separations. Every separation brings new freedoms. It also brings grief because with every separation, something is left behind. Those separations are not only physical, but also intellectual and emotional. Listen to Emily Ann's story:

Toddler Emily Ann held up her arms to her grandmother when she wanted to be held. Shortly before she was two, she expanded her vocabulary rapidly and became more assertive about what she wanted. One day she stood in front of Gram and said, "Hoe do!"

Hoe do, hoe do. What is hoe do, Gram thought? When she wants to do something, she says, "My do!" Is she telling me she wants to go out in the garden? She has a toy rake and a hoe.

"Would you like to go outside?" Gram asked.

"Noooooo, hoe do!"

Gram couldn't figure it out. The almost two-year-old stood staunchly in front of her grandmother and fussed forlornly. The next week Emily Ann's mother called and said, "I figured out what hoe do means. I often say, 'Emily Ann, would you like me to hold you?' I asked her if hoe do means she wants me to hold her and she said, 'Yeh.'"

Why wouldn't this toddler hold up her arms in the old baby signal when her grandmother didn't understand *hoe do*? Perhaps because learning to speak is a natural step in her individuation and the natural push to grow is so strong that she would rather grieve than regress to baby ways. Perhaps because her innate wisdom still knows that she must grieve each separation to be fully ready for the next step in growth or connection.

Adults Need to Grieve

Let us consider how attachment and bonding occur for adults. George Kohlrieser, from his study of attachment and bonding as the basis of his successful negotiations with terrorists and hostage takers, observes that if adults refuse to do their grieving, they cannot satisfactorily make the next connection.[1] Terrorists become so disconnected they can commit inhumane acts. Only when someone is able to establish some connection with them can they release hostages or surrender.

Grief can enhance connection when people grieve freely together, or it can cause a deep rift when someone turns away from the grief and so turns away from others.

When Anna's family lost their home in a flood, friends and neighbors came together to grieve and to help each other. They built a stronger community than they had before the flood.

It seems easy for people to reach out when the grief follows a natural disaster: the flood, the tornado, the earthquake, the hurricane, even the lost ship or airplane.

It may be harder to listen to the story and to give comfort when the grief is for a personal trauma.

When Jeremy's mother was killed in an auto accident, Jeremy's dad couldn't stand to face the loss so he destroyed all of her things, including the pictures of her. He never mentioned her again, and if Jeremy started to talk about her, his father walked out of the room. Jeremy felt as if he had lost both parents.

Fleeting, deeply searing, or someplace in between, grieving feels awful. It is not one of the happy emotions. Sometimes it is mixed with relief or even joy, but the grief part still feels awful. Physically, emotionally, spiritually awful. Someone or something is missing! Maybe that is why we let grief break connections.

Maybe that is why we wish for magic. *Please, fairy godmother, wave your wondrous wand and take my grief away. Restore my loss. Let me be as I was.* But, if we listen to the voice of the wise one, she does not say, *Of course, my child. I will remove all of your pain. I want you to be comfortable forever.* Instead she tells us that pain cannot be taken away, that it must be walked through, and that we had better persevere and be about it. She knows that grief is a giant that stalks us unless we work through it. She knows that the giant is really our own anger, our sadness, and our fear of the unknown. She tells us to recognize our dream, not to let it go, but to transform it to a higher level.

She reminds us that tribal people would have gathered us into healing rituals, familiar rituals that one had already participated in while helping others. But, for some of us, familiar tribal rituals cannot be. Or we believe they cannot be. Many of us live in a strange, disconnected tribe, so we have to create our own rituals in our families, with our friends, or in our safe groups. Although grieving is an internal, personal experience, it is enhanced by connections with others. We can tell the story of our loss to the hazelnut tree only so many times. Sometime we need the response of another human being. One who is empathic and does not hurry us. One who walks beside us, not pushing and not holding back. A friend who understands that grief is not logical. Grief has its own path and each of us must follow it, a path that may seem straight ahead one time and a labyrinth the next. A friend who will know, but not remind us before we are ready, that the path of grief, purposefully followed, leads to enlightenment. A friend who knows that grief work is the work of the soul.

Who Said Lock the Door?

If accepting the knock on the door and following the journey of grief is so important, why lock the door? A compelling reason, of course, is the wish to avoid the pain. Another is the culturally supported pursuit of pleasure.[2] If, as some say, the organizing principle of our age is consumption, we could hardly expect loss to fit comfortably with that.

In addition, in this land where both natives and immigrants have experienced great hardships, there must have been times when it seemed as if grief was a luxury that could not be given the time and energy that it called for, so it was turned off, squashed, denied, without the recognition that it would resurface in other ways. Those messages are with us still, in our literature, in our movies (Can you imagine John Wayne grieving?), in our families, and in our heads. If we are in a situation where we can't stop right now to let grief in, we can say, "Not now, grief. Later." But later better come as soon as possible or there will be a price to pay.

Identify the "don't grieve" messages in your life and in your head. Read the following list and check the ones you have heard. Circle the ones you believe. Add more.

- You'll get over it.
- Don't make a big deal of it.

- Let it go.
- Keep a stiff upper lip.
- Don't get so upset.
- You have nothing to be mad about.
- These things happen.
- Don't question it.
- You can have another baby.
- You can adopt.
- Don't speak of it outside of the family.
- Don't speak of it at all.
- Stop acting like a baby.
- Save your grief for something worthwhile.
- Serves you right.
- You wouldn't have had this loss if you hadn't done something stupid.
- Now I bet you wish you had taken better care of . . .
- It's been six months now. Isn't it time to get on with your life?
- Stop moping.
- Shit happens.
- People can't live forever.
- He was old. What are you complaining about?
- Nobody lives forever.
- Don't cry.
- Don't break down.
- Don't be a wuss.
- It's God's will. Just accept it.
- You're okay; put a smile on your face.
- You have cried long enough.
- It wasn't a person, after all.
- I'll buy you a new puppy.
- Men don't cry.
- Boys don't cry.
- Be a man.
- Tough it out.
- It'll all work out.
- Friends come and go.
- Life's a bitch; then you die.
- Forgive and forget.
- You didn't need that anyway.

- That's not important.
- Don't tell me about it.
- You're lucky she didn't suffer.
- My case was worse.
- You didn't want that anyway.
- You've got your eyesight, haven't you?
- You can find a new family.
- There is too much to grieve. Don't open it up.
- Others: _____

  _____

  _____

All of these messages say don't grieve, don't recognize your feelings, do shut down and, therefore, hamper your ability to connect next time around.

Think about the unfortunate model that Jackie Kennedy presented for the nation at President Kennedy's funeral: Stand tall, dress well, look beautiful, don't cry or don't let your tears show, don't break down. No doubt she was following the rules she had been given by her family or by her image advisors. Think how helpful the message would have been if she could have shown us how to cry at a husband's funeral and how to support children's sad feelings.

Think about your own rules. Some of your messages may already be included in the list. If you have others, write them down. Then rewrite all of the messages to support the grief process.

- ~~Don't make a big deal of it.~~
- Make as big a deal of it as you need to.

- ~~Men don't cry.~~
- Wise men cry.

- ~~Tough it out.~~
- Feel all of your feelings.

- ~~It's been six months now. Isn't it time to get on with your life?~~
- You can take as long as you need to grieve your loss.

- ~~You're lucky she didn't suffer.~~
- I'm sorry you lost your mom.

"Don't Grieve" Messages Hurt

Think about specific times your grieving has been discounted.

Walter remembered his grandpa's funeral and how choked up he felt when his dad said, "Stop crying. You have cried enough."

Jana recounted that she had loved the old blue car. When it was replaced by a shiny new brown one, everyone else in the family was excited and they wanted her to be glad to see old blue go. She wanted to sit in old blue and cry, but they told her that was silly.

Carmen's old uncle was at her house when she got a phone call with the news that her dear friend who was only thirty-five had been killed in an auto pileup. She went to her uncle in shock and asked for some comfort. He said, "Some people are not long livers," and clicked on the TV.

Carmen vowed not to share any more important things with that uncle. Connection broken.

Kendall, nine, was very quiet when she got home from school. Her best friend had decided to be best friends with someone else and Kendall was out. Her mother said, "Friends come and go. What made you think she would want to be your friend forever?" For a long time Kendall stayed to herself and was willing to make only tenuous attachments to new friends.

Clay grew up in a military family. Every time he bonded to a house or neighborhood, they moved. New room, new kitchen, new yard, new neighbor kids, new schools. Each time seemed to get harder. When he complained, his folks said, "You should be used to it by now, so get busy and pack your gear." After the sixth move, he decided not to care anymore.

If there is no relationship, there is no need to grieve. But decisions like these are apt to hang around and cause trouble in later connections. Now when his wife wants Clay to make some improvement in their home or contribute to a community project, he feels affronted. He can't understand why it is important. His wife's requests feel like nagging.

Think about whether the times your feelings were discounted

added to your grief or weakened some connections. All of these "don't grieve" messages are invitations to disconnect.

Let your heart grieve its losses so it can connect again. Open the door and let grief in. Otherwise you are apt to leave claw marks on everything you have to let go of.

The Trail to the Bluebird of Happiness

In the bluebird fairy tale, the one seeking happiness traveled the world, saw the sights, experienced the experiences, but didn't find happiness. When he finally returned home, he found the bluebird of happiness waiting for him in his own backyard. When Dorothy followed the advice of the Wizard of Oz to click the heels of her ruby slippers and chant, *There's no place like home,* she found her happiness.

If the tales are correct, if we all have to make our own happiness within the home that is ourselves, then learning to follow the path of grief is crucial, because unresolved grief not only affects us physically, but it also causes us to shut down emotions. The body is not built in such a way that we can selectively dampen sadness, fear, and anger without also diminishing the capacity for joy. Besides, the loss that was not grieved is still there, forming a hardball or festering. Only by resolving the grief and replacing it with a new connection can we be free to move on.

Whether the loss is people, relationships, position, self-image, dreams, or things makes no difference. The symptoms can be physical or emotional. Skin rashes, colds, pneumonia, cancer, depression, and post-traumatic stress are some of the symptoms that can be related to unresolved grief. Dr. Christine Northrup says, "The body keeps score."[3] It keeps score not only of its daily treatment of nutrition, exercise, rest, exposure to toxins, but also stress. The burden of carrying losses causes stress.

In addition, shutting down grief leaves a hole—a hole that turns to depression or begs to be filled with food or work or sex or drugs or gambling or power or something that gets way out of balance. Those substitutes never really fill the hole, and they can cause great damage to our bodies and our lives.

The only true healing balm for the hole is the soul work of becoming reconnected with others, with ourselves, and with our dreams, our highest wishes. That is the trail to the bluebird of happiness.

> *The careful experiencing of the grief process is a form of preventive medicine.*
> —*Elaine Childs-Gowell*

What We Grieve

The broken beads

Anya started to weep as she felt the smooth touch of beads rolling down her body and heard the chatter as they hit the hardwood floor and rolled in all directions. This is too much. It's just like my life. A year ago I felt secure, like my beads, and now the thread holding my beads is broken and they are just like me, scattered. Unstrung. I'm divorced, I lost my house, and the new apartment owner won't let us keep our cat. Timmy has been diagnosed ADD, and I don't know about his new school. My best friend at work has been transferred, and the car is making clunking sounds. My mother keeps telling me I should go to a grief support group. I can't. I wouldn't know what to grieve. I don't have time. I suppose it will cost a mint to get the car fixed. *Anya scrambled to pick up the beads, but they slipped through her fingers and rolled off the table.*

Anya has been hard hit by a bunch of losses. If she doesn't grieve them one at a time, they will keep rolling around like the beads.

Many kinds of bonds can be broken and cause grief. Some people are closely bonded to place. Leaving a home and a neighborhood, even if one has chosen to, brings grief for familiar things left behind. Losing a pet that one is bonded to is also deep. The diagnosis of a chronic condition in a child is hard in two ways. First, there is the stress of not knowing what the diagnosis holds for the future. Second, there is the loss of the dream of having a healthy, normal child. Attention deficit disorder, deafness, asthma, a deformed limb, a child who is odd looking, too small, or any of a hundred other surprises, involve a double grief—the loss of the normalcy and the loss of the dream. The loss of a person, by transfer, misunderstanding, betrayal, death, or divorce, can mean loss of a connection that was an important part of one's life fabric. A couple who wishes to conceive a child and fails to needs to be comforted not blithely told, *You can adopt.* The miscarriage of a fetus or the death of a baby can be discounted by others who say, *You can have another.* That denies the importance of honoring this small dear life and grieving its passing.[4]

Betrayal

Betrayals are especially hard to handle when they feel like an assault on the person. When a trusted friend or co-worker reveals a secret, damages a reputation, or embezzles funds, grief can be deep. Perhaps the hardest betrayal is the death of a child. The deep human expectation is that children will outlive their parents so the loss of a child is said to be the most difficult loss to mourn. It feels like a betrayal of some kind of universal order—of how things *should* be. In the book *A Broken Heart Still Beats,* Anne McCracken and Mary Semel have collected the words of many bereaved parents as they record this grief that has no words.[5] Another deep human expectation is to be raised by your birth parents. Children who are orphaned, adopted, or whose parents deserted or divorced often feel betrayed in a deep, nameless way and need special love and support while they grieve that unmet expectation. Incest is another betrayal that often takes the help of a therapist to grieve and recover from.

Deeply held beliefs

Deeply held beliefs or important desires that are challenged or that don't materialize are another kind of loss that needs healing.

Freda, a devout Christian for sixty years, was deeply disturbed when the new minister suggested that Mary, the mother of Jesus, may not have been a virgin and that it didn't matter. Freda was deeply shocked: I have always been taught to believe in the virgin birth. It is key to my faith. If I can't believe in that, what can I believe? *Freda was not helped by her family's debate about why the minister might be wrong or right. She needed to grieve what she felt was an assault on her faith. She needed the care, support, and empathy of her family to help her with her loss.*

Sandra and Barry were deeply grieved that the children each of them had brought to their marriage were not blending. In fact, they were fighting.

Sandra and Barry needed to grieve their dream so they could use their energies to help each person in the family.[6]

Warren is despondent about being retired. He assumed that when he was old, people would respect his opinions. They don't seem to. Even his own children patronize him. He doesn't know how to be a wise old man in a culture that doesn't want any wise old men. His dream is shattered. A book chock-full of helpful information about becoming a spiritual elder is Zalman Schachter-Shalomi's From Age-ing to Sage-ing.[7]

Dreams

A divorce, even if it was chosen, has many losses: loss of the person, loss of the love, and the loss of the dream, whatever that was. Perhaps the dream was of being married to that person for life or of living happily ever after. If the divorcing couple has children, the grief about the divorce can be reactivated with each incident of helping the children to adjust. If there is animosity following the divorce, the grief continues and needs to be attended to regularly, or it will become like many broken strings of beads. But, however difficult, it is important to grieve the old dream and move on to a new one. If you haven't thought of lost dreams as needing to be grieved, you might like Ted Bowman's helpful book *Loss of Dreams: A Special Kind of Grief.*[8]

The following list can help you identify some of your lost dreams. Look at the categories suggested in the list and then write some of the specific dreams you have lost.

- Family dreams—the family members you wanted, but never had; the family member who left too soon; the family member who did not, could not, meet your expectations.
- Career dreams—the career you wanted; the career that was only partly satisfying.
- Relationship dreams—the fellow workers, friends, lovers who did not meet your expectations.
- Loss of things—the things that you wanted but don't have; the things you dreamed would always be in your life that were lost.
- Role losses—the dream of being the boss, the president, the beloved one, the parent, the honored one.

- Fulfillment—the urge to become fully who you are that is disallowed by rigid sex roles or arbitrary class, ethnic, or racial boundaries.
- The body part or function—that you never dreamed of losing.
- The dream of how life would be—that was shattered by the accident, the war, the changes in the greater society.

Grieving any or all of these losses can make you more free, more able to build satisfying connections with others. Start with one. A small one. Go gently. Stay underwhelmed. Use the guided imagery exercise in chapter 21, pages 195–197, to help grieve the loss of dreams.

Walk the Path of Grief

Sometimes the grief path is a straight line. Other times it is a maze. Sue Murray likes to compare going through the stages of grief with the way toddlers learn to climb stairs. They go up one or two steps, sit awhile, and go back down. Eventually they make it to the top of the stairs. Sometimes they need support and help. Mostly they need the time and freedom to do it their own way.[9]

Rituals that support grieving are helpful. Elaine Childs-Gowell's wonderfully helpful little blue book, *Good Grief Rituals*, is chock-full of activities you can do with others or by yourself.[10] She suggests listing all of the things you need to grieve and then allocating fifteen minutes to an hour a day to do grief rituals. Limiting the time puts a fence around the grief and, if the grief is not recent and fresh, lets you live the rest of the day without the grief burden.

The reason for attending to old losses as well as new is that until they are grieved, they do not go away. Elaine Childs-Gowell says:

> If I do not do my grieving about the old hurts and insults, then, when I am faced with a here and now grief experience, I will end up having to dredge up all that old energy along with the current experience. When my mother died, I was surprised and pleased to find that my grieving for her was quite easy because, some years before she died, I had done my grief work vis a vis the hard times we had had together when I was growing up. Her death produced a clear, clean, and present grief for me.[11]

Here are two examples from the book *Good Grief Rituals* that enlist nature as a cleansing helper.

A burial

There is a tradition in North American Indian culture that suggests that if you have a grievous matter to deal with, go out into the woods or to a place where you will be private and dig a hole in the ground near a tree or bush. Pour all of your feelings into that hole. When you are quite satisfied that you have your spirit emptied of the foul stuff, cover the hole and thank the tree for listening and thank Mother Earth for receiving your grief. Then go about your business feeling better about yourself and more connected to the universe. Thank the tree or bush for witnessing your grief process.[12]

You can actually dig in the earth or you can do this digging in a visualization.

A waterfall

This is one of my favorite rituals for self-cleansing and releasing the pain of loss:

Find yourself in a quiet place and deepen your relaxation by following your breath, quietly and evenly. Imagine that you are walking through a deep forest on a mountain you have been climbing for some time. You notice the path has now turned into a gradual slope and you find yourself going down into a valley. As you climb down you become aware of your futility and pain. You feel deep sadness or anger at the loss you have suffered. You feel very burdened by your grief. It is a hot day and you are becoming very warm when you come upon a waterfall deep in the rocks, spilling into a wide pool. Listen to the sound of the splashing water. You remove your clothes and climb down into the water, feeling its cool, refreshing flow against your skin. Step under the waterfall and feel the water splashing down on your body and head. As you stand there, allow the splashing water to pour down over your head and body, taking with it all of your pain, cares, and burdens. See and feel the pain washing out of your body, the water cleansing all of your sorrow. When you step out of the water, allow the sunshine to dry you and feel every cell and tissue in your body fill up with the sunlight until you feel full of light, refreshed and renewed. Reclothe yourself and retrace your steps bringing yourself back to the place in which you started your ritual.[13]

Let Grief In

You can do this by yourself, by recalling it, or you can record it on audiotape and let the tape guide you, or you can ask a good friend to read it to you.

> *Let grief in. Welcome it, resent, it, rage against it, hate it if you like, but let it in. Join it. Walk with it. And come out the other side ready to connect with the next part of life.*

Chapter 19

The Journey of Grief

There is no right way to grieve—there is just your way.
—RUSTY BERKUS, *TO HEAL AGAIN*

Grief has so many faces! Sometimes, as the couple moves along the journey of a mutual grief, he is angry, but she is sad. Or he is fearful and she says it isn't important. Which one of these responses is about really grieving? All of these, and more. Grief has many faces.

The Stages of Grief

Are there stages that people go through during the time of grieving? Yes, but the sequence and the duration of each stage can be highly individual. A look at suggested stages can remind us of what we have been through and prepare us for the future. In 1975 Elisabeth Kübler-Ross, in her pioneering work on the necessity for doing grief work, introduced us to the idea of thinking about stages of grief.[1]

George Kohlrieser offers nine stages.[2] You can look at each of these stages and recall which ones you did when you grieved some important loss. You may have done them in a different order. You may have experienced some stage not included in this list. No matter. Use the ideas to explore your own way of grieving. Notice that the examples include the grieving of objects and beliefs as well as pets and people.

1. Denial—an immediate response to loss; denial is healthy for a short time because it offers protection and a bit of time to adjust before the full impact of the loss hits. It is sometimes called shock. *When Hannah was told that her dog had been run over by a car, she shook her head no and said, "That couldn't be.*

He was here with me fifteen minutes ago." Denial that continues for days interferes with the grieving process. Continued denial can stop grief cold, push the symptoms into the personality or the body, and cause illness.

2. Protest—the angry response to having to give up that which is assumed, depended upon, comforting. *Ross reached into an empty pocket and realized his wallet had been stolen. "Damn! I hate that! Some stupid idiot got a wallet with almost no money, but now I have to cancel all my credit cards. I don't have time to do that. I hate that."* Violence can occur during this period if people lash out to punish or to take the law into their own hands. *When Tammy "stole" Ginny's boyfriend, Ginny broke into Tammy's locker and poured honey in her jacket pockets.*

3. Sadness—the physical response of pain in the stomach and the chest, tightness in the throat, burning eyes, tears, and crying. *Tessa attended the good-bye dinner for her friend who was moving away, but Tessa didn't feel like eating. Her stomach hurt and the food tasted awful.*

4. Fear—the result of facing our separateness, of facing ourselves without this valued thing or person we lost. *After Fred lost his job, he worried that he would never find another. Ginny worried that she would never find a new boyfriend. Fear and sadness can trigger a period of depression.*

5. Intellectual acceptance—the mind accepts the loss but keeps feelings at a distance. *When Angela was told that she would soon be stone deaf, she sighed, then straightened her backbone and said, "I'll learn sign language and I'll learn to read lips."*

6. Emotional acceptance—that deep recognition of the loss—that body, mind, and soul integration of the meaning of the loss, the recognition that the loss is real and that you can live without your valued something. *As Angela's hearing deteriorated, she savored the last sounds of the wind, the doorbell, a book dropped on the floor, her lover's voice, music. She was flooded with sadness, but she planted the sounds deep so she could conjure them up after she entered the world of silence.*

7. New attachments—the stage of returned vitality and readiness to move on. This is an essential step in grieving. It involves truly making a new attachment, not using it as a poor substitute for the old attachment. This often brings up another round of grief for the old attachment, but if the earlier steps

were well done, this visit is shorter and less intense. It may involve more nostalgia or relief than deep grief. *Although Annie and Kevin hated to leave their circle of friends and relatives in Milwaukee, the new job in Minneapolis looked too good to pass up. They moved in the fall, determined to make the new state their home. Each weekend they talked about something they missed and then set out to explore a new part of their city. When old friends came to visit, they talked nostalgically of old times, but soon they were also showing off their new neighborhood. Annie persuaded her folks to get e-mail so they could communicate easily. By April, the couple were solid in their jobs and they felt at home. But June found them disappointed in the gardens at their new home and missing the parade of blossoms they had arranged at their old place. After a brief bout of what they called "flower grieving," they were designing annual beds and planting shrubs they had never tried before. They had made a successful attachment to a new place.*

8. Forgiveness—moving beyond the anger and sense of loss to forgiveness of the assault, of the loss, or perhaps of the unfulfilled promises of the attachment. *Sarah and her travel partner Vivian were planning a hiking tour in Scotland when Vivian was injured in an auto accident that left her immobilized. Sarah raged at the thought of her friend confined in a wheelchair and angrily canceled their trip. After Sarah grieved the loss of traveling with her favorite partner, she was able to accept that Vivian's accident was in no way directed toward her. Forgiving means letting resentment go; when Sarah did this, she was able to empathize fully with Vivian.*

9. Gratitude—the reclaiming of satisfaction and joy for the positives before the loss and even for the lessons of the grieving process. *When Betty was divorced, her primary social group did not accept the divorce and she lost all of her friends except one. One friend of over ten years stood by Betty and listened to many stories about Betty's pain. At the same time the "friend" was having an affair with Betty's ex-husband. When Betty found out, she felt deeply betrayed and stopped all contact with the "friend." After finishing grieving the betrayal and the loss of her friend, Betty was able to say, "This takes away my friend, but it does not take away the good experiences we had during the years before the divorce. I can still cherish those. Also, it is helpful to have learned*

again that friends may not be forever, and for every friend lost, there are six wonderful people out there waiting to become friends."

These are stages of grief. We go through them in any order, for differing lengths of time. We visit some of them only once. Others we loop back through as many times as we need to.

Make the list of things that you need to grieve: an auto accident, loss of a body part or a capability, a child living in chronic pain, a relationship, a betrayal, an embezzlement, a house, a view, a picture, an election, going to war, losing buddies in a war, not going to war.

Anyway you choose to do it, gather up all your losses, be they people, pets, places, abilities, dreams. Put your list of losses in a sturdy chest or a beautiful basket, and vow to fully grieve each loss, one by one. And what is the right way to grieve? Your way is the right way.

Anything Works If You Do It

*Maia had been a member of a helpful grief support group for two years following the death of her husband. She was asked whether she wanted to take over leadership of the group. A gifted therapist who has helped many people recover from the ravages and delayed grief of incest, Maia said she would think about it. She asked the current leader, "In all of your many years of experience in helping people grieve, what have you found that works?" The response was, "Anything works. Everything works, as long as you **do** the grieving! The only thing that doesn't work is not doing it."*

What are some of those ways to grieve? What does the person traveling the grief path do? There are many different routes:

Jonathon created a memorial in honor of his father. On the day it was dedicated he felt finished.

Lois told the story of her husband's death to everyone who would listen. She cried through the whole story. After a few weeks she had cried enough. She said she felt better, and she went about the task of distributing his things to people who would want them.

Adam never cried in front of other people, and he didn't talk about his wife's death much. But he wrote her a letter every day. Just before he went to bed, he read it to her by candlelight. He stored the letters in the old hatbox in which she had kept her sentimental treasures. After a while the letters got shorter and less intense. Finally, he stopped writing them. But when he had a wave of sadness, he would take one of the letters out of the hatbox, read it to himself, and think about the years they had together.

Terry's job as a manager in a large manufacturing plant sometimes included the task of firing people when orders were down. Terry regretted the hardship this imposed on his workers and their families. He knew that letting people go is part of most management jobs, but it did not fit his image of himself as a manager. The day after firing workers, he would have a sick stomach with much vomiting. Not a very good way to handle his grief? Perhaps not, but at least he got the stress out of his body. Wonder what would have happened if he had allowed himself a long, hard cry.

Melissa had always wanted a doll house. Following her divorce, she listed all of the things she needed to grieve. As she felt completed with each one, she bought herself one tiny piece of doll furniture. If that particular grief welled up again, she moved the little chair, or whatever represented that loss, from the shelf to her dresser to remind her to go ahead and feel the feelings and then move on.

Marnie took her time. After Brad's funeral she asked her friend Claudia to come and help clear his clothes out of the closets. Claudia arrived on the appointed day, but Marnie said, "I'm not ready yet. Thanks for coming. We are going to play today instead. That is what I need."

Widow Ellie, in her eighties, lost her ability to walk and to care for herself, but her mind remained razor sharp. Her executor promptly sold her condominium to get money to pay for the nursing home. Ellie was not ready to give up the dream of returning to her home. When she realized that she didn't even know what things had been gotten rid of or where the rest was in storage, her distress was deep. She needed more time to grieve her lost health before she started to grieve her lost home.

Not all of grieving is sad. Laughter finds a place.

The day that Al, a Norwegian immigrant, died, Jean noticed that the highway crew had left a pile of birch saplings in the ditch. Al was a woodsman and Jean wanted to decorate the church with the birch trees for the funeral.

She asked a friend to help; they tied the trees to the trailer hitch and drove the car slowly toward the house. The waiting relatives were perplexed. When Jean opened the door, her cousin asked, "What are you doing? It looks as if you were sweeping the highway." Jean's spontaneous response was, "Well, you see, there is this old Viking tradition that when a full-blooded Norwegian dies you have to sweep the path that the body came home on." They believed her. For a while. During the days of mourning, whenever the birches were handled or mentioned, someone burst into laughter about "the old Viking tradition."

Laughter eases grieving.

When Tanya was faced with a divorce she did not want, she took comfort from a little book filled with silly illustrations and tongue-in-cheek humor, Breaking Up: From Heartache to Happiness in 48 Pages, *by Yolanda Nave.*[3]

Sometimes sadness and joy are mixed.

When Casey's friend, who had suffered long, died, Casey was relieved that her friend's pain was over but was still very sad to lose her.

Monty was glad he did not get the job promotion he did not want, but he also grieved because the competitive part of him hated being passed over.

You can think of many other unique ways that you or others have helped grief take its course.

Rebuilding after the Grief

When the grief cycle is completed, and it takes however long it takes to go through the holidays and the anniversaries, the rebuilding will already have started. The broken beads have been picked up from the floor and the pearls have been saved. Trust has been restored if it has been re-earned. The life force is moving through the body and the soul like the sap nourishing the hazelnut tree. It is time to reach beyond the cloud to the new dream, to solidify new connections, to find new satisfying places to belong. Anniversary dates or a certain song or a particular odor can trigger a wave of grief, but if the grief was for a loved one, those waves gradually become a reminder to cherish the relationship. Do whatever you need to do to complete the circle so you can learn your soul lessons and make new connections.

Chapter 20

I'll Buy You a New Puppy: Helping Children Grieve

Those who do not know how to weep with their whole heart don't know how to laugh either.
—GOLDA MEIR, *PHOENIX*

Allowing Children to Grieve

One of the greatest gifts we can give our children is to help them learn how to grieve. With that golden gift they will be able to transform their losses into riches and their sorrows into strengths. Never try to lock the door on a child's need to grieve. Buying a new puppy before the child has mourned his beloved dog shortchanges the child. Adult efforts to spare a child pain by denying or minimizing a loss doesn't work well for the child. It creates mistrust instead of connection.

Mallory and Marc had families that attended to the grief process. When the dog died, Mallory's family planted a tree in his honor. It was always referred to as Brownie's tree. When the cat died, Marc's family buried it beside the path, in the location the children chose so they could remember it whenever they passed that spot. After the burial, each child told a story about the pet.

Many of us need to learn how to offer children support for their grief.

Lorraine, a warm and caring child-care provider, decided to spare the children in her care the painful feelings about the death of the old dog Logan. Twenty-month-old Emma had been especially attached to this gentle spaniel, and when she couldn't find him she demanded, "Where Wogan?"

Lorraine said, "Logan died last night. Now come and see the new toy I have for you." Emma allowed herself to be distracted, but on the way home she told her daddy, "Wogan die." Since her father did not know the dog's name, he was unable to figure out his little daughter's urgent message. Every few days Emma tried again: "Wogan die, Wogan die!" Finally the dad found out that Logan was the dog's name. "Oh, you've been telling me the dog died. Oh, honeygirl, I'm sorry." For the next few months in the midst of any activity, Emma would suddenly say, "Wogan die." When asked about it, Lorraine explained, "Oh, Logan died months ago. He was old and I didn't want to disturb the children so I just told them Logan died and then we went on with our day."

This loving caregiver, in her effort to spare the children, deprived them of the crucial learning that when you lose something dear, you honor both the loss and the lost. Children need rituals. It helps them feel secure in a world they don't yet understand.

When Kathy's beloved cat, Essie, died, she let the children in her care see and touch the cat. Together they buried it in the backyard. Some of the children cried. Kathy talked with the children about Essie and how they would miss her. The children painted a rock with beautiful colors and placed it as a marker. When the parents came to pick up the children, Kathy helped each child tell his parent about what happened to Essie. Kathy sent a note about Essie with the child who was picked up by a taxi driver.

If Emma's dad had understood the *Wogan* message the first time, he could have explained children's need for timely ritual to Lorraine. He also could have attended to Emma's loss: *You really liked Logan, didn't you? Do you miss him? Yes, he is in the backyard, but he isn't alive anymore. He can't bark or wag his tail, but his bones will be there for a long time. I'm glad Logan was your friend.*

Gradually Emma learns through this experience, and many more, that she is separate, that she can't keep what she values just because she wants it, that separations bring grief, and that she can bond again and live a joyful life anyway.

Bonding and codependence are not the same. It is important to keep our individual worth centered in ourselves, even in our most intimate bonds. Being strongly bonded to people, things, goals, and beliefs gives us energy and brings us satisfaction, but our lives depend on ourselves, and when we lose one of our valued entities, we need to grieve fully so we will be able to attach to new sources of energy and satisfaction.

When you think children are too young to understand, use small words, give simple explanations, be straight.

No Secrets

There is a Yiddish proverb that says, *Truth is the safest lie.* The chart on pages 186–187 provides information about how children react to grief at different ages. In the long run, secrets usually undermine trust and weaken the family system. When someone in the family circle dies, take children of any age to the funeral.

Liam was four when his grandmother died. In an effort to spare his feelings, the family left him with a babysitter during the funeral and told him Grandma had gone away. Liam waited and waited for her return and became anxious when other family members went away because he feared they, too, might not return. If Liam had attended the funeral, he might not have understood what was going on, but he would have a basis for asking questions.

Lana, also four, attended the funeral of her grandmother who had been cremated. On the way home, she said, "When will Grandma come to play with me again?" Her dad held her gently and said, "Grandma isn't coming again. That's what dead means. But we have her picture and her voice on tape, and we will talk about her as often as you want. We can draw pictures about things we did with her. I'll miss her. I bet you will too. But Grandma isn't sick anymore." And Dad explained his beliefs about the afterlife.

For children five and older, being part of the funeral preparation can be very demystifying, particularly if they can create some of their own rituals.

Six-year-old Will had already lost a pet and moved from one house to another. From experiencing those two big losses, he had begun to learn how to grieve big losses. When his grandfather died suddenly, Will was included in the activities of the following days. He went to the funeral home, was present at the choosing of the casket, went to the florist, looked at the pictures of the bouquets, went to the home of his cousin where people had brought in food and were comforting the crying widow. During the visitation period at the funeral home, which involved an open casket, Will roamed the building but returned often to lean on the edge of the casket and stare at his grandfather's body. He had already been told that the body would be stiff and cold. He was neither encouraged to nor dissuaded from touching. He did touch, then ran to his mother and said, "Grandpa's not stiff; he's hard. Does that happen to everybody when they die? Do they get hard?"

Later he tugged on his mother and said, "Take me to Mr. Belts." The funeral director had made friends with Will when they had met earlier. Mother took Will into the director's office and told Mr. Belts that Will wanted to speak with him. The tall, friendly man stood up to his full height, walked around his desk, and said, "What can I do for you?" The six-year-old said, "The box Grandpa is in is way too deep. It doesn't need to be that deep; he's not that thick. What is underneath it?" Mr. Belts smiled and said, "Get your cousins if they want to come, and I'll take you downstairs into the vault and show you."

The cousins, who were slightly older, had been withdrawn from the casket, not wishing to talk with people, mostly sitting by themselves; they now followed eagerly. The director took the children into the vault, lifted the lid on a casket, showed them that there was a mattress, that below that was a spring, and below that was empty space. The older children were silent. Will asked, "Why is there all that space? Grandpa doesn't need it." The director said, "It may seem silly to you, but some families like to see the casket looking big. Perhaps they are thinking about how big that dead person was in their life." Then Will said, "But why is there a mattress? He can't feel anything." The director smiled and said, "Well, I think the mattress is to make the survivors, the people who are still alive, feel better. That's why it looks soft; that's why it is a pretty color. You are right; your grandpa doesn't feel anything. But it is good to do some things that will help the people who are left feel better." Will asked if Mr. Belts would lift the spring and let him stand in the casket. He needed to know all he could about Grandpa's casket. The older cousins didn't even giggle nervously. They were too busy letting the directness of the six-year-old and his need for concrete information help them on their journeys.

For the next ten years Will experienced the death of an immediate family member every two years. When he was sixteen and his parents went to his school for a regular school conference, one of his teachers said, "We need to talk to you about Will and death." His parents were startled. "Why, what about Will and death?" they asked.

"Well, it turns out that Will is the school's best grief counselor and we

hope you don't mind. This year children in two different families have lost a parent. In both cases those children had never attended a funeral and they had no idea what to expect. The one who was most helpful to them was Will, and we want you to know that we appreciate what he does." That evening Mom brought up the subject, "Will, Mr. Davis told us that when kids have lost a parent you are the one who is helpful in talking with them."

"Oh, really?" Will said.

"Yes, what do you say to them?" Mom asked, curiously.

"That's easy. I tell them what is going to happen, the whole thing. Some kids have never been to funerals. I tell them there are a lot of rules about funerals so even if you think you know them all, you probably won't. Whenever something happens and you don't know what to do, just sit down and cry because then somebody will come and take care of you and tell you what to do next." Will's dad asked, "Will, how did you learn to do that?" Will looked at his dad with an expression of disbelief and said, "Dad, it's nothing special; it's just that our family has had so many funerals, we all had to get good at it."

It is not our wish that children would have to "get good at" dealing with deaths. It is, however, fortunate when a child, by whatever means, learns how to grieve. This child had the good fortune to be in a situation that supported his grieving and the good sense to learn the lessons. (A book for adults helping a child grieve the loss of a parent is J. William Worden's *Children and Grief: When a Parent Dies*.)[1]

One can only hope that the children who are experiencing unnatural deaths in their families in the war-torn parts of the world are getting the support they need along the way and will have the support they need later on to process those griefs and be able to transform those losses.

Continuing Losses

Will's story is about a death that is a sudden and complete loss. Many children's losses are continuous, but the principle of sharing, guidance, being able to talk about it, having people to rebond with is the same. There are many kinds of continuous losses. Living with a family member who has a chronic illness, having a chronic illness or disability, divorce, being orphaned, being adopted, and constantly moving are some examples. This is the process that occurs for children who are living in homes with alcoholism or other addictions. If they attend

Alateen, they find that they are not alone, that they have a place to tell their stories and not be discounted, and that they have peers with whom they can share coping skills. Sending a child to Alateen does not mean that the parent should not confront his or her addiction and recover from it. It means that the child can receive support from Alateen as well as from the family in recovery.

Double Separation

Sometimes a child will become anxious and the parent will not know what caused the child's distress. When that happens, look for delayed distress or double distress. In her book, *Learning to Say Goodbye: Starting School and Other Early Childhood Separations*, Nancy Ballaban tells the story of a three-year-old girl who enters a new day care, kissing her mother good-bye and moving into the new situation with confidence and enthusiasm.[2] Weeks later she becomes tearful and inconsolable when her mother leaves, and the mother is not able to identify anything unusual that would have precipitated this new behavior. The fact that the little girl's family had moved three months before and there had been excitement and busyness and maybe no attention to grieving had left a reservoir of unresolved grief in her. Only when she became comfortable in her new home and with her new child-care provider did the three-year-old feel safe enough to express her grief.

Honor the Child's Need to Grieve

Never discount a child's grief. Discounting means making the grief somehow less. Discounting occurs in one of four ways, or at four levels. The first level says there is no need for the grief because the event is not one that should be grieved: *You don't need to grieve about moving because we had to move for Daddy's job.* Or: *Embassy families move. That's just how it is.*

The second level discounts the importance of the grief: *I don't know why she would be grieving for that old house because our new house is better; her room is bigger and more cheerful.*

Discounting a grief because there seems to be no help for it is the third level: *Nobody knows how to help children grieve; they just have to work it through.*

The fourth level is that of personal impotence: *I see that my child is grieving. I would like to help her, but I don't have a clue what to do.*

Parents and child-care providers both need to take a position of empowerment: *I will notice that there is a loss. I will attempt to discover how serious this loss is to this child. There are things that can be done to help children deal with loss. I will find out what they are and I will do them.* (There is more about discounting in chapter 2, pages 14–18.) One of the ways we help children grieve is by using the time-in puzzle pieces. We **attend**, we pay attention to what the grief seems to be about. We also **ask:** *Do you want to tell me about it? Do you want to tell me what you liked about your old house? Do you want to tell me what you miss about your old house?* Another way to use time-in with grief is to use the **act** puzzle piece: Perhaps spend more time with the child, maybe time doing happy things but also unstructured time, just being with the child, hanging out, allowing the time and safety for the hurts to surface. Offer touch, pats, messages, cuddles, hugs, kisses, even with big kids who say they don't need it. The parent can say, *Well, I need it. I want to sit beside you while we talk about your loss. . . . No, I won't. . . . All right, then I want to sit beside you while we watch a TV show.*

Rituals

Another way that parents take **action** is by creating rituals to honor the loss and to honor the grieving. Use the healing rituals described in chapter 18 on pages 167–169. Use a book. For little children, coloring books like Marge Heegaard's The Drawing Out Feelings Series can help kids deal with death, divorce, illness, and remarriage.[3] A workbook like Carole Gesme's *Help for Kids! Understanding Your Feelings About Having a Parent in Prison or Jail* can help children who have a parent who is incarcerated.[4] Her *Help for Kids! Understanding Your Feelings About Moving* guides children through a series of steps for saying good-bye to the old places, the old friends, the old situation, and hello to the new.[5] Younger children can play out some of their grief with toys, a family of dolls, two houses, a moving van or truck. Use a storybook. There are many children's books about helping children with divorce or separation and other losses.[6] Read the book yourself first and don't use one that glosses over the grieving. Don't use a book that in any way lays blame for the loss or the responsibility for dealing with the loss solely on the child.

For older children, for teenagers, don't depend on their assessment of the grief, particularly around a death. Their need to be cool or their unfamiliarity with the grieving process may cause them to say no, they don't need to do this; they don't need to do part of this; they'd rather stay in school. Stewart's grandpa died suddenly the week of school exams.

Stewart chose to skip the preparations for the funeral and take his exams. He was confident and convincing, and his parents agreed. His exam grades were two levels below what he had expected. The depression that he experienced afterward lasted for weeks.

Stewart had lost his birth father when he was two, and the unresolved grief from that was triggered by the death of his grandfather. Perhaps if he had been able to go through every step of the funeral preparations, to have experienced all of the support given to the family by the community, to have been present and allowed to cry if he was able to, as often and as long as he needed to, he would have resolved some of his old grief.

It is particularly traumatic for adolescents when a friend dies. Fortunately, many schools offer counseling to students after the death of a classmate. Marilyn Gootman's book *When a Friend Dies: A Book for Teens About Grieving and Healing* is written for teens, but is helpful to adults as well.[7]

Grief support groups can be helpful to children and to families. There may be an excellent local program in your area. Or you may turn to a widespread organization such as Rainbows.[8]

Little Losses

Death is the big loss, but remember, any loss can have a powerful impact on children. A child who has lost a favorite toy through your carelessness can be comforted by your sincere regret: *How can I make it up to you? I want to make it right,* may be more comforting than your offer to buy a new one. If he has lost a favorite toy due to his own carelessness, the question is, *How can you make this up to yourself?*

When the Child's Loss Is Also Your Loss

Sometimes it's difficult to focus on helping a child grieve because you are grieving the same loss. Contributing to that difficulty is that the parent and the child may work through the grieving path at a very different pace. The adult may be deep in sadness. The child may, for comfort, have temporarily returned to denial and be unsympathetic to the sadness. The parent may have moved to acceptance, and the child may still be experiencing anger and fear. Think how easily that could happen around a divorce.

It is often helpful to have someone outside the family talk with the child about the loss. If the child is old enough to understand, talk about the grief path and the fact that Mommy or Daddy is feeling sad right now and that the child will feel sad at another time or vice versa. Adults who are unable to support a child through the stages of grieving need to take a long look at their own process and where they are with their own grieving. Perhaps they are denying part of their own journey. If so, they need to correct that because this is unfair to the child. If good friends and books are not sufficient, seek the help of a support group or a professional. Unresolved grief wrenches the soul.

Developmental Stages and Children's Response: A Grief Chart

The following chart was developed by the Annie Tran Center for Grief and Loss in Prosser, Washington.[9] Children and their parents who have experienced a death, divorce, or most any loss are helped at this center.

All children, even the youngest, will respond when a significant loved one dies. As caregiving adults, we can be most helpful when we understand how children perceive death and be willing to meet them on that level of understanding. Love the children for whom you are making lasting impressions. It is only from love that we can give love, and our love is the greatest gift we can give a child grieving the death of a loved one.

While the following information is not comprehensive, it does provide some basis of understanding and can serve as a helpful guide to those of us who are privileged to walk with children on their journey through grief.

Be willing to walk with children on their grief path. When we can *hold* the child's grief without taking it upon ourselves or into ourselves, without taking ownership of it, we are free to feel deep empathy. We can stay focused on the child's need rather than on our need.

We empathize with his grief and help him work through it. We do not try to take it away from him even if we are grieving the same loss. We help children stay connected with their own soul growth as they wrestle with their loss. We let the journey strengthen their connection with us.

Approximate Developmental Age:	*Grief reactions:*	*Approach:*
Infant to 2 years	General distress, sleeplessness, shock, despair, protest. Child responds to parental grief.	A consistent nurturing figure. Include in funeral rituals.
Ages 2–5	Confusion, agitation at night, frightening dreams, regression. Children often understand that a profound event has occurred. May seem unaffected. Repeated questioning. Child's understanding of death is limited.	Simple, honest words and phrases. Reassurance. Securing loving environment. Drawing, reading books, playing together. Include in funeral rituals.
Ages 5–8	Wants to understand death in a concrete way, but thinks it "won't happen to me." Denial, anger, sorrow. General distress, confused, disoriented. May behave as though nothing has happened. Desire to conform with peers. May ask questions repeatedly. May need physical activity on a regular basis.	Simple, honest words and phrases. Answer questions simply and honestly. Look for confused thinking. Offer physical outlets. Reassurance about the future. Drawing, reading books, playing together. Include in funeral rituals.

Approximate Developmental Age:	Grief reactions:	Approach:
Ages 8–12	Shock, denial, anxiety, distress. Facade of coping. Finality of death understood, phobic behavior, morbid curiosity, peer conformity. May need physical activity on a regular basis.	Answer questions directly and honestly. Reassurance about future. Create times to talk about feelings. Offer physical outlets. Reading. Include in funeral plans and rituals.
Adolescents	Shock, anxiety, distress, denial, anger, depression, withdrawal, aggression. May react similarly to the way adults do but have fewer coping mechanisms. May feel young and vulnerable and need to talk.	Allow and encourage ventilation of feelings; encourage peer support. Groups are helpful. Appropriate reading. Involve other supportive adults. Maintain consistent environment. Include in funeral plans and rituals. Encourage involvement of family.

Chapter 21

I Don't Know What to Say: Helping Adults Grieve

Did you call Al?
No.
Why not?
I wouldn't know what to say.
But he just lost his son.
Yah, I know.

—JEAN ILLSLEY CLARKE

Sometimes we don't know what to say to a friend who is grieving because we didn't learn the words. We want to connect, but we don't know how. We need a flash card that gives us options:

- I'm sorry.
- My heart goes out to you.
- There aren't any words, but I'm here for you.
- I hold you in my heart.
- Know that I am thinking about you.
- You are in my prayers.
- This is tragic. I'm so sorry.
- This is really awful!
- I want to hear about it when you are ready to talk.

Sometimes we don't know what to say because we are scared the same thing might happen to us. Sometimes we can't talk because what happened activates a loss we haven't grieved. Or we may be afraid of adding more pain by saying or doing the wrong thing; so we do nothing. Other times we are embarrassed about sympathizing because we are celebrating that it didn't happen to us.

How to Help Others Grieve

The following are ways we can support others in their grieving. The list may give you some ideas or may trigger other ideas that work for you.

Listen

We can listen, really listen to the story as many times as the person wants to tell it.

Once a week Janet listened to Margaret tell of the shock of her cousin's suicide. Janet noticed that each time the story was a little less detailed, a little less intense. After six weeks Margaret said, "I don't need to tell it today. Let's talk about something else."

Give gifts

We can give gifts. Flowers, cards, books, food, or offers of help are thoughtful gifts for a person who has just experienced a deep loss. It's important to remember that a gift offers comfort, not a replacement. *I'll buy you a new ring* to the woman who has just lost her treasured wedding ring can be the same "don't grieve" message as *I'll buy you a new puppy* is to a child who's just lost a pet. Instead: *I'm sorry you lost your ring. I brought you a blooming plant to remind you that I love you.* Later on a new ring might be appreciated.

Support their place on the grief path

We can track where the person is on the grief path and provide support there.

Carter seemed to be moving along after his divorce, but this day he is revisiting anger. He storms around the room and smacks his fist in his hand as he tells his friend Dylan how disgusting, awful, mean, vindictive, and destructive his ex-wife is. Dylan listens and nods. He refrains from saying, "Okay, you've gone on long enough." He does not argue or reason. He lets Carter ventilate, even if the accusations are not all true. When Carter quiets, Dylan asks, "Carter, what is the one thing that we could do right now that would both help the situation and help you feel better?"

Let them grieve as they want to

We can let people grieve the way they want to grieve.

Reverend Rita Morales was in her office on a Tuesday morning when a parishioner she had seldom seen slipped in. "What can I do for you?" Rita said.

"I need some grief counseling. I just found out a dear friend was killed in an auto accident," the parishioner replied.

"All right, what shall we do? Would you like me to read from the Bible?" she asked.

"No, I just want to tell you how unfair and awful it is and kick your wastepaper basket and make lots of noise and cry."

Rita turned her body openly toward the grieving parishioner and listened as the woman stormed and wept. Suddenly the woman stopped raging and knelt before Rita. She said, "I think my heart is breaking. Will you put your hand over my heart and heal it with your hand, not with words?" Rita laid a loving hand on the woman's chest and prayed silently. After a few minutes the woman gently removed the hand, stood up, said a calm thank you, and was gone.

Touch can be a powerful healer at times of loss.

Don't say, "I know how you feel"

We can express empathy, that quality of being fully there for the other person. The *Oxford Dictionary* says that to empathize is to fully comprehend. But it doesn't say *what* is fully comprehended. When we empathize with another person who is grieving, we need to attend to the depth of the grief. But if we say, *I know just how you feel,* we risk offending. Grief is personal. *You can't possibly know how I feel; you are not me!*

We can say, *I know how I felt when I lost a friend, my house burned, my cat died, I was divorced . . . It was tough.* But we do not know how the other person feels. And we must be especially careful if we have not had a similar experience. If we have never had a cat die, a house burn, or been divorced, there is no way we can wrap our minds around the many kinds of grief that can surround that experience.

We need to be especially careful when comforting someone who has lost a child. Not only is the child lost to that person, but the great contract in the sky that says parents are to die first has been broken. If we have not lost a child ourselves, the best we can say is, *I can't know how you feel because I have not lost a child, but my heart is with you.* Some people who have lost children find comfort in books. There are some examples in the notes at the end of this book.[1]

Attend to the dream

We can look at a lost dream. *After Travis left for college his cat Ivan got feline leukemia. When Ivan started to suffer and the vet said the cat would slowly die, Travis's mom had the vet give the cat a lethal injection. During the winter holidays, Travis moped and mourned the loss of his pet. His mom justified her action, explaining over and over again how sick Ivan had been. Travis was not comforted. Finally he hung his head and growled, "I was going to pick him up after I graduated from college and start house-keeping with him."* A dream is a dream and the loss of any dream, large or small, leaves a hole and the hole hurts. In Ted Bowman's book *Loss of Dreams: A Special Kind of Grief,* he describes lost dreams:

> A loss of dreams relates to images or pictures of our personal world that we create and to which we attach strong emotional invest-ment . . . the way things are supposed to be. . . .
>
> . . . If we don't know that we have experienced a loss of dreams or have words to describe our experience, it will be hard, very hard, to grieve that loss and, as a result, we may find our grieving of other losses unfinished or tainted by an overlay of something mysterious which we can now call loss of dreams.
>
> Some people take their grief and turn it into a cause. They become the advocates for others like themselves, taking on hospitals or drunk drivers, the divorce courts, or an unsafe workplace. Such transforma-tion of energy and attention can be healing . . . as long as it is not done at the cost of grieving the loss of dreams. Action can serve to aid us in avoiding our grieving or it can be the outlet for grieving. Check yourself and your process.[2]

Tell a story

> *The power to dream arises from a drive of creating itself. We search for the next world and in the process of searching (dreaming) the next world is created.*
> —*Nate Eppley*[3]

To help another person grieve, we can tell a story of hope. It could be about our own or another's experience, but it must end with the transformation to a new dream, new attachments, new connections. It could be a fairy tale, as there is lots of wisdom in fairy tales and myths. It could be a story you created for a specific loss. Here is one I made up for women about divorce that could be used for many losses. Before you read this or another story, tell the person to whom you are reading to get comfortable, preferably with eyes closed, and to let the story in.

The Colored Bird

Once upon a time or yesterday there was a young girl who lived far away or close by. She was a dreamy girl or an outgoing girl, a tall girl or a short girl, a dark girl or a light girl, and she had her own special kind of intelligence. In her knowing part, she knew that she had an important contribution to make. She thought about how she would offer her gifts to the world, a little or a lot, quietly or dramatically, but she always assumed that when she did, it would be in the right way and at the right time for her. And so she made her home and took care of the people in it. Things were going not so well or very well when slowly or suddenly her world turned upside down and she said, *"Ouch, that hurts. I didn't expect it. This is not what I bargained for. This is not how it is supposed to be."* So she sat on a tuffet and cried and cried until she felt a gentle nudge on her shoulder. A little bird, brown or black or yellow, sat on her shoulder and spoke softly into her ear: *"You are right. This is not what you bargained for. But it is—it is this way. So there are two things you must do. Only two, but you must do them both. First, list all the things you lost and grieve them, every one. Get off your tuffet and find some folks to help you do that. Do not do it alone! You can do it fast or slowly, quietly or with a great gnashing of teeth and thrashing about. But you must grieve every loss or they will make you sick.*

"Second, you must carry on—you have a special kind of intelligence and an important contribution to make. And if you do both of those things, grieve your losses and carry on, another bird will come to sit on your shoulder. Not a brown or black or yellow bird, but the bluebird of happiness. Now go and do what I bid you!" And so the little girl from once upon a time or yesterday, who lived far away or close by, did what the little bird said, and the bluebird of happiness came to her many times. More than she expected.

Let the person listening to this story sit quietly as long as she wants to. Do not ask questions or offer interpretations. Let her think her own thoughts.

Here is a story I offer for men about lost career dreams. Before you read, ask the person to whom you are reading to make himself comfortable, preferably with his eyes closed, and to let the story in.

The Boy Who Would Be the King

Long ago in the days of dragons, or just yesterday, there lived a young boy who dreamed of being the king. He lived in an unusual kingdom where the crown was not passed down by divine right, but by selection. When the king got old, there would be a great search across the land to find the man who would be the next king. The lad dreamed of being the king. He would be a powerful monarch who would rule wisely and be much loved by his people. So this young lad who was very tall or not so tall, heavy or slim, dark or light, quick of tongue or slow to speak, studied his lessons and did his chores and practiced the arts of being kingly. He didn't know exactly what those arts were, but he was pretty sure that one of them was to protect the people of the kingdom from dragons.

Now a dragon named Ofed lived in the hills nearby, so the lad spent days and weeks observing Ofed and learning dragon ways. Eventually Ofed and the lad became friends and they spent many hours together. Sometimes they fought each other; sometimes they just talked about why dragons and people have such a hard time getting along. Gradually, the lad began to feel confident that as king he could handle the dragons in the hills.

But, there was another dragon. The one inside the lad called anger or fear or greed or sadness or shame. That one was harder to handle. It often got him in trouble, so he fought with it and tried to hold it down, but that only made it grow stronger.

As the years passed, the lad did what lads do. He became a man, he did his work, he took care of his family, and he was loyal to his friends. He did a very good job or an all right job or a not-so-very-good job, but he always felt restless because he wanted to be the king.

Then one day his world turned upside down. He learned that the new king had been selected, and he had not been chosen. Not chosen? How could that be? This he had wanted. This he had waited for.

At first the angry dragon rose inside of him. He roared and cursed and blamed the selection committee. He even blamed the king! Then he grew depressed. He neglected his family and his friends and wouldn't tell them what was wrong. Then he pretended he had never wanted to be king at all. But that didn't help either.

Now the man hadn't seen the dragon Ofed for a long, long time, but he thought he might feel better if he went and had a good old-fashioned fight with Ofed, so he dragged himself across the valley and up the hill. He bellowed a challenge for Ofed to come out for a terrible battle.

Ofed came out, but he didn't circle to start the fight. Instead he put a massive taloned paw on his friend's shoulder and with a gentle but irresistible shove, forced him to sit down. Then he rumbled very firmly, *"My friend, it is time for you to wake up. You have wanted to be the king; you have prepared to be the king; you have waited to be the king. You are not going to be the king. That is the way it is.*

*"Now you must grieve the loss of your dream of being the king. Get out of your funk and find people who will listen to the story of your lost dream, people who care about you and will support you. Tell your story enough times so it starts not to hurt so much. Begin by telling it to me every day this week. Then figure out all the things you do well and build a new vision of your life. Let your family and friends back in. Make them part of the vision. If you do not do both of these things, the angry dragon within you will eat you alive, and you will become a walking dead man. If you do both of these, and you must do both, the anger and restlessness will pass and **you** will become the kind of king that you were always meant to be."*

So the man who was very tall or not so tall, heavy or slim, dark or light, quick of tongue or slow to speak did his grieving and made his vision. With his friend Ofed, he found a way to help dragons and people get along. Gradually or very quickly the restlessness faded away and anger became his friend. And in the time that followed, right away or after a long time, he became much loved and admired because the people were no longer afraid of the dragons. And there were those who said he made a greater contribution to the people and the kingdom than even the king had made.

The person listening to this story may want to be silent for a time after hearing the story. Do not ask questions. Let him think his own thoughts.

Offer a Healing Ritual

When we wish to help others in their grief, we could offer to do a healing ritual for current losses or for old unhealed hurts. We can use one we already know, we can make up one, or we can use one from Elaine Childs-Gowell's book *Good Grief Rituals*.[4]

Healing rituals can be physical activities or visualizations. Here is my rather long visualization, but it is a powerful ritual and can be used to heal wounds from any old loss, large or small, at any age. Read it aloud or read it onto an audiotape so your friend (or you) can use it again and again for any number of old losses.

This guided imagery, called "Grieving an Old Loss," will let you create an image of what should have happened for you when you first experienced your grief. In this guided imagery, you will be asked first to visualize the people whom you would like support from, and then to visualize them coming to you and hearing your pain, and then to visualize the gifts you would have liked to have received. If that feels and seems like something that would have been helpful to you, you can experience that now, even though you may not have had it earlier.

Will you make yourself comfortable in the way that is comfortable for you? You may want to lie down; you may want to get a cushion.

As you are getting your body ready and closing your eyes and starting to breathe deeply, think about some of the messages that told you not to grieve. Think about times when people ignored your need to grieve. Think about some of the unhelpful things people said, such as *Are you still doing that?* or, *When are you gonna be through with that?* or, *Well, my loss was bigger than your loss!* or, *The statute of limitations has run out on that.* Realize that we live in a culture that, because it doesn't know how to handle grief well, tells us to please not have it. If you ever picked up any of those messages and thought you should believe them, forgive yourself for that right now. Bathe yourself in forgiveness. Then let the awareness come into your mind that there are many stages of grief, and there are some griefs that are with us always. Long years after, we may revisit them for a short time with a poignant feeling. Then be aware that, when we have allowed ourselves to feel all of our feelings, we can get to a time when that poignant feeling is one of brief longing, but no longer one of deep pain. Give yourself permission to see that in the future without having to hurry toward it.

Now think of the particular grief you are going to mourn today. Just one. One. Now be in a room, not this one, but a room or some other space that you know and that is large enough and comfortable enough. I will call your space a room. Look around your room. Smell your room. Hear the sounds in your room. And now see the people whom you want there. Maybe they are people who did support you at the time. You can also put there some people whom you wanted support from but who didn't know how to give it. Today they will know how. They will be able to come to you fully and give you what you need.

So see your people.

And now from a distance, looking at your room with your people and yourself, hear yourself telling them your story about your grief, and that this time you are telling them all the parts of the story . . . and that there is enough time . . . and that they are attending . . . and that you are telling the things that you didn't remember to tell . . . or that you thought it wasn't safe to tell. Look at your room from a distance and see yourself telling with people listening. Notice that they are there as long as you need them.

And now see that quite some time has passed, and they have listened to your whole story. You have told your whole story. Now see them moving into groups. See them making clusters of three or four people. Feel the one person you chose to sit beside you while those clusters go off to decide upon their gifts to you. Feel the comfort of the person beside you. Know deep in your bones that grieving is not to be done alone. Feel that person beside you.

Now notice that the clusters are starting to come back. Some of the people have things in their hands that you can't see yet. And now you are standing up and the first cluster is approaching you. See who is in it . . . take the things they are offering . . . let the other clusters come in the order in which they want to come. They are bringing whatever you want: cards, flowers, songs, poems, books, laughter, hugs, dances, a pin, a ring, love.

And now notice whether all of the groups have come to you or whether there are still more groups to come. As you notice that, look beyond your groups and see that there are more comforting groups out there, more than you could count, more who are there ready to hear your story and ready to give gifts to you. Many more than you knew were there. More than you can see.

And now know that this is your room and these are your people . . .

and these are your gifts . . . and you can bring the gifts back here with you. . . . This is your room, and it will always be there. You can return to it later as many times as you want to, and the people will be here with their gifts. So, know that the room is yours and you can visit it anytime, before you go to sleep at night, when you are on a walk, when you are spending some time alone, when you're by a very good friend who will sit quietly with you while you visit your room. You can come here as often as you want to. Any time you need some soul healing. You deserve this comfort.

And now hold the gifts, see the gifts, hear the gifts, bring the gifts back with you as you say good-bye to your room for now and slowly move yourself fully back into this room here, today.

All right. Stretch gently or give yourself a little shake. Move fully into your adult self. Stand up, straighten your back. You may want to be by yourself now. You may want to journal. You may want to talk with someone. Do whatever will help you keep the healing power of this experience. Don't be surprised if it is easier to make or deepen connections now that you have your room and your gifts and your new healing of this old grief.

With an Open Heart

You can invent many more ways to support other people's grief journeys. It is important to offer help with an open heart, to keep your grief separate from theirs, and to offer hope. This is your gift of time, energy, and love or friendship to help them be able to connect more fully with others in the future.

Remember that joy and sorrow are neighbors, and if sorrow is in your house today, joy is outside, waiting to come in.

Chapter 22

Beyond the Frozen Winter of Grief

It's good to be back in life.

— MAGGIE LAWRENCE

When grief is no longer fresh and when old connections have been honored and new connections are being made, the day comes when, as one friend said, "It's good to be back in life." Then sooner or later comes the time of surprise. The time one thought could never happen. The time when the memories are there, but the cutting edges have been dulled and golden moments return. Listen to how this daddy calls up the wise one within himself after the death of a pet and a friend's accident to help his child understand about golden moments.

"Dad, what are golden moments? What do you mean gold? Gold won't bubble up from Chipper's grave, or Gary won't get a gold leg!"

"No, my child, this kind of gold is not about money or jewels or even paid-up credit cards. These riches are about something much more precious, something that is inside of you and me. It means that our hearts get bigger. After you have grieved for Chipper and are ready for a new hamster, you will find that your heart will be big enough to love two little furry animals. They will be alike in some ways, and you will love that. Some ways they will be different, and you will also love that. A new pet will not replace Chipper. He was your friend and he will always be in your heart. But after a while you won't cry for him anymore. You might be sad for a moment now and then, but mostly you will remember all the fun you had. How he giggled when you fed him and the special times like when he crawled underneath your birthday presents and we couldn't find him and we thought he was going to miss your party."

"But what about Gary? The doctor said his hurt leg might stop growing. How can his heart get bigger?"

"Maybe it won't for a while. He may be very angry and sad. He might be scared that he won't be able to run as fast as you other boys. And maybe he won't. But, after he does his mad and his sad and his scared, he will find other ways to have fun with you, and he will have a special feeling called empathy—he will have a special way with all creatures that have a physical problem to overcome. If he does his grieving well and finds his new strengths, you and he may become even better friends. Be kind to Gary and help him now, but don't worry about him. Gary is strong and courageous, and I predict that his heart will grow bigger."

"Daddy, do you feel sad sometimes?"

"Sure do. Remember I told you your grandma died before you were born. I was so sad she never got to meet you. She would have thought you were wonderful. But that was not to be. Now when I think of her, I feel sad and glad at the same time."

"How can you do that, Daddy?"

"Well, you know I sing in a choir. You've heard us sing. In some of the songs there is a high part called an obbligato. Katie Williams sings those beautiful high notes just like your grandma used to, clear and true, and when I hear Katie's voice soar way above the rest, I get sad tears in my eyes, and I'm also glad because Katie reminds me of my mom and it's like I touch her for a moment. The wonderful things in your life are never really lost if you choose to keep them."

"But Daddy, wouldn't it be better if we never had to hurt?"

"I don't know son, because that's not possible. You see, grief is a mystery teacher and each of us has to figure out what the lessons are for us. But this I know: After we grieve, we are stronger. Always remember, whenever you lose something or somebody or some dream, take time to say good-bye so you'll be ready to say hello to the next one. Especially to the new dream. Nothing ever was that was not first a dream. So connect with your new dream, and tell me about it whenever you want to."

Beyond the frozen winter of grief there is a different understanding, new energy, and the ability to connect in more profound ways.

Some people use their losses to fuel their energies for new dreams and important causes. Nobel Peace Prize–winner Elie Wiesel, concentration camp survivor, has become a spokesman for Holocaust survivors and an advisor to presidents.[1] Respected and revered, Bruno Bettelheim, another Holocaust survivor, put his hard-earned understanding into the service of children and families.[2] Candice Lightner started MADD, Mothers Against Drunk Driving.[3] Most of us don't do things that are as noticeable as those. But we do what we can in our situation and with our talents.

After a while you learn that even sunshine burns if you get too much. So you plant your own garden and decorate your own soul, instead of waiting for someone to bring you flowers. And you learn that you really can endure, that you really are strong. And that you really do have worth and that you keep learning. With every good-bye you learn [to] let your heart grow bigger.
                —Author unknown

SECTION **V**

Reaching Out—
Reaching In

Chapter 23

Did I Do Something to Offend You? Clear Boundaries — Clean Connections

Good fences make good neighbors.

—ROBERT FROST, "MENDING WALL"

Fences

Robert Frost is frequently credited with the saying "Good fences make good neighbors." In his poem, it is his neighbor who makes that assertion while the two men are repairing a wall, replacing stones the winter's freezing and thawing have displaced. Frost challenges this assertion with "Something there is that doesn't love a wall."[1] So which is it? Do good fences make good neighbors or does something in nature abhor a fence? I think both.

Our personal boundaries are our edges, our skin, or the energy line where our personal spaces end. How we respect the edges of others and how others respect our edges have a great deal to do with the quality of our relationships and with our ability to establish and maintain connections.

Listen to some ways we indicate that we are protecting our own boundaries or having difficulty with the boundaries of other people:

- "He has a concrete mind, all mixed up and firmly set."
- "She is so pushy, she steamrolls over everyone."
- "He is hard to reach."
- "She blows with the wind; she will never take a stand."
- "He is always ready to take offense."
- "She is so codependent, she has to ask someone else what her opinion is."

Healthy personal boundaries are strong enough to protect us and flexible enough to let others in when we want to. One of the jobs of parents is to provide babies with enough closeness, enough skin contact, enough immediate response so the infant will be satisfied and trustful that the adults are available and will be ready to start the long journey toward building her own boundaries, toward the place of respect for self, others, property, and nature.

The template for the individual's way of relating in groups is laid down in the family setting. Here the child first learns how to make connections, how to judge their appropriateness, how to identify and evaluate boundaries and to figure out the norms of a group. Children who grow up in a family where the teachings about boundaries were too haphazard, too rigid, or lacking, may face a daunting number of situations in childhood and adult life where they need to learn new skills in order to be accepted in a group. Fortunately, people can learn new skills at any age. Sometimes that is easy to do. Other times it is very challenging.[2]

In her soon-to-be-published book *Get Off My Foot: Boundaries and the Relationship Dance,* Joan Casey explores the implications of healthy and unhealthy personal boundaries.[3] You can use her two charts to help you identify areas of your life in which you use healthy boundaries and areas where you may use one of the unhealthy approaches.

Boundaries: Where You & I Meet
Boundary Dilemmas—Defenses

RIGHT (closed) overprotects self inflexible, unyielding little or no spontaneity insensitive, tough no room for negotiation "My way or the highway"	INVISIBLE (open) unable to protect self doesn't set limits pushover, victim feels wounded, misunderstood, or used incongruent internal/external says "yes" while feeling "no"
DISTANT (far) retreats egocentric, aloof, cold loner, vacant disconnected do for self—not others physically or emotionally absent "Leave me alone" messages	ENMESHED (overlapped) approaches do for others—not self feels partner's feelings, clone overly involved, smothering no opinions of one's own loss of own identity "You and I are the same" i.e., You
INTRUSIVE (boundaryless—sending out) acts forces things onto others unaware of intruding upon others clumsy—physically, verbally does not react to others' cues invasive, bulldozer, pushy, loud, rude can be sneaky or invasive w/sexual energy	HYPER—RECEPTIVE (boundaryless—taking in) reacts hyperaware of others' cues without identity/chameleon "How am I supposed to act?" tense, overly receptive to data hypervigilant, waits for data/cues "Peace at any price"

RIGID

Boundaries: Where You & I Meet
Healthy Boundaries—Boundary Solutions

FIRM (non-negotiable) solid, firm protects self sets clear limits says "no" clearly maintains own limits/values knows what is right for self does not marshmallow	FLEXIBLE (negotiable) open, not rigid maintains sense of self respects own & others' values willing to try others' styles open to other idea/styles willing to change if requested may accept alternative if offered
DISENGAGED (introspective) present centered giving to self identifying with self pulling own energy inward spending time alone focusing on experience with self	ENGAGED (empathetic) interactive grounded & open healthy symbiosis gives support and nurturing takes in support and nurturing actively sensitive to others spending time with others connection with others
ASSERTIVE (proactive) confrontive playful visible sends out energy sets rhythm, "makes waves" appropriate intrusiveness physical if necessary takes action	ADAPTABLE (yielding) sensitive to others uses feedback loop in rhythm with others chooses ways to blend looks for & uses cues appropriately willing to try on others' styles/ideas gathers clues to alter behavior adapts while maintaining own values

You may notice some ways you want to improve your personal boundaries to maintain strong connections within the family. But the family is also affected by the way we observe the boundaries of other groups. For example, strong connections within a friendship group or a work group will often benefit our family members: *Dad's workmate was willing to introduce Junior at a hobby club Junior was interested in.* On the other hand, a boundary violation in groups outside the family can have dire implications for the family: *Mom's family suffered when she was imprisoned for embezzling from her employer.*

Beyond the Family

Let us look at the relationship between boundaries and connections in groups beyond the family. Since I grew up on a farm, I know that good fences make good neighbors. I hated getting up in the night to chase loose livestock belonging to some careless neighbor. On the other hand, there are times when fences keep us apart. For example, the **unless** fences: *You may not enter here unless you are this color, this wealthy, this nationality, this accomplished.*

Remember the verse attributed to Saint Thomas.

> He drew a circle to shut me out.
> Heretic, rebel, a thing to flout.
> But love and I had the wit to win.
> We drew a circle that took him in.

So let's think about how our circles of boundaries can hamper or help our connections inside and outside of the family.

At first glance, we may not see a strong relationship between boundaries and connections.

Actually, boundaries and connections are closely related. The boundaries of a group signify where that group begins and ends, and the norms— the rules about behaviors within the group—define what connections are appropriate.

Sometimes we leap across boundaries to make creative connections. But when we leap across boundaries, to connect in ways that are not appropriate in that setting, we can cause trouble not only for ourselves and our families, but for many others as well.

Common Boundaries

A boundary is an edge, a definer. Let us think first about some common boundaries. Look at the diagram of concentric circles below. In the middle is self and at the outer edge is the universe. In order to consider the boundaries bordering his relationships, Hiram, a middle-aged man, filled in some information about the people and experiences he has in various groups. He arranged the groups in order of their current importance to him. Notice that he put his circle of friends before the work circle and community beyond that. A person who loves her work might put work before friends. A person whose values are more fully expressed in community involvement might put that before work. Notice that some people show up in more than one circle. Joe is both a friend and a work colleague. Hiram's brother Al is active in Hiram's political party on the community level. Tom, a fishing buddy, is a member of Hiram's church. Rick, active in the same professional organization as Hiram, is also a Vietnam War vet. Joe, Al, Tom, Ned, and Rick all show up in more than one level of the circle diagram.

Group Boundaries in Hiram's Life

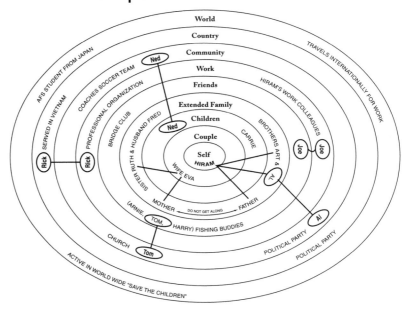

Adapted from *The Structure and Dynamics of Organizations and Groups* by Eric Berne.[4]

The boundaries of the **self** include the skin, which is the edge of the physical self, and the personal bubble, which is the edge of the private space that we are comfortable letting only certain people enter. We also have an emotional bubble, which our family, friends, and close colleagues come to recognize as the boundary around certain beliefs, values, or experiences that are sacred to us and not to be joked about.

For Hiram, the space next to himself includes his **spouse** or **partner**. With this person, Hiram has a deeply bonded connection. He shares much, but not all of himself. Although the couple have deep bonds with the **children**, the kids are in the next circle because the couple were together and bonded before the children arrived and hopefully will be after they are grown, whether the grown children remain at home or not. Some things should remain within the couple boundary because it is not appropriate to cross that boundary with children or anyone else. For example, the parent role dictates that neither parent complains to a child that a partner is not good in bed. Children do not need parents who are confidants. They need parents who are confident. Children don't need parents who are friends; they need parents who are friendly.[5]

In the next space is Hiram's and Eve's **extended family.** This is a flexible boundary. When an extended family member is in dire need, the children may be required to put their needs and wishes on hold temporarily. But when the extended family member makes a demand that would harm the children, the parents pull up the drawbridge and say, *Sorry, we can't do that.*

Extended family members who are connected in other groups need to remember where they are. If Hiram and his brother Al use every family gathering to go off by themselves to talk politics, their connections with the rest of the family members will be stressed.

The boundary between extended family and **friends** can be a wonderfully elastic one. A friend may be designated "as family," but the boundaries about how much they are part of family are either specifically or intuitively clear.

Clara knows she will be included in Hiram's holiday celebrations as she has been for years. The children say, "Clara is family." Clara enjoys this connection, but she does not expect, for example, to be consulted on decisions concerning the family welfare or to receive an equal part of the family inheritance.

Making appropriate connections with colleagues within the **work** world can significantly affect a person's career success. If Hiram won't connect with his colleagues, it will be difficult for him to be an effective team player. On the other hand, if he makes friends with a colleague and lets the friendship influence decisions about work, or if he uses work time to do friendship-related activities, he has crossed the border between colleagues and friends and will get in trouble for it or at least will be a less effective worker.

Joe's daughter was in a drug treatment center that expected Joe to participate in family meetings four times a week. Hiram's son was in treatment two years before. The hours Hiram and Joe spent during work time talking about the treatment procedures were resented by fellow workers and made both of them less effective in their jobs. They should have limited those conversations to lunch or break time.

Connections within the larger **community** may cross boundaries to include colleagues, friends, and relatives. In Hiram's case, he will need to be aware of which set of community boundaries are operative at the moment. In the middle of a meeting at church, he does not ask his **friend** Tom about their weekend fishing plans or about his children's activities. He will talk to Tom about those subjects during the coffee break or on the way to the parking lot. Since the norms of his church encourage families to know about each other, Hiram could announce at the end of the meeting, *I'd like to announce that Tom's daughter, Carolyn, has the lead part in the Children's Theater production of* Cinderella.

One's emotional attachment to one's **country** may fall anywhere from a very loose connection to a tight bond. In some countries, allegiance to the motherland or fatherland is very strong. This tight bonding to place can be a great source of certainty, stability, and identity. It can motivate people to fight for their country, their native land, and that is good or bad, depending on your position in relationship to them. On the other hand, excessive nationalism can lead to wars and exploitation of others. The citizens of the United States generally do not overtly express strong bonds to their country and have constitutional rights to criticize it in words, song, and action. This may help to keep us clear sighted about our shortcomings, but it can also deprive us of a solidity of identity that people who are strongly bonded to their country seem to have. Hiram and Rick are aware of these pulls as they struggle to have their and other Vietnam vet's experiences validated by their families, friends, and the rest of the culture. One time they took their concern to their professional group and asked permission to poll the members to find out if others were also Vietnam vets. There were several and the intensity of their response threatened to take over the meeting. When Hiram and Rick invited everyone to visit the traveling Vietnam War Memorial Wall and named a time when they would meet people at the wall, the group returned to the professional work at hand. Hiram and Rick succeeded in connecting two of their groups without violating the norms of either.

The physical boundaries of the United States are clear and well defined. Furthermore, there are many norms and boundaries that define what we do and don't do individually and in our families because we are American. If you, from any country, think you are not much of your culture, travel to a country that has a different ethnic, religious, economic, and governmental base. Notice differences in family customs. Notice the myriad ways you see, hear, perceive, and interpret things in a way that is different from your hosts.

Our connections within the **world** circle are changing dramatically. We will all need to re-examine our nationalist positions as we recognize our global connectedness. The national boundaries of the past will have different meanings as we move further into the information age. The Internet has made it easy for information to cross all kinds of boundaries. Worldwide groups routinely cross or circumvent national boundaries. The financial world, the business world, the major religious establishments, terrorist organizations and other underground organizations, as well as the information world cross national boundaries in powerful ways.

Boundaries That Exclude

Boundaries are serious stuff. Without them any group becomes an unwieldy crowd. Properly drawn, boundaries help any family and society run smoothly. Improperly or too rigidly drawn, they can stifle individuals or exclude whole groups from the mainstream of the society.

It is possible to draw tight boundaries around class, religious, ethnic, sexual orientation, or nationality groups. Tight racial boundaries could look like this and could prescribe relationships in specific ways. For example, members of the excluded "out" group could be allowed to function as members of a team in the workplace but are not in the more intimate "friends" category.

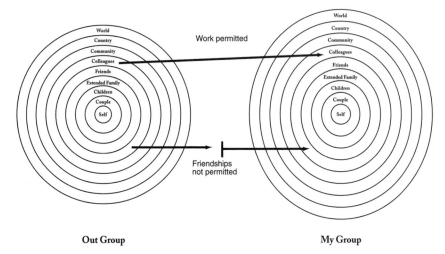

Out Group   **My Group**

Or, an individual member of the excluded group could be a friend, but the entire group, as a class, is not allowed to interact with a certain community group of the dominant culture.

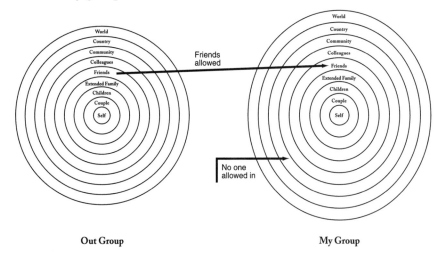

Out Group   **My Group**

Boundaries are about connection and the need to belong, to have reliable connections within known boundaries. This need is so great that youth and adults who are excluded or feel excluded will go looking for places to belong even if the price is high and the consequences are dangerous.

Did I Do Something to Offend You?

The son of a family of recent immigrants to the United States was at odds with his family and shocked by the rigid racial boundaries in his school and the community. When his distressed parents challenged his decision to join a gang, he said, "Look, I don't belong in this family because your heads are still in the old country and I'm here. I can't belong at school because I'm on the bottom. In the gang I belong. I know who I am." When challenged about the violence the gang is known for, he replied, "The violence is not important. It's not why I joined. It's just a way of proving you are worthy to belong. It just happens to be there. I belong there and you can't stop me from going there."

It Is Easier to Stay Connected If You Know What Is Expected

Some of the norms of some groups are clearly spelled out: No smoking in the school building. Commercial deliveries at the back door. Open from 9:00 to 5:00 weekdays and 9:00 to 12:00 Saturdays.

With the possible exception of the military and some religious communities, many norms about what to do and what not to do within the boundaries of a group are informal. You have to learn the norms by noticing, by asking, by making mistakes, and maybe by being told what you did was wrong or maybe by experiencing the silence that tells you to be embarrassed about something, though you may not know what. No wonder children like house and school rules made clear and posted. It is easier to stay connected if you know what is expected.

Teaching Children about Boundaries and Norms

Every group has norms about what relationships and behaviors are acceptable in that group. Although there is pressure from inside a group and sometimes from the outside to behave according to the group's norms, the individual is responsible for maintaining proper connections within a set of boundaries. No one can force an individual to respect the group's norms, but in some cases, flaunting a certain boundary can be cause for punishment or exclusion from the group by censure, shunning, divorce, firing, extradition, litigation, imprisonment, or impeachment.

We can think about the habits children need to develop about boundaries in two ways. On the personal level, if the child is too suggestible, too easily led by others, he needs to develop stronger personal boundaries, to learn to set his own limits and protect himself. If, however, the child intrudes upon others, moves in like a bulldozer, it is time for lessons about respect and empathy.

Marta helps herself to her sister's clothes, toys, and books. If Marta wants to play, she has a hissy fit if her sister won't play right then. Time for enforcement of strict house rules: Ask before you use someone else's things. Respect each other's time and space.

Children need to learn how to notice the cues that help them recognize the norms of a group. They also need to be taught to evaluate those norms against family values and to think about when they need to change groups or how they might get a group to change norms.

Community Support

Teaching children how to observe boundaries and recognize norms is a major responsibility for parents and all adults. Children who live in a community where all adults expect and teach the norms for all children are lucky.

When I was growing up years ago, if I misbehaved, the neighbors didn't call the police. They usually didn't even call my parents. They put a hand on my shoulder and said, "Enough of that." Or they said, "Come with me; you don't belong here." Or, "Time for you to go home."

When I was raising my children in a suburban area with mostly at-home moms, they seldom told me when my kids misbehaved, but they gossiped with each other. When I sent kids home, I was told I was too harsh. Maybe I was. But raising kids without support is hard, and it is easy for parents to become too harsh or to give up and become marshmallows. I expect I did some of both.

Now, if my grandchildren misbehave, the neighbors are more apt to call the police than to tell the child to behave. Getting connected with the police by being picked up for misbehavior is not the kind of connection most parents want their children to have with law enforcement officers.

It is much easier for children if their parents have found or created at least one supportive social group. At best, it can take a long time and lots of effort for children to learn group norms in the informal way that they are taught. When families lack the support of the village that it takes to raise a child, it is not only harder for the parents, it is much harder for the children and any help that parents can offer is important. Try **attend, act, ask,** and **amend.**

Changing the Norms

It takes a long time and real effort to change norms in some groups. The easiest place to change a norm is in the family. If the adults agree and are consistent, household norms can usually be changed in a few weeks or months.

It was the norm at the Steven's house for everyone to drop outdoor clothes on the bench in the entryway and books and packages on the table. It was also the norm for the mother to nag about that, but for nobody, including her, to change the habit. One day she announced that clothes would be hung up in the closet and books and packages could be left on the hall bench, and she changed her habit. She hung up her coat and put her packages on the bench. She did not nag. The children continued to drop their stuff as before. In this case, she found that modeling was not enough so she put a large box in the back hall and told people that any clothes left on the bench or books left on the table would be removed to the box. She carried things to the box consistently. It takes time and energy to change a norm! She did not mention it again, but a few weeks later she removed the box. It was no longer needed. The family had changed that norm.

In large organizations some norms change gradually to conform to changes in the general culture. Casual dress on Friday is one example. Sometimes people from outside a group attempt to change that group's norms or boundaries by marches, protests, and boycotts. In other cases, changing norms takes determined effort by powerful people within the group. In some cases laws have to be passed to support the change. The armed services of the United States have changed the sex norms during the last few years, and we have been able to follow that difficult process in the media.

When Boundaries Are Violated

When people argue about whether a behavior was okay, they are often arguing about whether it was okay where it was done. For example, taking food from the refrigerator without asking is okay at home. Doing that at a friend's home is a breach of etiquette. Taking food from the grocery story without paying is an illegal offense. Telling your mate she has bad breath is appreciated. Telling your boss she has bad breath could get you in trouble. Having sex within the marriage or partnership is okay. Having sex outside the marriage or partnership depends on the values of the individual and the norms of that circle. Having sex with someone of unequal status in the workplace is not okay. It can lead to censure, lawsuits, or loss of jobs. Rape is never okay!

The consequences of violating norms range from the slight rebuff of raised eyebrows, to being shamed, to the life-changing consequences of going to prison.

Use the diagram on page 217, "Your Boundaries Group," to begin to think about your boundaries and your family's boundaries. On the empty circles, fill in words that describe the groups within the boundaries of your life. Some of them may look like Hiram's; others may be very different. Students, at any age, would designate a circle for school. If you have powerful enemies, they might occupy a separate circle. Or they would be a subgroup within the work circle if you work with an enemy. If they are outside of your nation, they would be in a subgroup in the world circle.

As you look at your boundaries, think about what they mean in your family and in your life. You may want to read more about boundaries.[6] Are the norms of your groups healthy and supportive? Do they allow you to make the kinds of connections you want? Do you need to be more active in some of your circles? Do you need some new groups?

Every group has boundaries. Every set of boundaries has norms. Norms tell us how we are expected to connect within those boundaries.

Your Boundaries Group

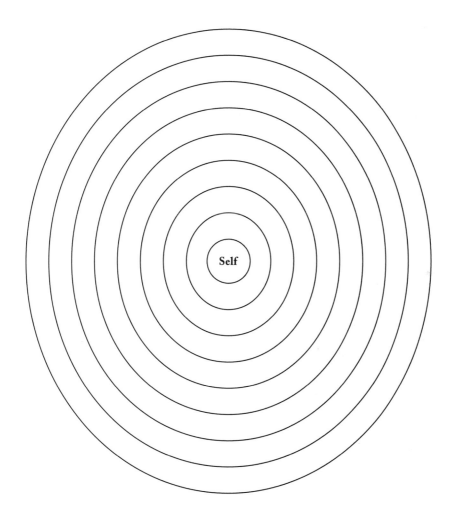

Chapter 24

Time-In for Yourself

Why me? the young one asked.
Who else? the wise one answered.
— THE OLD WISE ONE

It all starts with you. It's hard to be connected with others if you are disconnected with yourself. You are the center of the circles. How you connect within each of the other boundary sets depends on how well you are connected with yourself.

Try using some time-in for yourself.

Ask: Am I taking the time to know myself and to care for myself well? Am I connected with the right dreams for me? [1] Am I doing the healing I need to do? Am I sure enough of who I am, my true self, so I can connect with others without dominance or codependency? Am I allowing others to connect with my true self, the best that is in me? Am I making my life a celebration of the good things in me?

Attend: Observe. Feel. Think. About your sense of self, your self-esteem, your worth, your uniqueness, your gifts. Think about staying connected with your dream, with your spiritual self. Be careful of competition. Be competitive when competition adds verve to your life, but be careful not to let competition use you. Remember the old Italian proverb, "Once the game is over, the king and the pawn go back in the same box."

Act: Choose one way to start to take better care of yourself, or hold yourself accountable, or make amends to someone else, or celebrate your uniqueness, or strengthen a wanted connection. Find some friends who will support you. Keep these motivating slogans in mind:

- Do it.
- Then choose another action.
- Do one action at a time.
- Live one day at a time.
- Stay underwhelmed.

Amend: Can you think of an instance where you have shorted yourself, or gone without in order to play the martyr, or neglected to experience joy, or lost your connection with your true self and done something you were ashamed of? If so, figure out a way to make amends to yourself. Imagine yourself in a world of abundance and give yourself what you really need—not want, need. Replace the martyr with the willing helper. Make amends with yourself for breaking the bond with your true self and doing the shameful act. That is as important as making amends to another.

Easy?
Sometimes.
Do you ever get it all done?
No. Life goes on.
It looks really hard. Is it?
Only if you make it so.
Only if you try to be perfect.

Remember that insisting on perfection usually means giving up excellence[2] and that the important work of the world is done by people who are not perfect, but are good enough.[3]

- good enough parents
- good enough spouses or partners
- good enough siblings
- good enough sons and daughters
- good enough friends
- good enough co-workers
- good enough leaders
- good enough followers
- good enough humans

All of these "good enoughs" make for connections that are good enough. And good enough is plenty. So take some time-in for yourself, get your needs met, and create joy.

If you want something you've never had, you must do something you've never done.   —*Author unknown*

Notes

PREFACE

1. Jean Illsley Clarke, "Time-In: To Discipline Is to Teach,"*WE Newsletter* 15, no. 1 (1996). 16535 9th Avenue North, Minneapolis, MN 55447; 612-473-1840.

2. Jean Illsley Clarke, *Time-In: When Time-Out Doesn't Work* (Seattle: Parenting Press, 1998).

3. John McCord, "Questioning the Value of Punishment," *Social Problems* 38, no. 2 (May 1991).

4. Joanne M. Joseph and Irwin Redlener, *The Resilient Child: Preparing Today's Youth for Tomorrow's World* (New York: Insight Books, 1994).

5. David Walsh, *Selling Out America's Children* (Minneapolis: Fairview Press, 1994); Robert N. Bellah, Richard Madsen, William M. Sullivan, Ann Swidler, and Steven M. Tipton, *Habits of the Heart: Individualism and Commitment in American Life* (Berkeley, Calif.: University of California Press, 1985).

6. Sylvia Ann Hewlett and Cornel West, *The War Against Parents: What We Can Do for America's Beleaguered Moms and Dads* (Boston: Houghton Mifflin Company, 1998).

7. Thanks to Sheri Goldsmith for permitting the publication of her letter.

8. Abraham Maslow, *Motivation and Personality* (New York: Harper and Row, 1954).

9. Most, but not all humans, start with the physical union of a man and a woman. But, no matter whether the ova and sperm make that first connection in bodies, test tube, or petri dish, the seminal coming together of the receptive ova and the purposeful sperm in dramatic connection makes unique life possible.

10. Only recently have teaching stories been written down. For most of human history, wisdom was passed from one generation to another by stories. In this book, when the essence of the old wisdom is presented it will be attributed

to *the old storyteller*. When reference is made to the deepest wisdom of an individual, it will be attributed to *the wise one within*.

11. Jean Baker Miller, M.D., and Irene Pierce Stiver, Ph.D., *The Healing Connection: How Women Form Relationships in Therapy and in Life* (Boston: Beacon Press, 1997).

12. Deborah Tannen, *You Just Don't Understand: Women and Men in Conversation* (New York: William Morrow and Company, 1990).

13. See Peter L. Benson, *The Troubled Journey: A Portrait of 6th–12th Grade Youth* (prepared by Search Institute, Minneapolis, for RespecTeen, 800-888-3820).

14. Edith Hamilton, *Mythology: Timeless Tales of Gods and Heroes* (Boston: Little, Brown and Company, 1942).

INTRODUCTION: WHY A BOOK ABOUT CONNECTION?

1. Thanks to Sue Murray, Maggie Lawrence, and Todd Pointer for adding becauses.

CHAPTER 1: TIME-IN, TIME-WITH, TIME-OUT: LOOKING AT TIME IN A NEW WAY

1. See chapter 8, "What about Time-Out?," for productive ways to use time-out.

2. Laura Shapiro, "The Myth of Quality Time," *Newsweek* (12 May 1997).

3. Jean Illsley Clarke, *Self-Esteem: A Family Affair Leader Guide* (Minneapolis: Daisy Press, 1981). This book has six exercises that point out how this kind of indirect language invites children to believe they are powerless rather than responsible for their behavior, that they contribute to and shape "how the day goes."

4. Jean Illsley Clarke and Connie Dawson, *Growing Up Again: Parenting Ourselves, Parenting Our Children*, rev. ed. (Center City, Minn.: Hazelden, 1998), chapters 16–19. See also David J. Bredehoft, Sheryll A. Mennicke, Alisa M. Potter, Jean Illsley Clarke, "Perceptions Attributed by Adults to Parental Overindulgence During Childhood," *The Journal of Family and Consumer Sciences Education* 16, no. 2 (1998).

5. Edward T. Hall and Mildred Reed Hall, "Hidden Differences: Studies in International Communication," *How to Communicate with the Germans* (Hamburg, West Germany: Stern Magazine, 1983).

6. William J. Doherty, *The Intentional Family: How to Build Family Ties in Our Modern World* (Reading, Mass.: Addison-Wesley, 1997).

CHAPTER 2: ATTEND

1. See the section about "Putting in Coventry" chapter 15, pages 132–133; this section describes a form of shunning used as punishment.

2. Martin Buber, *I and Thou* (New York: Charles Scribner's Sons, 1970).

3. Peter L. Benson, *The Troubled Journey: A Portrait of 6th–12th Grade Youth* (prepared by Search Institute, Minneapolis, for RespecTeen, 800-888-3820).

4. Jean Illsley Clarke and Connie Dawson, *Growing Up Again: Parenting Ourselves, Parenting Our Children*, rev. ed. (Center City, Minn.: Hazelden, 1998). There is theoretical background in *Cathexis Reader* by Jacqui Lee Schiff et al. (New York: HarperCollins, 1975).

5. Lyndall Shick, *Understanding Temperament* (Seattle: Parenting Press, 1998).

6. Carol Watson, *Run, Yell & Tell! A Safety Book for Children* (Missing Children Minnesota, 1993; P.O. Box 11216, Minneapolis, MN 55411, 612-521-1188).

7. Jean Illsley Clarke, Carole Gesme, Marion London, and Donald Brundage, *Help! For Kids and Parents About Drugs* (Minneapolis: Daisy Press, 1993).

8. Geoffrey Canada, *Reaching Up for Manhood: Transforming the Lives of Boys in America* (Boston: Beacon Press, 1998).

9. Elizabeth Murphy, *The Developing Child: Using Jungian Type to Understand Children* (Palo Alto, Calif.: Consulting Psychologists Press, 1992).

10. Olga Silverstein and Beth Rashbaum, *The Courage to Raise Good Men* (New York: Penguin Books, 1994).

11. Thanks to Mark Allister for pointing out the hazards of constant photo opportunities.

CHAPTER 3: ASK

1. Thanks to Carole Gesme for sharing the idea of using flash cards.

2. Jean Illsley Clarke, *Self-Esteem: A Family Affair* (Center City, Minn.: Hazelden, 1998), chapter 8.

3. Phyllis Reynolds Naylor, *King of the Playground* (New York: Atheneum, 1994).

4. Chick Moorman, *Parent Talk: Words That Empower, Words That Wound* (Merrill, Mich.: Personal Power Press, 1998).

5. Thanks to Laurie Hamilton for providing information on the freeze response.

6. Jean Illsley Clarke, *Time-In: When Time-Out Doesn't Work* (Seattle: Parenting Press, 1998).

7. Ruby K. Payne, *Poverty: A Framework for Understanding and Working with Students and Adults from Poverty* (Baytown, Tex.: RFT Publishing, 1995).

CHAPTER 4: ACT

1. Betty Hart and Todd R. Risley, *Meaningful Differences in the Everyday Experience of Young American Children* (Baltimore, Md.: Paul H. Brookes Publishing, 1995).

2. See "Ask to help the child gain power: fight, flee, freeze, fix, or flow" in chapter 3, pages 34–35 or in Jean Illsley Clarke's *Time-In: When Time-Out Doesn't Work* (Seattle: Parenting Press, 1998).

3. Laurie A. Kanyer, *The Journey of Becoming a Mother: Tools for a New Mother's Emotional Growth & Development* (Golden, Colo.: The Love and Logic Press, 1996).

4. Elizabeth Jones and Gretchen Reynolds, *The Play's the Thing: Teachers' Roles in Children's Play* (New York: Teachers College Press, 1992).

5. Beverly I. Fagot and Mary Gauvain, "Mother-Child Problem Solving: Continuity Through the Early Years," *Developmental Psychology* 33, no. 3 (1997): 480–488. Their research indicates that mothers' disapproving looks may slow cognitive development.

6. Sylvia Fair, *The Bedspread* (New York: Macmillan Children's Books, 1982).

7. Try classic books on development such as Louise Bates Ames and Frances L. Ilg, *Your Two-Year-Old: Terrible or Tender* (New York: Delacorte Press, 1980) or more current books such as the photo-filled series *Your Child at Play, Birth to One Year; One to Two Years; Two to Three Years; Three to Five Years*, by Marilyn Segal (New York: Newmarket Press, 1998). Or try Jerri Wolfe's books, *I'm Two Years Old! Everything Your Two-Year-Old Wants You to Know About Parenting* and *I'm Three Years Old! Everything Your Three-Year-Old Wants You to Know About Parenting* (New York: Pocket Books, 1998).

8. Jean Illsley Clarke and Connie Dawson, *Growing Up Again: Parenting Ourselves, Parenting Our Children*, rev. ed. (Center City, Minn.: Hazelden, 1998). The overindulgence research is also reported in the *Journal of Family and Consumer Sciences Education* 16, no. 2 (Fall 1998).

9. Ibid.

10. Stephen A. Small and Gay Eastman, "Rearing Adolescents in Contemporary Society: A Conceptual Framework for Understanding the Responsibilities and Needs of Parents," *Family Relations* (October 1991), 455–462;

Stephen A. Small and Tom Luster, "Adolescent Sexual Activity: An Ecological, Risk-Factor Approach," *Journal of Marriage and the Family* 56 (February 1994).

11. Michael Schulman and Eva Mekler, *Bringing Up a Moral Child* (Reading, Mass.: Addison-Wesley, 1985).

12. Blake Bowden and Jennie Zeisz, "Eating with Teens Improves Their Level of Adjustment," *The Brown University Child and Adolescent Behavior Letter* 13, no. 10 (October 1997). From a presentation by Blake Bowden, at the 105th annual meeting of the American Psychological Association, Chicago.

13. William J. Doherty, *The Intentional Family: How to Build Family Ties in Our Modern World* (Reading, Mass.: Addison-Wesley, 1997).

14. George Holden, *Parents and the Dynamics of Child Rearing* (Boulder, Colo.: Westview Press, 1997), 54.

CHAPTER 5: AMEND

1. You can read about discounting in chapter 2, pages 14–18.

2. Diane Chelsom Gossen, *Restitution: Restructuring School Discipline* (Chapel Hill, N.C.: New View Publications, 1996).

3. Jean Illsley Clarke, *Time-In: When Time-Out Doesn't Work* (Seattle: Parenting Press, 1998).

CHAPTER 7: TIME-IN FOR DISCIPLINE

1. John McCord, "Questioning the Value of Punishment," *Social Problems* 38, no. 2 (May 1991).

2. Samuel P. and Pearl M. Oliner, *The Altruistic Personality: Rescuers of Jews in Nazi Europe* (New York: Free Press, 1988).

3. Alice Miller, *For Your Own Good: Hidden Cruelty in Child-Rearing and the Roots of Violence* (New York: Farrar, Straus, Giroux, 1983).

4. Harriet Heath, *Using Your Values to Raise Your Child to Be an Adult You Admire* (Seattle: Parenting Press, 1999).

5. Madelyn Swift, *Discipline for Life: Getting It Right with Children* (Fort Worth, Tex.: Stairway Education Programs, 1998).

6. Barbara Coloroso, *Kids Are Worth It: Giving Your Child the Gift of Inner Discipline* (New York: William Morrow, 1994).

7. Diane Chelsom Gossen, *Restitution: Restructuring School Discipline* (Chapel Hill, N.C.: New View Publications, 1993).

8. Jean Illsley Clarke and Connie Dawson, *Growing Up Again: Parenting*

Ourselves, Parenting Our Children, rev. ed. (Center City, Minn.: Hazelden, 1998).

CHAPTER 8: WHAT ABOUT TIME-OUT?

1. Otto Weininger, *T. I. P. S.: Time-In Parenting Strategies* (Binghamton, N.Y.: esf Publishers, 1998).

2. Ibid., 31.

3. Lyndall Shick, *Understanding Temperament* (Seattle: Parenting Press, 1998).

4. Peter Ernest Haiman, "'Time Out' to Correct Misbehavior May Aggravate It Instead," *The Brown Child and Adolescent University Behavior Letter* 14, no. 10 (October 1998).

5. Mary Sheedy Kurcinka, *Raising Your Spirited Child* (New York: Harper-Collins, 1992).

6. Madelyn Swift, *Discipline for Life: Getting It Right with Children* (Fort Worth, Tex.: Stairway Education Programs, 1998).

CHAPTER 9: THE ROLE OF RULES

1. Peter L. Benson, *The Troubled Journey: A Portrait of 6th–12th Grade Youth* (prepared by Search Institute, Minneapolis, for RespecTeen, 800-888-3820).

2. Example sheet adapted from pages 79–80 of *Growing Up Again: Parenting Ourselves, Parenting Our Children,* rev. ed. by Jean Illsley Clarke and Connie Dawson (Center City, Minn.: Hazelden, 1998).

3. Ibid., adapted from page 80.

4. Thanks to Barb and Bill Kobe for this rules poster for a family with a three-year-old and an infant.

5. Clarke and Dawson, *Growing Up Again.*

CHAPTER 10: NOW WHAT? WHY KIDS MISBEHAVE

1. Susan Beekman and Jeanne Holmes, *Battles, Hassles, Tantrums & Tears* (New York: Hearst Books, 1993). This book is chock-full of wisdom about resolving conflict.

2. Read Mary Sheedy Kurcinka's, *Raising Your Spirited Child* (New York: HarperCollins, 1991); and Lyndall Shick's, *Understanding Temperament* (Seattle: Parenting Press, 1998).

3. David Walsh, *Selling Out America's Children* (Minneapolis: Fairview Press, 1994).

4. William J. Doherty, *The Intentional Family: How to Build Family Ties in Our Modern World* (Reading, Mass.: Addison-Wesley, 1997).

5. Kathryn M. Hammerseng, *Telling Isn't Tattling* (Seattle: Parenting Press, 1995).

6. Holly E. Brisbane, *The Developing Child: Understanding Children and Parenting* (New York: Macmillan/McGraw-Hill, 1994), 452.

7. "Mindworks," 6 March 1997, *Minneapolis Star Tribune.*

8. Jean Illsley Clarke and Connie Dawson, *Growing Up Again: Parenting Ourselves, Parenting Our Children,* rev. ed. (Center City, Minn.: Hazelden, 1998).

9. Jean Illsley Clarke, *Time-In: When Time-Out Doesn't Work* (Seattle: Parenting Press, 1998).

10. Madelyn Swift, *Discipline for Life: Getting It Right with Children* (Fort Worth, Tex.: Stairway Education Programs, 1998).

CHAPTER 11: WHY DO CHILDREN RESPOND DIFFERENTLY?

1. Lyndall Shick, *Understanding Temperament* (Seattle: Parenting Press, 1998). This is an easy-to-use book designed to help parents recognize and respond to children's differing personality styles. For a more theoretical treatment of the seminal work done by Stella Chase and Alexander Thomas, read *Prevention and Early Intervention: Individual Differences as Risk Factors for the Mental Health of Children* by William B. Carey and Sean C. McDevitt, eds. (New York: Brunner/Mazel, 1994).

2. Linda S. Budd, *Living with the Active Alert Child* (Seattle: Parenting Press, 1990, 1993); Mary Sheedy Kurcinka, *Raising Your Spirited Child* (New York: HarperCollins, 1991).

3. Mary Cahill Fowler, *Maybe You Know My Kid: A Parent's Guide to Identifying, Understanding and Helping Your Child with Attention Deficit Disorder* (Secaucus, N.J.: Carol Publishing Group, 1990).

4. Kurcinka, *Raising Your Spirited Child.*

5. Elizabeth Murphy, *The Developing Child: Using Jungian Type to Understand Children* (Palo Alto, Calif.: Consulting Psychologists Press, 1992).

CHAPTER 12: LOOKING AT DISCIPLINE IN A NEW WAY

1. Thanks to Joan B. Lourie for her article "Cumulative Trauma: The Nonproblem Problem," *Transactional Analysis Journal* 26, no. 4 (October 1996) and for encouraging me in private conversations to expand upon this material for parents, to help us get it right the first time around.

2. For additional information on recycling, read Jean Illsley Clarke's *Self-Esteem: A Family Affair* (Center City, Minn.: Hazelden, 1998) or Pamela Levin's *Becoming the Way We Are* (Pompano Beach, Fla.: Health Communications, 1988).

3. William Pollack, *Real Boys: Rescuing Our Sons from the Myths of Boyhood* (New York: Random House, 1998).

4. Stanley I. Greenspan, *The Growth of the Mind: And the Endangered Origins of Intelligence* (Reading, Mass.: Addison Wesley Longman, 1997).

5. Berry T. Brazelton, *Touchpoints: Your Child's Emotional and Behavioral Development* (Reading, Mass.: Addison-Wesley, 1992).

6. Joanne M. Joseph and Irwin Redlener, *The Resilient Child: Preparing Today's Youth for Tomorrow's World* (New York: Insight Books, 1994). Or select from the many books on resilience at your local bookstore. Or use the USDA's National Network for Family Resiliency (NNFR) at phone number 515-294-7244, e-mail: x1stout@exnet.iastate.edu, or Web site: http://www.nnfr.org/about.html.

CHAPTER 13: WHEN THERE ARE PROBLEMS
USING TIME-IN TO DISCIPLINE

1. Jane Brody, *Jane Brody's Nutrition Book,* rev. ed. (New York: Bantam Books, 1987).

2. Elizabeth Jones and Gretchen Reynolds, *The Play's the Thing* (New York: Teachers College Press, 1992).

3. Ed Fischer, *101 Fun Hugs* (Ed Fischer, 57 Viking Village, Rochester, MN 55901, 507-281-5119, 1992).

4. Bill Chandler, *25 Things You Can Do to Feel Better Right Now* (Redmond, Wash.: Andante Publishing, 1993).

CHAPTER 14: WHAT ABOUT MY ANGER?

1. Philip J. Greven, *Spare the Child: The Religious Roots of Punishment and the Psychological Impact of Physical Abuse* (New York: Alfred A. Knopf, 1991).

2. Ronald G. Slaby, Wendy C. Roedell, Diana Arezzo, and Kate Hendrix, *Early Violence Prevention: Tools for Teachers of Young Children* (Washington, D.C.: NAEYC, 1995).

3. Rollo May, *Power and Innocence: A Search for the Sources of Violence* (New York: C. C. Norton, 1971).

4. Fred C. Clark, "Anger and its Disavowal in Shame-Based People," *Transactional Analysis Journal* 25, no. 2 (April 1995).

5. Linda S. Budd, *Living with the Active Alert Child* (Seattle: Parenting Press,

1990, 1993); Mary Sheedy Kurcinka, *Raising Your Spirited Child* (New York: HarperCollins, 1991).

6. Adapted from Jean Illsley Clarke, *Time-In: When Time-Out Doesn't Work* (Seattle: Parenting Press, 1998).

7. Robert K. Cooper, *Health & Fitness Excellence: The Scientific Action Plan* (Atlanta, Ga.: Houghton Mifflin, 1989).

8. Harriet Goldhor Lerner, *Dance of Anger* (New York: HarperCollins, 1985).

CHAPTER 15: WHAT ABOUT SHAME?

1. Thanks to Anna L. Fussell for her helpful conversations as well as for *Sounding One's Song: Shame, Self-esteem, Creativity and Spirituality* (Minnetonka, Minn.: Change Navigators, 1996); Change Navigators, 3824 Willmatt Hill Rd., Minnetonka, MN 55305; 612-935-2280.

2. Gershen Kaufman and Lev Raphael, *Coming Out of Shame: Transforming Gay and Lesbian Lives* (New York: Doubleday, 1996); Donald L. Nathanson, *Shame and Pride: Affect, Sex, and the Birth of the Self* (New York: W.W. Norton and Company, 1992); Donald L. Nathanson, *The Many Faces of Shame* (New York: Guilford Press, 1987); John Bradshaw, *Healing the Shame That Binds You* (Deerfield Beach, Fla.: Health Communications, 1988); Vicki Underland-Rosow, *Shame: Spiritual Suicide* (Shorewood, Minn.: Waterford Publications, 1995).

3. Thanks to Susan Legender Clarke for sharing the story about Coventry.

4. Read Alice Miller's *For Your Own Good: Hidden Cruelty in Child-Rearing and the Roots of Violence* (New York: Farrar, Straus, Giroux, 1983) and *The Drama of the Gifted Child: How Narcissistic Parents Form and Deform the Emotional Lives of Their Talented Children* (New York: Basic Books, 1981).

5. Thanks to Bernard Saunders, co-author of *Ten Steps to a Learning Organization* with Peter Kline (Arlington, Va.: Great Ocean Publishers, 1993), for sharing his method of stopping bullying.

6. Dan Olweus, *Bullying at School: What We Know and What We Can Do* (Cambridge, Mass.: Blankwell Publishers, 1993); Ronald G. Slaby, Renee Wilson-Brewer, and Kimberly Dash, *Aggressors, Victims, and Bystanders: Thinking and Acting to Prevent Violence* (Newton, Mass.: Education Development Center, 1994); Education Development Center, Inc., 55 Chapel St., Newton, MA 92158.

CHAPTER 16: WHAT IF A CHILD DOESN'T CONNECT?

1. Jean Illsley Clarke and Connie Dawson, *Growing Up Again: Parenting Ourselves, Parenting Our Children*, rev. ed. (Center City, Minn.: Hazelden,

1998); Gregory C. Keck and Regina M. Kupecky, *Adopting the Hurt Child: Hope for Families with Special-Needs Kids: A Guide for Parents and Professionals* (Colorado Springs, Colo.: NavPress, 1998).

2. This affirmation is reprinted from Cheryl Kilvington and Robert F. Brunjes, *Affirmations for Your Healthy Pregnancy* (Minneapolis: Affirmative Press, 1992); Affirmative Press, 5115 Excelsior Blvd. #413, Minneapolis, MN 55416, 612-546-9311.

3. Clarke and Dawson, *Growing Up Again*, 218–219.

4. Robert Karen, *Becoming Attached: First Relationships and How They Shape Our Capacity to Love* (New York: Oxford University Press, 1998).

5. John Bowlby, *Attachment and Loss. Vol. 1: Attachment* (New York: Basic, 1982); *Attachment and Loss. Vol. 2: Separation* (New York: Basic, 1973); *Attachment and Loss. Vol. 3: Loss, Sadness and Depression* (New York: Basic, 1980).

6. Mary D. S. Ainsworth, *Infancy in Uganda: Infant Care and the Growth of Love* (Baltimore: Johns Hopkins University Press, 1967).

7. Daniel A. Hughes, *Facilitating Developmental Attachment: The Road to Emotional Recovery and Behavioral Change in Foster and Adopted Children* (Northvale, N.J.: Jason Aronson, 1997).

8. Foster Cline, M.D. and Jim Fay, *Parenting with Love and Logic: Teaching Children Responsibility* (Colorado Springs, Colo.: Pinon Press, 1990); *Parenting Teens with Love and Logic: Preparing Adolescents for Responsible Adulthood* (Colorado Springs, Colo.: Pinon Press, 1992).

9. Mary Pipher, *Reviving Ophelia: Saving the Selves of Adolescent Girls* (New York: G. P. Putnam's Sons, 1994).

10. Olga Silverstein and Beth Rashbaum, *The Courage to Raise Good Men* (New York: Penguin Books, 1994); Geoffrey Canada, *Reaching Up for Manhood* (Boston: Beacon Press, 1998); William Pollack, *Real Boys: Rescuing Our Sons from the Myths of Boyhood* (New York: Random House, 1998).

CHAPTER 17: FAMILIES DON'T BLEND: SOMETIMES THEY BOND

1. Michael J. Murphy, author of *Popsicle Fish: Tales of Fathering*, and psychologist for the Massachusetts Department of Corrections, wrote in *The Brown University Child and Adolescent Behavior Letter* 13, no. 9 (September 1997): 8: "My informal research, based on interviews with thousands of male inmates, indicated that about four out of five had no consistent caretaking male figure in their lives. . . . When a desperate single mother asks me how she can fill the father-void in her son's life, I offer the usual litany: Big Brothers, Boy Scouts, uncles, coaches. But the silent truth is that for many young men, the closest thing to a father they will ever experience is the prison. . . .

The prison offers limits, structure and rewards for good behavior, all managed and provided by older men. Another terrible truth is that many young men thrive in prison; it is only in the community, where there are no surrogate parent figures guiding every decision, that failure, and renewed punishment, await. . . . What has disappeared from the lives of the majority of Americans is the 'good enough father'—the guy who consistently represents an ethic of hard work, discipline and silent love. He may have had faults aplenty, but he had one great asset: He was there. When he disappeared, along with him went the thousands of moments in which he modeled appropriate behavior and impulse control, and filled in the space in a child's mind when he or she said the word 'father.'"

2. Jean Illsley Clarke and Connie Dawson, *Growing Up Again: Parenting Ourselves, Parenting Our Children,* rev. ed. (Center City, Minn.: Hazelden, 1998).

3. Emily Visher and John Visher, M.D. *Stepfamilies: A Guide to Working with Step-Parents and Children* (New York: Brunner/Mazel, 1978). Also read *Old Loyalties, New Ties: Therapeutic Strategies with Stepfamilies* (New York: Brunner/Mazel, 1988); *How to Win as a Stepfamily* (New York: Brunner/Mazel, 1991); *Therapy with Stepfamilies* (New York: Brunner/Mazel, 1996); and *Stepfamilies: Stepping Ahead,* 2nd ed. (Baltimore, Md.: Stepfamilies Press, 1989).

CHAPTER 18: LET GRIEF IN

1. George Kohlrieser, from a workshop in Zurich, Switzerland, July 1998. Special thanks to George for stimulating me to think about this topic in new ways and for his willingness for me to share his insights.

2. Neil Postman, *Amusing Ourselves to Death: Public Discourse in the Age of Show Business* (New York: Penguin Books, 1985), 86.

3. Christine Northrup, *Women's Bodies, Women's Wisdom: Creating Physical and Emotional Health and Healing* (New York: Bantam Books, 1998).

4. Sherokee Ilse, *Empty Arms: Coping After Miscarriage, Stillbirth and Infant Death,* rev. ed., Ed. Arlene Applebaum (Maple Plain, Minn.: Wintergreen Press, 1990).

5. Anne McCracken and Mary Semel, *A Broken Heart Still Beats: After Your Child Dies* (Center City, Minn.: Hazelden, 1998).

6. See chapter 17, "Families Don't Blend: Sometimes They Bond."

7. Zalman Schachter-Shalomi, *From Age-ing to Sage-ing: A Profound New Vision of Growing Older* (New York: Warner Books, 1995).

8. Ted Bowman, *Loss of Dreams: A Special Kind of Grief* (Ted Bowman, 2111 Knapp St., St. Paul, MN 55108-1814, 651-645-6058, 1994).

9. Thanks to Sue Murray for offering this analogy.

10. Elaine Childs-Gowell, *Good Grief Rituals* (New York: Station Hill Press, 1992).

11. Ibid., 7.

12. Ibid., 33.

13. Ibid., 76, 77.

CHAPTER 19: THE JOURNEY OF GRIEF

1. Elisabeth Kübler-Ross, ed., *Death, The Final Stage of Growth* (New York: Simon and Schuster, 1975).

2. Thanks to George Kohlrieser (from a workshop in Zurich, Switzerland, July 1998), for his willingness to share this material.

3. Yolanda Nave, *Breaking Up: From Heartache to Happiness in 48 Pages* (New York: Workman Publishing, 1985).

CHAPTER 20: I'LL BUY YOU A NEW PUPPY: HELPING CHILDREN GRIEVE

1. J. William Worden, *Children and Grief: When a Parent Dies* (New York: Guilford Press, 1996).

2. Nancy Ballaban, *Learning to Say Goodbye: Starting School and Other Early Childhood Separations* (New York: New American Library–Dutton, 1985, 1989).

3. Marge Heegaard's The Drawing Out Feelings Series: *When Someone Very Special Dies; When a Family Is in Trouble; When Something Terrible Happens; When Mom and Dad Separate; When Someone Has a Very Serious Illness; When a Parent Marries Again* (Minneapolis: Woodland Press, 1993). Woodland Press, 99 Woodland Cir., Minneapolis, MN 55424; 612-926-2665.

4. Carole Gesme, *Help for Kids! Understanding Your Feelings About Having a Parent in Prison or Jail* (Minneapolis: Pine Press, 1993).

5. Carole Gesme, *Help for Kids! Understanding Your Feelings About Moving* (Minneapolis: Pine Press, 1991).

6. For ages preschool through grade three: Laurene Krasny Brown and Marc Brown, *When Dinosaurs Die, A Guide to Understanding Death* (Boston: Little, Brown and Company, 1996); Tomie de Paola, *Nana Upstairs and Nana Downstairs* (New York: G.P. Putnam's Sons, 1973). For grades K through four: Judith Viorst, *The Tenth Good Thing About Barney* (New York: Atheneum, 1971); Joan Fassler, *My Grandpa Died Today* (New York: Human Sciences Press, 1971). For grades two through five: Benette W. Tiffault, *A Quilt for Elizabeth*

(Omaha, Nebr.: Centering Corporation, 1992). For grades five and up: Eric E. Rofes and the Unit at Fayerweather Street School, *The Kids' Book About Death and Dying: By and for Kids* (Boston: Little, Brown and Company, 1985). For all ages: E. B. White, *Charlotte's Web* (New York: Harper, 1952).

7. Marilyn E. Gootman, *When a Friend Dies: A Book for Teens About Grieving and Healing* (Minneapolis: Free Spirit, 1994).

8. Rainbows is an international, not-for-profit organization founded to help children and teens cope with the emotional pain of divorce, death, and other family loss. Today it also serves single parents and other adults. For more information, call Catholic Charities, 800-266-3206.

9. Thanks to Shirley Knox for making this material available from the Annie Tran Center for Grief and Loss, P.O. Box 481, Prosser, WA 99350; 509-786-7100 or 509-453-8110. It was developed by Shirley Knox and Vicki Meyer, grief specialists.

CHAPTER 21: I DON'T KNOW WHAT TO SAY: HELPING ADULTS GRIEVE

1. Sherokee Ilse, *Empty Arms: Coping After Miscarriage, Stillbirth and Infant Death*, rev. ed., Ed. Arlene Applebaum (Maple Plain, Minn.: Wintergreen Press, 1990); Anne McCracken and Mary Semel, *A Broken Heart Still Beats: After Your Child Dies* (Center City, Minn.: Hazelden, 1998); Nicholas Wolterstorff, *Lament for a Son* (Grand Rapids, Mich.: William B. Eerdmans Publishing, 1987).

2. Ted Bowman, *Loss of Dreams: A Special Kind of Grief* (Ted Bowman, 2111 Knapp St., St. Paul, MN 55108-1814; 612-645-6058, 1994), pages 16, 19, 28.

3. Nate Eppley offered this contribution about dreams following a workshop on grieving dreams in Fort Wayne, Indiana, 1998.

4. Elaine Childs-Gowell, *Good Grief Rituals* (New York: Station Hill Press, 1992).

CHAPTER 22: BEYOND THE FROZEN WINTER OF GRIEF

1. Dorothy Rabinowitz, *Dimensions of the Holocaust*, 2nd ed. (Evanston, Ill.: Northwestern University Press, 1990).

2. Bruno Bettelheim, *A Good Enough Parent: A Book on Child-Rearing* (New York: Alfred A. Knopf, 1987).

3. MADD, Mothers Against Drunk Driving. National organization: 511 East John Carpenter Frwy, #700, Irving, TX 75062, 214-744-6233 or 800-777-6233.

CHAPTER 23: DID I DO SOMETHING TO OFFEND YOU?
CLEAR BOUNDARIES—CLEAN CONNECTIONS

1. From "Mending Wall" from *The Poetry of Robert Frost,* edited by Edward Connery Lathem, © 1958 by Robert Frost. © 1967 by Lesley Frost Ballantine. © 1930, 1939, 1969 by Henry Holt and Co., Inc. Reprinted by permission of Henry Holt and Co., Inc.

2. For a spoof on the rules for behavior in "Southern Society," read Maryln Schwartz's *A Southern Belle Primer: Or Why Princess Margaret Will Never Be a Kappa Kappa Gamma* (New York: Doubleday, 1991).

3. Joan Casey, *Get Off My Foot: Boundaries and the Relationship Dance* (forthcoming); Boundaries, 9038 Fourteenth Avenue Northeast, Seattle, WA 98117; 206-284-2126.

4. Eric Berne, M.D., *The Structure and Dynamics of Organizations and Groups* (New York: Grove Press, 1993).

5. Thanks to Ada Alden, Ph.D., parent educator, for this quote.

6. Charles L. Whitfield, M.D., *Boundaries and Relationships: Knowing, Protecting and Enjoying the Self* (Deerfield Beach, Fla.: Health Communications, 1993); Anne Katherine, *Boundaries: Where You End and I Begin* (Center City, Minn.: Hazelden, 1991); Jan Black and Greg Enns, *Better Boundaries: Owning and Treasuring Your Life* (Oakland, Calif.: New Harbinger Publications, 1997). New Harbinger Publications, 5674 Shattuck Ave., Oakland, CA 94609.

CHAPTER 24: TIME-IN FOR YOURSELF

1. Our dreams, our own myths, our stories shape our lives. Two books that offer especially helpful ways for us to examine our own myths and stories are *Scripts People Live: Transactional Analysis of Life Scripts* by Claude M. Steiner (New York, Grove/Atlantic, 1990) and *The Stories We Live By: Personal Myths and the Making of the Self* by Dan P. McAdams (New York: Guilford Press, 1993).

2. Thanks to Carol Kuechler for offering this succinct way to remind us of the hazards of being a perfectionist.

3. There is much helpful information for people who want to take better care of themselves in *Growing Up Again: Parenting Ourselves, Parenting Our Children,* rev. ed., by Jean Illsley Clarke and Connie Dawson (Center City, Minn.: Hazelden, 1998).

Index

About the Author

Jean Illsley Clarke holds an M.A. in Human Development and an Honorary Doctorate of Human Service. She is a parent educator and teacher trainer and the author of *Self-Esteem: A Family Affair* (Hazelden) and *Time-In: When Time-Out Doesn't Work* (Parenting Press) and coauthor of *Growing Up Again: Parenting Ourselves, Parenting Our Children* (Hazelden). She is the 1995 recipient of the Eric Berne Memorial Award in Transactional Analysis in parent education. She lives with her husband, Dick, in Minneapolis, Minnesota, near their children and grandchildren.

Clarke and her colleagues conduct workshops for people who want to facilitate group learning experiences based on *Self-Esteem: A Family Affair* or *Growing Up Again*. She has developed leader guides which provide a systematic approach to the use of these books in group sessions. Inquiries about the leader guides and other support materials may be directed to Clarke, care of Hazelden.